POSITIONING TO WIN

POSITIONING TO WIN

PLANNING AND EXECUTING THE SUPERIOR PROPOSAL

James M. Beveridge

Edward J. Velton

CHILTON BOOK COMPANY   RADNOR, PENNSYLVANIA

LIBRARY OF CONGRESS CATALOG CARD NO. 81-66638
ISBN 0-8019-7112-8
DESIGNED BY JEAN CALLAN KING/VISUALITY
MANUFACTURED IN THE UNITED STATES OF AMERICA

3 4 5 6 7 8 9   1 0 9 8 7 6 5 4

Contents

Preface

Positioning To Win applies a proven marketing discipline to all types of proposals—big and small, high-technology and no-technology, systems and service, solicited and unsolicited. The authors originally developed their approach for high-technology application, and it is admittedly an aerospace industry fallout. But where else, except in an industry where the winner gets billions and the many losers struggle for survival, might such a disciplined approach to proposal development be formed? That harsh and lucrative environment forces the bidder to create a superior offering through an evolutionary discipline and then package it in a better set of words.

When *Positioning To Win* becomes your approach to the attaining-new-business process, the customer will respond. You have substantiated every claim. Substantive marketing, wherein you demonstrate that the proven features of your approach provide verifiable benefits for your customer, is your ultimate output. Competitive convergence, wherein you merge your innovative concepts with your customer's perceptions, is the process and the discipline.

Competitive convergence requires you to develop approaches that are superior because they contain the benefits sought by your customers. You will have worked with and listened to the ultimate experts, your customers. Their perceptions are the only ones that count. If your first approach doesn't provide the needed benefits—as they perceive them—you modify your approach until it does. That's competitive convergence, easy enough to grasp as a good idea but very difficult to implement as standard practice.

This is the third in a series of books about disciplined marketing. In 1964, JMBeveridge and Associates, Inc., began an international seminar series on aerospace marketing for management. The seminar, with its companion text, *The Anatomy Of A Win*, has now been given for more than eighteen years. Tens of thousands of people have attended, including most of the officers of almost all of the significant aerospace companies. *The Anatomy of A Win* was, and is, J. M. Beveridge's personal philosophy about the integrated attaining-new-business effort in the aerospace industry. It covers the entire effort, not just proposal development. Jim's philosophy clearly works, for in his consulting practice he has successfully supported the winning companies on specific major aerospace program efforts whose sales total tens of billions of dollars.

There's no question that proposals don't in and of themselves produce a win. But in formal procurements, especially those of the Department of Defense, the National Aeronautics and Space Administration, and, increasingly, other government agencies and commercial firms, the proposal has indeed become the heart of the effort. So in the winter of 1977, Jim began a collaboration with Edward J. Velton on a second book concerned entirely with the proposal process. Ed had created one of the first proposal-development groups in the country at General Dynamics' Convair Division in San Diego. His forte was the implementation of Jim's discipline, and he excelled at it. Ed's disciplined application of Jim's philosophy tripled Convair Division's win ratio, and over the last seven years that Ed worked there, it was at least double the industry average.

Their book, *All You Should Know About Creating Superior Proposals But Somehow Never Fully Understood*, was published by JMBeveridge and Associates, Inc., in the spring of 1978, and it immediately became the aerospace industry standard. The book institutionalized the discriminator, the Aha!, and the Ghost story, cautioned against the Oh-Oh!, and avoided the Ho-Hum.

A discriminator is something that makes your design, concept, approach, offering or proposal different—in the eyes of the customer—from any other competitor's. Those differences may be strengths or weaknesses, anything that must be addressed to tilt the evaluation in your favor. Aha!s are your strength features, the ones you emphasize. Ghost stories are the medium with which you expose your competitor's weaknesses (or perhaps with which he exposes yours). Oh-Oh!s are the weaknesses you must neutralize. Ho-Hum!s are issues or approaches that just don't make any difference in the competition.

Companies that applied this discipline did indeed create superior proposals, and their customers rewarded them with greatly increased sales. It soon found application in fields far beyond proposal development, but it was heavy going for companies outside of the aerospace industry because the examples and language were aimed at engineers.

With much encouragement from nonaerospace people, the authors continued the thrust they had begun toward a universal application of the discipline. They first tested and proved their philosophy and recommended actions in the real world, then set them down in final form.

This book, *Positioning To Win*, shows how the competitive convergence discipline can be applied to your product line, for your customer complex. To position to win, you feature your unique strengths (and your competitor's unique weaknesses), neutralize your own weaknesses, counter the other fellow's strengths, and exploit the customer's hopes, fears, and biases while using the competitive convergence discipline to evolve a superior approach.

You probably are doing at least some of these things intuitively right now. But it is quite possible to develop the sort of discipline that harnesses your intuitive creativity and avoids hit-or-miss results. *Positioning To Win* will show you in detail, with real-world examples, how to achieve substantive marketing as a way of life.

Summary

The Only Good Proposal Is a Winner

To position to win, every step in the marketing process must be concentrated on a win. Your whole object is to differentiate yourself in every way possible from the rest of the pack—your competitors. You start by identifying all of the discriminators in the competition, anything that could distinguish you or a competitor from the rest. Basically, discriminators are strengths or weaknesses that are unique to someone in the competition, as perceived by the customer. As we will see later, these strengths and weaknesses don't have to be real. If the customer thinks they are real, then you must address them. Getting a good handle on the competition through the use of discriminators is the start of *Positioning To Win*.

Identifying the discriminators in a competition in itself doesn't position to win. You have to do something with those discriminators to realize your competitive potential. We define that as the total capture and complete use of the discriminators in your proposal, presentation, brochure, advertisement, or offering in a manner that influences the evaluation in your favor. We feel that if you practice *Positioning To Win* perfectly, you could win up to 90 percent of the competitions you enter. That's tough to do, but we've had years of better than 80 percent, which isn't too far off.

To actualize this potential, *Positioning To Win* offers a selective approach that directs you to products, propositions, and arguments that your customers may perceive as clearly superior. The key word here is *may*. You have a chance to influence the customer's perceptions, and indeed, if you don't, there is no chance to win. You must establish contact with him early and see him often. You check out the status of your going-in (initial) approach to see if it has the potential of evolving into the superior approach. If it does, you work it out with the customer, always yielding in the end to his perceptions. There is no "reality" in this life, only perceptions of reality, and your "reality" surely had better be your customer's perception of "reality."

In evolving the superior approach, you begin by listing all of the characteristics and approaches of your competitors, including your own. You are just one of the crowd at this point. Now you take the first step to break away and take over the lead (or get out of the competition) by eliminating from this list all common characteristics and approaches. Similarities don't distinguish you from the bunch; differences do. You are looking for discriminators. You keep this up until you have only those things that are going to matter in the competition. And don't forget to include your customer's hopes, fears, and biases in drawing up that final list; these may be the most important factors of all.

Next, you analyze how you will use those discriminators as influencers to feature your strengths and your competitor's weaknesses, neutralize your own weaknesses, counter the competitor's strengths, and—at all times—exploit the customer's hopes, fears, and biases.

You can't get far in this process without substantive marketing. This is the discipline of substantiating that the proven features of your approach provide concrete benefits for your customer. Obviously this works only for the superior approach. It bombs with a Ho-Hum approach and immediately exposes anything that might be categorized as garden variety. If you don't provide substantiation for every claim you make, your arguments are hollow.

When you have done all of this, you will undoubtedly find some shortcomings in your approaches, and this is where we separate the winner from the losers. The winner abandons his going-in approach for something better. He practices competitive convergence; that is, he merges his innovative concepts with the customer's perceptions. The winner isn't going to go down with a losing approach. He (or she) realizes that he isn't the final authority. He understands that usually what benefits the customer and what the customer wants are one and the same. He isn't going to try to push off his "hobby shop" ideas on the customer. He listens to the ultimate expert, the customer.

The last half of this book is dedicated to proposal implementation. It deals with getting what matters up front for maximum effect by using argumentative headlines and competitive theses. It describes the proposal challenge and the importance of team selection and organization in the winning process. We take you through the real world of proposal development. Using examples, we walk you through the right ways to produce proposals. We present the classic approach, the challenging-the-discriminators approach, and the hybrid approach. Next, we look the real world in the eye and deal with the imperfect backing-in approach. Lastly, we touch on that elusive, frustrating approach—the closet approach. The closet-proposal writer wants to do things his way and in the process always blows the big one, the program you most wanted to win.

In learning to position to win, you come to understand that you haven't been losing because of incompetence, but because of arrogance. Hardly anyone will tolerate incompetence, but arrogance is another matter. We tolerate it in the smart ones and even come to expect it from the experts. That's fine, so long as it wins. But when it results in putting a technical discipline above winning, something is wrong. Arrogance loses far more competitions than incompetence. And don't forget, it doesn't do you any good to be right if you lose. You can't help anyone as a loser. There is nothing more tragic than competent potential winners choking on their own arrogance. The fundamental rule of *Positioning To Win* is to give your customers what benefits them.

1

The Discriminator Discipline

Life is a series of proposals and counterproposals. Some are requested, some unsolicited. Some are formal, and some are informal. You are reading a proposal right now, for the purpose of this book is to sway your thinking and motivate you to action.

You propose a raise to the salary committee for one of your people. Winning that proposal is important to you because it will help you keep that person motivated. You propose an addition to your facilities because you need it to do your job better. Winning that proposal is also important to you. You propose the expenditure of company funds in order to develop hardware that you think is important in capturing a certain market. Just as you need to sell your proposal to the customer who represents that market, you also need to sell it to your management to spend the funds in preparation for a bid when the time comes. Even the most ivory-towered scientist must concern himself with the process of positioning himself to win in each of his necessary proposal efforts. In developing an idea, he cannot proceed effectively unless he proposes it, sells it, and gains acceptance and support from those who work with him, those who work for him, and those for whom he works.

Indeed, winning a complex proposal in response to a formal Request For Proposal is not much different from winning any of the many other informal proposals which concern us every day. For your proposal to be accepted, you have to know what you want, you have to understand what motivates the decision makers, you have to understand your opponent's strategy, do all your homework, and then make all your arguments simple and logical, calculated to appeal to the motivational patterns of your customer. These fundamental steps apply when you want your spouse to cook your favorite breakfast, your children to set the table, the fellow across the street to lend you his fishing cabin for the weekend, your boss to add two more people to your overworked staff, or your customer to buy your product. These are all proposal situations, and you hope that you will win in each case.

However, the nature and content of proposals are changing. Once we were able to sell cars and mopeds and refrigerators and travel packages and all sorts of products and services with only vague claims presented by macho men and sexy women. There was little effort involved in proposing that your spouse fix breakfast while you got ready to go to work. Our traditional roles limited choices and expectations.

But then we became more enlightened. We began to question the past and challenge the future. It slowly dawned on us that Duz may *not* do everything or that Maxwell House might *not* be good to the last drop. More economic freedom, more education, more communication, and more choices began to change our lives. Then came government watch groups and inflation and more technology and more competition. And out of this emerged a far more sophisticated, enlightened, and educated customer.

Technology increasingly affects all levels of marketing, so

much so that without special expertise you can't effectively compete in today's markets. Customers are more sophisticated, more informed, and far more demanding. They recognize that they have a choice, and they want products that provide the most benefits to them, their family, or their company. Inflation has severely reduced everyone's buying power, from the biggest company to the individual family, yet at the same time, largely because of a tremendously expanding technology base, competition for this reduced buying power has skyrocketed. Sellers have to make a rational proposal in order to close the sale.

Customers have a bewildering number of choices available to them, and many of them are very good choices indeed. But even when customers extend their buying power to the limit, they can buy only a small percentage of what they think they need. And because of this, they want to know all the facts, instead of the baloney, when they go out to buy.

Vague claims by macho men and sexy women won't sell in this environment, at least not consistently and in large quantities. Even the blue-collar workers of today are quite knowledgeable about the relative merits of competing products. TV and instant news coverage have given everyone a data base upon which to form opinions. In many ways, the instant exposure of today's news media has had a greater effect on sales than much of the advertising. If an automobile company has to recall a car to make it safe, the whole country knows about it that same night. When an airplane crashes, or one company sues another, or a new product hits the streets, the public knows about it instantly. The news industry needs a constant supply of copy. The need is so great that its appetite exceeds the number of sensational news items available and invades the business world.

We all "care enough to send the very best," but we now know that the very best is a constantly changing commodity. Thus positioning to win requires that you substantiate the claims you make. Everybody has "a team of highly trained professionals" and a product that "works twice as fast" or that "will last a lifetime." You can be sure if it's Westinghouse, but the problem is you are not exactly sure what it is you can be sure about. The real key to selling your customer is making him believe that the features of your product or service translate into meaningful benefits to him. An engineer calls this substantiation or validation, and his disciplined reasoning process directs him to question anything that is not substantiated or validated with hard facts. Indeed, there is a formal process in Department of Defense procurements where proposals move from a Concept Formulation Phase (a pipedream) into a Validation Phase (does it really work and can it meet the claims we've made?), and then into a Prototype Production Phase (so it worked in the shop; can you actually build some at reasonable costs with just ordinary people?), before the product is produced in quantity. Wild claims have to be proven before billion-dollar commitments are made to achieve supposed benefits.

Leaf through any magazine and see for yourself how most of the advertising claims for the products are vacant and hollow. Most are unvalidated, and they leave you feeling at least vaguely uncomfortable. We are promised "lots more with L&M." Perhaps they are talking about "lots more" taste. But the Surgeon General has determined that smoking is hazardous to your health, and it is entirely possible that what you get "lots more" of is cancer and emphysema!

The company that produces the analgesic with the combination of ingredients now advertises some nonsense about an extra, seemingly miracle ingredient. The ad used to imply that there was no question that this product was better. Now the FDA tells the company that it can't make unsubstantiated claims. The unfortunate truth of the matter is that there is little evidence that this "extra ingredient" is useful at all, and it could indeed be harmful, as could ingesting anything that's unnecessary in the first place.

Today, many buyers reject unsubstantiated claims; tomorrow, most will. And even if the buyer is insensitive to the quality of those claims, the Feds aren't. If it isn't true, you probably can't claim it. If you have been playing the substantiation game, the Feds will sooner or later catch up with you and force you to reveal the basis of your claims. The mouthwash and electric-shaver folks found this out, and so have many others. Even more important, your customer will demand that substantiation before he will buy your product over your competitors'.

Cadillac once sold nicely because it was indeed the top of the line. And Frigidaire once so dominated the marketplace that its name was synonymous with refrigerators. But now even the most uninformed consumer knows that there are alternatives to both Cadillac and Frigidaire, and consumer magazines publish convincing, validated data impartially enumerating finite differences that translate into real benefits for each of us who use competing products.

The key word is differences, not similarities. You don't buy something because it is the same as something else. You buy it because it is different. It's smaller, larger, prettier, more durable, simpler, more sophisticated, shorter, longer, heavier, lighter, faster, slower, cheaper, or longer lasting. No major product or service is significantly any different than those offered by the competition. What closes the sale is some relatively small perceived difference, something special that makes one product or service unique. Once you have that thought firmly established in your approach, you will begin to attack the marketplace with differences, or DISCRIMINATORS. How you choose to exploit these fundamental perceived differences or discriminators is the very heart of a disciplined marketing approach.

By thinking differences or discriminators, you begin to assess what it is that you have to offer compared with the other choices that may be available to the customer. You can single out a few of these discriminators and make the customer aware of their existence. The customer might not even recognize discriminators, so you may have to educate him. If there are no significant differences, you'll have to lead him to perceive a difference so that he can justify his buying decision.

Working with the fundamental concept of discriminators, you have the catalyst for generating innovative concepts. Thus if one fellow is selling long johns with buttons, another fellow, trying to enter the market, may feature zippers, while yet a third competitor may be selling a Velcro closure. Each offers definite advantages and has certain disadvantages as well. Buttons are sure but slow, zippers are fast but may get stuck, and Velcro is both sure and fast but is rough to the touch. The process of using the discriminator discipline to pick a superior offering is what we call COMPETITIVE CONVERGENCE.

Substantive marketing and competitive convergence through the discriminator discipline is an aerospace industry innovation, and we have used it for many years to produce billions of dollars of sales. Interestingly enough, though an aerospace marketing effort may involve several years and many billions of dollars of investment in pre-award risk capital, require a twenty-volume, four-foot-high proposal and a stupefying amount of bureaucratic complexity, the whole thing still is aimed at one simple question. It is the very same question even the simplest advertisement for the most unsophisticated product has to answer: "Why should I buy from you?"

Believe it or not, the more sophisticated the product (such as a hugely complicated military weapons system), the simpler the answer you have to supply to that question! Literally hundreds of people may be involved in the evaluation of an aerospace proposal, dozens will be involved in the executive decision process, and at least a significant handful will have to bless and sprinkle it before the decision is made known to the world, and that's why the decision will favor the proposer who can provide a simple, clean, easily defensible, clearly articulated, emotionally satisfying, thoroughly convincing answer to that deceptively simple question, "Why you?"

Why you, indeed! Why not the other person instead? There is one sure thing that happens in every award: While someone wins, someone else loses. That means the customer has to go through a comparison process, and that process means examining the discriminators. Thus the discriminators are a fundamental part of the process of determining who will win and who will lose. Every discriminator you select through the discriminator discipline will answer the question, "Why you?"

One simple test we have learned to make in percolating

the vitamins out of all the horse manure that makes up the classic response to the government's bureaucracy is to think through a simple, short, response that the decision maker can comfortably tell the losers. He needs a response to protect him from the losers' slings and arrows when he proudly announces a winner. If you have trouble finding that reply, you will have trouble coming up with a win. And if you are looking for that response, you are going to find it in a discriminator.

To find that discriminator, you have to put yourself in your customer's shoes, take on the customer's hopes, fears, and biases, and dispassionately look at what you have to offer compared to whatever somebody else has to offer for the same requirement. In cases where you have several years to get ready (because the customer's need for a new aircraft, submarine, tank, gun system, or data center evolves over a period of time), you go through many designs and discriminator exercises to try to reach an optimum solution.

You start with some preconceived notion of what the customer will need and what you will be able to offer through your investment in technology. We call this your GOING-IN APPROACH. Losers stick with their going-in approach and try to mold the customer to fit what they have to offer. Winners constantly modify their going-in approach in a competitive convergence with their customers' final articulation of their requirements based on all the options available to them, all the hopes, and fears, and biases they bring to the evaluation tables, all the realities of their budget and their politics, and a hundred and one other factors. Some of these factors lead each customer's thinking in a direction that will be helpful to you because of the unique factors that you, and you alone, bring to the party.

HOW TO MAKE THE
DISCRIMINATOR DISCIPLINE WORK

Begin the competitive process by looking for discriminators. Discriminators are INFLUENCERS that a reasonable, knowledgeable, and dispassionate evaluator could/would/does perceive as noticeable differences in the offerings of the various competitors. We say *could* because it may be necessary to educate customers to perceive differences they may not now perceive. We say *would* because it is reasonable to suppose that the customers would perceive these differences because they are talented and and are known to have certain hopes, fears, and biases that will color their views of facts. And we say *does* when you have done enough homework to confirm independently that what you think the customers perceive is what they indeed do perceive.*

Start by listing every discriminator you think the customer may perceive, big or little, profound or trivial, obvious or subtle. It is important to explore all aspects of perceived dif-

---

* When you have a customer as complex as a huge government agency, you quickly learn that there is no such thing as "the customer." Instead, there is "the customer complex." Indeed, there is no such thing as "the United States Air Force." There is the Strategic Air Command. And there is the Tactical Air Command. There is the Air Defense Command. And there is the Logistics Command. There is Headquarters. And there is Air Staff. And, believe it or not, a whole host of other "U.S. Air Forces," all of whom will get their oar in to muddy the waters before a decision is made. Then there are the civilians who are at the executive level of the Air Force and the various functions in the Department of Defense and their staffs. And then, of course, Congressmen and their staffs. And the fellow in the White House and his staff. Truly, it is quite complex. And believe it or not, we have developed an orderly, rational process for making this whole thing work—a rather predictable process, in fact. We bet our companies on it almost routinely as a normal course of business! That orderly rational process will work for your product line too, because it works even better when you can more easily define and predict the customer. What you need is a logical process to sort the whole mess out.

In the case of aerospace, you start the process by getting a handle on the many alternatives that are available to this customer complex. Next you weave your way through the customers' generation of their requirements to less than articulate statements of what this customer complex thinks it wants. And finally you address a far less than perfect and often very biased evaluation process that selects you as the winner. What the consistent winners soon learn is that there is no such thing as a fact. It is only the customer's perception of facts that counts. This is a hard lesson for engineers. Their world tends to be black and white. But reality is grey. It takes a great deal of disciplined thinking to sort facts from fiction, good data from bad, articulated needs and stated evaluation criteria from what will actually happen in the procurement process, and stated budgetary constraints from those that eventually evolve (and thus change all the tradeoffs you've been making). Often-changed priorities and rapid changes in the world geopolitical situation only add a little more spice to this soup.

ferences—managerial, financial, geopolitical, philosophical, and so on. The list grows, and it changes often as both the program and the design mature. A discriminator is a unique characteristic. If both you and your competitor are good plumbers, that's not a discriminator, even though plumbing may be the number-one evaluation criterion in selecting a winner. Discriminators are differences, not similarities.

Classify your discriminators into several categories. If a discriminator is only ordinary (a Ho-Hum), relegate it to a catchall heap that you will use to weave in the garden-variety boiler plate to guarantee a complete story. But you must recognize that you haven't got much leverage with a Ho-Hum discriminator. If the discriminator turns out to be a special strength (an Aha!), you have found a leverage point. It's unique and meaningful to you, so no doubt it will also cause the customer to sit up and take notice. Aha!s or the lack of Aha!s quickly indicate just how well equipped you are to enter the competition and be perceived as having something special.

An Oh-Oh! discriminator is one that hurts you. It's a definable difference between you and the other folks, a difference that the customer could perceive as a weakness. It can be either real or imaginary. You have to work to neutralize the Oh-Oh! by changing the facts (or the perception) that created it in the first place. And finally there is the Ghost discriminator. The Ghost (help, help a Ghost!) is your medium for revealing the other fellow's Oh-Oh!—his weaknesses, real or perceived. You will have to expose each one so that the customer will begin to feel uncertain in going to your competitor. We will talk about this in more detail later, but for now remember that a Ghost doesn't necessarily have to be real. It only has to be imagined, suspected, or just left as an unknown or unanswered worry.

When you work with your discriminators, remember that there is no such thing as an absolute truth. Truth is in the eye of the beholder. There is only one beholder, and that is the customer. The customer may be a vast complex in which many people have a say. In that case, the beholder is the customer complex. If you can figure out who really counts in that complex, you can weight his perception more than the other people in the complex. When you get away from government agencies and large firms, the customer usually becomes an individual. Even if you can't put your finger on the exact person or group that makes the decision to buy, you have a rough idea of who these people are and how they feel. You also have a clear understanding of who they aren't. They aren't *you*. Don't get your perceptions mixed up with those of the customer's. There is no reality, only perception, and in the case of marketing, you can rely only on the perception of your customer.

DISCRIMINATORS ARE COMPETITIVE INFLUENCERS

Discriminators are the perceptions (facts and/or beliefs) that separate you from your competition. Discriminators are your ammunition when you enter the battle. In other words, you will use them as influencers in your competitive thrusts. The fellow who best captures all of his competitive potential by properly using these competitive influencers while substantiating his position with validating arguments comes out the winner.

There are four kinds of influencers, and each is worth examining in detail. We call them FEATURES, NEUTRALIZERS, COUNTERS , and EXPLOITERS. We will touch on them very briefly here just to get you started. Then, in successive chapters, we will explore each influencer in detail.

- You *feature* your strengths and your competitors' weaknesses as perceived by the customer. Of course, when it comes to your competitors' weaknesses, you do your best to enlarge and strengthen that perception. Features are the highlights of your proposition. They tell the customer, "Why you?"
- You *neutralize* your weaknesses. In a way, your neutralizers are the other side of the coin. They deal with the question "Why not you?" in a positive way. They prove

that you don't have those weaknesses the customer suspected, and that you're really okay.

- You *counter* your competitors' strengths. Counters deal
  with the question "Why not the competitor?" in a negative
  way. They show that the strengths the competitors emphasize aren't that solid, and that the competitors really aren't
  okay.
- You *exploit* the hopes, fears, and biases of your customers.
  Sound underhanded? Not at all. Because you exploit these
  by presenting approaches that satisfy the hopes, calm the
  fears, and fit the biases of the customer. And while you are
  at it, you feature the inadequacies of the competitors'
  approaches in dealing with these hopes, fears, and biases.

The discriminator discipline provides the customer with a
superior approach because it requires you to direct your work
to his needs. You don't say, "Here are my approaches—what
do you think of them? Take 'em or leave 'em." Rather, you
consider all the influencers and use them to achieve a truly
superior approach. You then present your approach as a contrast to your competitors' garden-variety approaches in a substantiated, crystal-clear fashion. Competitive convergence and
substantiated claims help you sort out all the discriminators,
providing you with a very clear picture of how you stand
competitively. When you package the influencers you have
evolved through the discriminator process, you maximize everything that you have going for you, you minimize everything
that you have going against you, and you make sure that the
other fellow has been crippled as much as possible.

Finally, at any time in this evolving effort, you can package your discriminators into a short white paper that provides
you with a competitive thesis. You have a careful look at it
and know just about where you will stand when the moment
of truth comes.

Competitive convergence and substantiated marketing are
the key to positioning to win. They are the meat that flesh out
the skeleton of your thesis. Substantiation. That marvelous in-
depth wholly defended well-articulated easily understood

and emotionally moving stuff from which any persuasive proposition is made.

A FIRST LOOK AT SOME EXAMPLES

We see more and more attempts at positioning to win in television advertisements. In fact, some of these advertisements reveal all the features of unsolicited proposals. When empty claims are made, the missing substantiation is very noticeable. In 1979 and throughout 1980, we had the Chairman of the Board of a major automobile manufacturer in our living rooms every night, sometimes many times each night. He told us that if we were buying a car, we should compare his cars with other cars. That's all he wanted us to do. He implied that if we did it would be good for us, and certainly it would be good for him too. Obviously he felt that his sales would go up because we would find that his cars were as good or better than the competitions'. And at various times, to take care of those who were on the fence, he offered money if we bought one of his cars.

Where was the featured Aha! influencer? The television message was silent on that subject, and thus it implied that there really wasn't any. The message seemed to be that this guy's cars are every bit as good as any other cars. He didn't feature his competitors' weaknesses either. He ignored them. Nor did he attempt to counter their strengths. He made no attempt to neutralize his own weaknesses, not the least of which was that his company was going bankrupt! In his 1979 appearances, he banked everything on exploiting our desires to get a $300 rebate for buying his car, which might or might not be just as good as the competitors'. He subtly hinted that his car might be better, but he never made a strong claim. He even ignored the possibility that knowledgeable people might question whether a bankrupt company could honor a commitment to rebate $300.

While his proposal strategy was certainly simple, it did not seem destined to succeed. He put all his eggs in one basket. Exploiters are powerful influencers, but rarely are they enough to carry the day by themselves, especially where an expensive product is involved. There are too many other factors. And, indeed, his company ended up breaking the record for losses the next year.

Where was the neutralizer to the obvious ghost, (probably really an Oh-Oh!) that nothing was a bargain if its resale value wouldn't hold up? How will you get it serviced if the company fails to survive? What sort of an automobile would you be buying when the management of the company couldn't see far enough ahead to understand that for too long it had not been listening to the American public and had been ignoring unmistakable trends in the marketplace?

The company's product sales didn't increase that first year, but it is probably fair to say that it may have cut its tremendous losses somewhat. Eventually, this Chairman of the Board had to plead to Congress (and clearly reveal to all his customers) that if Congress adjourned without guaranteeing his company a billion dollar-plus loan, the company would surely go under. Again he used the exploiter to motivate the politicians. A rational, clear-thinking supporter of the free enterprise system would have the courage to recognize the awful pitfalls of guaranteeing a major loan to support a beleaguered company with a questionable product line and nearsighted management, and stand firm against the obvious threat of organized labor and the coming elections. But he counted on the absence of that courage in an election year. His perception of Congress and the Administration was of course correct, and that exploiter worked.

Another interesting exploiter was at work too, and surely he understood this well. His $300 rebate was bad for his competition. But there was something far worse that could happen, and he knew that they knew. In fact, it guaranteed their silent acquiescence for the congressional bailout. The whole market was soft already, and while the competition didn't need a competitor with a cost differential of $300 to cause them trouble, a bigger threat was a bankrupt competitor with tens of thousands of cars flooding the market at panic-liquidation prices. So there was an exploiter *against* the competition that the competition had to support! The bottom line was that he got his bailout. It gave him breathing room, a temporary stay of execution. And he had his exploiter going for him now with the active support of the Administration, the Congress, and his competitors! That's a marvelous job of marketing, isn't it?

In the long run, though, if he were to be successful, he would have to address the other competitive influencers just as aggressively as he did with the $300-rebate exploiter. Certainly he had to do something more to neutralize the public's continued concern over the possible bankruptcy Oh-Oh! And he had to own up to how and why the company got into the mess it was in and what he was doing to correct it, another required neutralizer on his continued Oh-Ohs! It was unlikely that he would get away forever with the Ghost he raised that government regulations hurt him more than the others. If that were the case, why weren't other little guys hurt more? And if the management had been listening as well as managing, it would have worked its way around that problem years ago. The public was too well informed and too intelligent to buy such a lame Ghost story. By not addressing reality, surely there was a danger that the public would lose even more faith in him and his company. By not being forthright, by not replying directly and fully to the real-world perception, he would forfeit his right to provide an explanation.

One option available to him addressed his Oh-Oh! head on: "Look, you all know we have troubles. Those troubles are . . . (one or two sentences). But we've corrected all that. Principally, we've . . . (one or two sentences). Now we make a good line of cars. In fact, they aren't all that different from the others. They have some unique features too . . . (one or two sentences about best features). You can take advantage of this situation by comparing our car with others and if—as we feel—you find our cars just as good, we'll give you a $300 rebate. We lose money, but selling off our inventory is essential to our future survival, and we do intend to survive! You get a real bargain. Even if the worst should happen, we've got enough spare parts to last for ten years. You still win, even if we lose. We've got some exciting things on the drawing board too . . . (one or two sentences about the future). Look us over; we're sure you will find our $300 sweetener makes buying one of our cars, which is as good or better than the competitors', a real bargain!"

Once he said all that, he had featured a strength—"Our misfortune results in your fortune, a $300 rebate for the same quality." He also neutralized a weakness—"We've taken corrective action, and even if we do go under you won't be without spares." And he exploited the customer's desires for the same quality for less money. The only thing missing is a counter. Apparently, he just didn't have a counter to his competitors' strengths.

If there are not at least some significant discriminators that make his cars better than the other fellows' (the $300 represents only a few percent of the cost of the car and a totally negligible amount when matched against a few years of operating expenses) then why even bother to look at his product? Even implied Aha! disciminators are helpful, such as, "let your local dealer show you some of the unique features we have . . ." or "the surprising benefits of our . . ." The saga continues, and history will record just how successful his messages become.

In the latter half of 1979, we saw a beautiful example of a counter on TV. Remember when Firestone took on the Sears battery? It was a pure counter. Everyone knows that Sears stands behind its products. And, for its battery, it spelled this out in the warranty. Firestone looked right into that recognized strength and claimed Sears' backing was second best. Here is how Firestone went about it: The ad opened with the Sears battery. The announcer read the 90-day warranty that Sears offered. Then there was a picture of the equally priced Firestone battery, and the announcer read its *lifetime* warranty. That's a lot longer than 90 days! It countered Sears' strength by showing it was weak relative to the warranty Firestone featured. In a pure and specific counter, you have to be good, and you have to know your product and the product of your competitor.

Most counters aren't that bold. They tend to be Ghosts

rather than organized influencers. Let's look at another of the Sears ads as an example of a nonspecific counter. You have seen the Allstate car insurance ad, "We've got a better deal." That's where the couple looks over its insurance for the coming year and questions whether it is more expensive than someone else's. A voice out of the blue says to come to Allstate and compare. And sure enough, Allstate has a better deal. Everyone smiles at one another and the ad ends on a light note, like the buyer offering the insurance man a peanut or the husband noticing that his wife is wearing a new hat. The whole world has turned rosy again. But who was the competitor and how much better was the Sears deal? The implication is that no matter who the competitor is, Allstate has a better deal. If you want to find out, come and talk to the friendly Allstate insurance salespeople.

Did everyone believe that? And is price the only concern in insurance sales? Possibly so for a lot of people. What the ad did was to keep Allstate in front of the public, and it gave an aggressive salesperson a "live one" to talk to about other insurance leads. Maybe that's all it wanted to accomplish. The tube still has a lot of ads such as this, and they have their place, but the trend is toward substantive marketing, the spell-it-out kind of proposition. Substantive marketing focuses on competitors collectively or one by one, whichever is the most beneficial to the competitor. It picks a feature and makes an item-by-item comparison. That kind of presentation registers with buyers and influences their next purchase. The more specific the marketing thrust, the more influence it has.

Many inventive ads of the past were built around mythical discriminators. These ads supported product lines that had no significant discriminators. There was no sound reason why an informed, unbiased, unemotional customer would pick one offering over another. But informed, unbiased, unemotional customers were a rarer breed. Millions bought cigarettes because they had "Lot's More," toothpaste because it had Irium, and pain reliever because it "has more of what doctors recommend" Lots more of what? What in heaven's name is Irium, and why do I need it? And of course the pain reliever has more aspirin in it than one of the other pills. They're simply different doses of the same thing!

Well, responses like that might have been the start of positioning to win. As the trend grows, the effectiveness of mythical discriminators fades into the past. The need for real discriminators is upon us—not only real, but the right ones, those that will sell your product by forcing you to evolve the superior approach. Having introduced the concept of the discriminator and having begun to suggest the leverage we can get out of features, neutralizers, counters, and exploiters, we will now explore each of these concepts individually. So let's go through it all over again, from the top.

2

Discrimination at Its Best

Over the years we have been conditioned to think of discrimination as bad. That's because most discrimination is practiced by one race or class against another race or class. The motives of this type of discrimination are selfishness, fear, and prejudice. But discrimination need not be bad: It just depends on what the discriminators are. In fact, discriminators can do a lot of good when they are motivated by higher concerns. There's nothing wrong with discriminating motives that separate the good from the bad, the superior from the inferior, and, in positioning to win, the winner from the also-rans. In marketing, discrimination is at its best when the motive is to select unique features that benefit your customer. You cull these features from the mass of ordinary features that, even though they may be important, don't distinguish you and your approaches from the rest of the herd.

Once you begin to isolate your discriminators and learn to

use them effectively, you are on your way to evolving your superior, winning approach. The first step in this process is to define the unique differences between you and your competitors as seen through the eyes of your customer. Before you can earn the respect and confidence of your customer, you have to take stock of where you stand in relation to your competitors. To succeed, you must be able to identify unique differences, or discriminators, and you have to do this as though you were your own customer.

In a competitive environment, if the customer thinks it is so, then it *is* so. It is not a matter of fact; it is a matter of perception. When all the marketing has been done and the moment of truth is at hand, if the customer perceives a difference between you and one of your competitors, then that's the way it is, regardless of whether or not it is true. And that's the reality you have to address.

To count, the discriminators have to be unique to you or your competitor. That's the very nature of a discriminator. You no doubt have many good (and bad) things in common with your competitors. You will have to evaluate them, of course, but they are the garden-variety factors (Ho-Hums) that all competitors address. You get your leverage with the customer's perceptions of differences, and that's what determines a win or a loss.

How and when do you go about determining these discriminators? And what do you do with the discriminators once you determine them? You determine discriminators by applying constant analysis, and you do this well in advance of the proposal. When you think you have begun to define a discriminator, you nurture it and massage it until it evolves into something significant—a *difference* between your product and your competitor's. This process requires interchange with the customer at all levels and in all disciplines, and you must do a lot of listening. By determining early what discriminators you might have going for you, you can begin to move a procurement in a direction that will benefit you and hurt your competition. But mostly you have to have an open mind if you really are going to use discriminators to evolve your going-in position to the winning approach through competitive convergence.

Indeed, in a proper market effort, you will be thinking discriminators in the earliest stages of proposal development. You will develop these early (maybe just potential) discriminators through customer interchange and generous amounts of your own discretionary funds. And you will sample often and independently to determine if what you think is a discriminator is indeed an Aha! or just a Ho-Hum. Remember, it is not just differences, and it is not just *any* differences. You are looking for significant perceived differences.

DETERMINE THE DIFFERENCES BETWEEN YOU AND YOUR COMPETITORS EARLY

Sometime in the process of developing your market, you will become involved in an obtaining-new-business effort, and you will consider at least the following items:

- Who is the customer, and who are the people who will be involved in the decision?
  Agency or company
  Names
  Positions
  Locations
  History and background
  Relationship with other agencies, divisions, and key customer personnel
  Hopes, fears, and biases
- What does the customer want to purchase, or what do you want to sell?
  Scope
  Objectives
  Tasks
  Statement of Work (SOW)
  Work Breakdown Structure (WBS)
  Deliverables

Quantities
Data requirements
Unique features
Background
- When will the opportunity materialize, and how long will it take to complete?
Request for Proposal (RFP)
Customer-funding
Program schedule
Schedule risks and uncertainties
- How firm is the business opportunity?
Requirement (approved?)
Funding (approved?)
Support (who and how important?)
Enemies (who and how important?)
Competing concepts or programs
History
- How does the customer want to contract for the work?
Type of contract
Terms and conditions
Unique factors
Payment schedule
Contracting officer or person
- Why do you want to pursue the opportunity?
Applicability to product line
Amount of dollars in the contract
Potential follow-on
Other factors
- How well prepared are you to pursue the opportunity?
Previous applicable contract or independently funded activity?
Knowledgeable people
Innovative approaches
Standing with customer
Contribution to creation of business opportunity and support of opportunity
Support of customer
Pre-RFP activities

- Who are the competitors?
  Names of companies
  People
  Approaches
  Ranking
  Relative standings with customer
  Unusual factors
- What do you have to sacrifice to win?
  If a proposal is required, what is the strategy (how can you win?)
  Going-in approach
  Technical efforts required
  Leaders and key-people requirements
  Facilities
  Dollars
  Other resources
  Proposal schedule and activities
  Proposal and program organization

This list amounts to a complete data repository, which you compile as early as possible, of everything you know about the business opportunity. At this stage, you may decide not to pursue the opportunity any further. If so, you have saved a bundle, and available resources can be directed to other opportunities. But if you decide to explore the opportunity, even at a low level of effort, then you get everyone at the kickoff meeting to tell what they know about the significant differences between you and the competitors. These should include your most knowledgeable technical, marketing, and management people. They are people who know and deal with the customer and the competition. If anyone should know who's who and what each is doing and who did what to whom in the past, it is this group.

Ask the group for a list of discriminators. Remember that discriminators are the seeds of a win. They highlight the strengths and weaknesses that are unique to the competition. You and your competitors use discriminators primarily as Aha!s (featuring your strengths) or Ghosts (featuring your competitor's weaknesses). This discriminator discipline is known as the DAG list, an acronym derived from Discriminator/Aha!/Ghost. DAG is more descriptive because it tells how you use discriminators and how to bring the feelings and attitudes of your customer into the act. Remember, it's not a matter of fact but of perception. It's what the customer thinks, or what you or your competitors can *make* the customer think. You are in essence considering all the customer's hopes, fears, and biases. A good Aha! from the customer means you have proposed something the customer likes. And when you or your competitor present a story that causes the customer to see a Ghost, you have exploited the customer's feelings, feelings that result from past experiences or future concerns.

We call the Ghosts or weaknesses that cause you fear, Oh-Oh!s. Thus, your DAG list is a measure of your potential for making your customer work for you. It will also tell you how well your competitor can make the customer work against you if the competitor competes hard and goes all out. It tells you what you have to correct if you want to win the competition. When you analyze your DAG list, you know the price you have to pay to win. And you will know how you stand at the start, relative to the competition, in the eyes of the customer. You can compare your approaches to what you know about your competitors' approaches.

This comparison is absolutely necessary before you can begin to evolve a superior approach. You have to know where you are and where you should be going before you can improve yourself. If you find yourself so far behind that there's nothing you can do that will make you competitive, you should probably not pursue the opportunity. That's much better than losing money on it because you never took the time to analyze where you stood and whether or not you could make yourself competitive.

Surprisingly enough, many business propositions go from cradle to grave without management knowing how the company stacks up against the competition. Most managements never sit down and figure out how their approaches benefit their customers. Most never take the time to analyze the benefits their customers seek. Often they simply take the off-the-shelf concept handed to them and propose it. That concept generally belongs to their most vocal and convincing engineer, salesperson, or market analyst. But most shocking of all, most proposals are so foggy that it's impossible to figure out what propositions they contain. You read the proposal from beginning to end and you wonder, "What did it say?" There were long sentences and big words and every once in a while a brief thread of logic. But that logic immediately got lost in the fog or got mixed up in rambling, convoluted thoughts. The reason is because you didn't start with an understanding of the importance of discriminators.

How can you possibly win if you don't know what you are proposing? You can't compare what you haven't analyzed with what your customer perceives about you and your competitors' offer. And if you can't do that, you can't compare the competing proposals with what the customer wants and from there develop a superior approach.

Let's summarize what we've just said about discriminators. You have to look for the real discriminators (forget the Ho-Hums) if you are to succeed. Start by listing the approaches and characteristics of all your competitors, including yourself, of course. The characteristics might include background, past performance, size and location, and related programs. The approaches also include technical, manufacturing, management, plans, and personnel. All in all, list everything that could matter in relation to the competition. But even after you have done this, you are a long way from isolating discriminators and using them to your advantage.

The first thing you do with the list of characteristics and approaches is to apply the customer's evaluation criteria to determine perceived strengths and weaknesses. Remember, you must apply the customer's evaluation criteria, not your own. About half of you will go astray right here if you aren't careful and disciplined. What comes out of this, in addition to the lists of real strengths and weaknesses for you and your competitors—the Aha!s, Ghosts, and Oh-Oh!s—are simple garden-variety (Ho-Hum) claims. These characteristics and approaches may be important to you, but if the customer doesn't rank them high, and if you can't change his perceptions about them, they remain strictly Ho-Hum. What you are looking for is what the customer perceives as strengths or weaknesses. But you still aren't there with discriminators.

What you have now is close and certainly important. But you are still in Ho-Hum territory from a positioning-to-win standpoint unless the strengths and weaknesses are unique to one of the competitors. If you list a strength but all of the competitors possess that strength, you won't be able to have much influence over the evaluators. The same is true of a weakness. You have gathered only Ho-Hums from a claims standpoint unless they are unique in the eyes of the customer. At this point, you are looking for that elusive discriminator, the strength or weakness that can become an influence in the evaluation. Whether or not it does become an influencer of course depends on what you do with it.

TWO SIMPLE EXAMPLES

To understand discriminators, let's take a look at two simple examples. If the discriminators were yours, you would feature them if they help you or neutralize them if they hurt you. For our first example, imagine that you are answering a Request for Proposal (RFP) for a thousand rowboats. There are only two competitors—you with a fiberglass rowboat and someone with an aluminum rowboat. To keep this simple, assume that the RFP asks for a rowboat size that is exactly what the two of you have to offer. So the decision is based only on the differences between fiberglass and aluminum, and you have to make it come out fiberglass or you will lose. To compete effectively, you start with discriminators. You want to know what you should feature and what you should neutralize. And certainly you need to get a handle on your competitor's strengths and weaknesses. Only then can you decide how you should counter or exploit them. You start out by drawing up a list of discriminators for your fiberglass boat (Figure 2-1).

FIGURE 2-1. DISCRIMINATORS SHOW FIBERGLASS' STRENGTHS AND WEAKNESSES

	You		Competitor	
DISCRIMINATORS	Strength; feature as Aha!	Weakness; neutralize this Oh-Oh!	Strength; counter to discredit	Weakness; feature with Ghost
Fiberglass shapes more attractive	X			
Aluminum must be assembled and riveted				X
Aluminum seams may leak				X
Fiberglass easy to patch	X			
Fiberglass has glossy finish	X			
Aluminum boat unpainted				X
Aluminum becomes hot to touch				X
Fiberglass boat is heavy		X		
Aluminum boat costs less			X	
Aluminum boat is noisier				X

First of all, your fiberglass boat can be molded into more attractive shapes than the competitor's aluminum boat. That's important from the standpoint of looks, since customers may place a high value on appearance. Moreover, aluminum boats have to be assembled in pieces and then riveted together. That makes the boats less attractive, and there is always the danger that the seams will allow leaks.

If you're a fisherman, you already know about the noise that accompanies every movement in an aluminum boat. All you have to do is shift your feet and you will scare every fish within casting range. And how about patching up holes? Anybody with rowboat experience knows that you're always banging them against rocks or dropping them. People also know that it is easy to place a fiberglass patch over the fiberglass. Fiberglass is tough too, and with the color mixed in, it looks terrific.

The aluminum boat usually isn't painted, and if it is, it is always hot or cold to the touch according to weather extremes.

Have you ever tried to put an aluminum boat in the water at high noon when it's 101 degrees in the shade? You had better wear gloves if you do. Fiberglass is just the opposite: it's easy to handle, and you won't get burned when you touch the boat.

But there are some problems too, and these problems must have clear answers if you want to sell those thousand boats. First, your boat is heavier than the aluminum boat, so it doesn't have the ease of handling that the aluminum boat does. How can you neutralize that weakness? Well, it's not a weakness if the customer doesn't perceive it as so. Perhaps you point out that for the size boat the RFP requests, 95 percent of the existing models use rollers and car loaders. These devices can handle the extra weight with no trouble. It's that toughness and style and color and ease of repair that's important.

You still have one more discriminator to neutralize, and it's a tough one. The aluminum boat costs less. There is just no way around this discriminator except to deal with it head-on. You admit your boat costs more, but you point out that it's also worth more. You can attempt to substantiate that it holds its value and even has appreciated in recent years. Point out the value of trouble-free operation and the security of a rugged, tough, durable hull. You have to compete hard here or you will have the customer admiring your offering but buying the aluminum boat.

Let's look at another simple example before we go on to a more involved case. Imagine that you make bicycles and are competing against a company that makes mopeds. You are both trying to sell large quantities of your products to a sports outlet. The sports company will probably buy some from each of you, but how many they buy from you will depend on how well you present your product. The sports company will use that presentation in its sales campaign to its customers, the many individuals who come in to make single purchases.

Here again, to compete effectively, start with discriminators. First, draw up a list of discriminators so that you will know right away where to put your emphasis (Figure 2-2).

FIGURE 2-2. DISCRIMINATORS LOOK AT BOTH SIDES OF THE COMPETITION

DISCRIMINATORS	You		Competitor	
	Strength; feature as Aha!	Weakness; neutralize this Oh-Oh!	Strength; counter to discredit	Weakness; feature with Ghost
Bicycle costs less	X			
Bicycle maintenance less expensive	X			
Bicycle is lighter	X			
Bicycle provides exercise	X			
Moped a liability if the engine stops				X
Moped is smelly, leaky				X
Moped fuel mixture costly, inconvenient				X
Moped is powered			X	
Moped is faster			X	
High accident rate for both		X		X

Your bicycle costs less than half of what the moped does. Because inflation has decreased everyone's buying power and people are short on cash, you want to emphasize the cost differential. You also want to point out that it costs less to maintain a bicycle than a moped. In fact, very few people take bicycles in for maintenance. They maintain them themselves. But most of the moped owners take their mopeds to be serviced regularly.

Another major strength is that a bicycle is lighter. You can make a good argument out of this fact. It's easier to store a bike or hang it up, but it's hard to do the same with that heavy moped. Then there is the value of exercise. You should drive that home hard. And be sure you make it clear that moped owners never even work up a sweat.

Don't quit now. Shift gears to the Ghost. In other words, play on the customer's hopes, fears, and biases. What if the darn moped breaks down? How do you get it home? You surely don't pedal it. That's just for advertising. How many times have you seen someone actually pedal a moped for any distance? Never! You can offset the lack of operator effort with the Ghost story about a breakdown far from home. Have you ever pushed a 150-pound moped five miles or through traffic or up hills? Of course not. And don't forget the pollution factor and the cost of fuel. Mixing the gas and oil together is a messy job, and mopeds invariably drip fuel on the floor. Wouldn't a bicycle be much cleaner? You bet.

It would be easy to stop here. In fact, most people would stop right here. But then they would only be competing part-way. If you want to get the lion's share of that order, you had better address your weaknesses too. One obvious weakness is that the moped is powered and the bicycle isn't. That means the moped requires little effort on the part of the operator. Mopeds go faster too, at least on level ground. These are your competitor's biggest strengths, and you have to concede those strengths to him. But you can use the high accident rates of mopeds to point out that the slight speed advantage is dangerous. What you need to emphasize here is the data that show moped accidents are more serious than bicycle accidents. And you end by conceding nothing more than a slight speed advantage when the bike operator is healthy.

These two examples are simple ones. It's obvious that if you did everything right in either case you would simply overpower the competition if they didn't compete just as hard. But you can also imagine that, even when the cards are stacked totally in your favor, you can still lose if you don't identify and address all the discriminators, particularly your strengths. That should prove the overpowering influence of discriminators. When used properly, they assure that the superior approach will win. They can also reveal your inferior approaches and drive you toward a superior approach by forcing you to drop or neutralize your weaknesses and adopt better approaches. You might play the two games in reverse and imagine yourself in the role of the competitors. What steps could you take to improve your position and to preserve your few going-in strengths?

Now that you have a feel for the competitive potential that

can be generated by using the discriminator discipline, it is time to move from simple illustrations to real-world competition. In Chapter 3 we conduct an exercise with a competition structured to produce many discriminators among the three competitors. We define the competition, draw up a discriminator list for each of the three competitors, and then write a competitive thesis (a white paper) for each of the competitors. What you will discover is that we come up with three almost equally strong competitive theses because we used the discriminator discipline to capture the full competitive potential for each of the three proposals. They all look good, and it will be hard for you to pick a winner.

3

A Real-World Competition

To get a handle on discriminators and how to use them, you need to study an exercise with a competition structured to produce numerous discriminators among many competitors. We have created a detailed competition designed to do just that. We realize that many readers will be tempted to skip it and go on to Chapter 4. However, unless you are the ultimate expert, we recommend that you resist the temptation and dig in for a thorough understanding of discriminators. Without that understanding, you won't get much from the rest of the book, nor from the self-practice exercises in the Appendix.

We will start by defining the operator, the customer, the competitive setting, and the characteristics of the three competitors. Having set this stage, we will present an overview of the Request for Proposal (RFP), just the things you need for this exercise. We will then draw up a discriminator list for each of the three competitors. And finally, we will write a competitive thesis, or white paper, for each of the three competitors. If we accomplish what we set out to do, we will come up with three equally strong competitive theses because we will have made use of all the discriminators.

The objective of this exercise is to show how the competitors can make the most of what they have to offer. When they do, they all look good. If one or more fails to go the whole way, those competitors will come out second best. The winner will be the one who does the most with his discriminators to evolve the approach that benefits the customer. And that competitor would have started with discriminators to develop that superior winning approach.

The companies we use as examples in this exercise operate and maintain recreational facilities for various organizations, such as military bases, government agencies, private clubs, condominiums, large companies, and schools. We will refer to the companies as *operators* and the organizations, whose recreational facilities they operate and maintain, as *customers*.

THE OPERATOR

The operator assumes responsibility for the operation and maintenance (O&M) and security of the facilities. Operation includes opening and closing the facility, monitoring the performance of the users—the customers' employees or members for whom the facility has been set up—and assuring the safety of the users, which can be a major task.

Customers have learned that operators who know the O&M business can run the facilities more efficiently and for less cost than those with no O&M experience. In the beginning, most customers operated the facilities themselves, often employing voluntary labor. Many found that this resulted in poor operations and membership problems. They found that by contracting for an operator they could not only get better service for less cost, but had a higher utilization of facilities and a better employee/membership relationship.

The customer in our example is a county in California. Twenty years ago the county built a shooting range for the benefit of the state and city policemen. The county operated the facility for the first three years. All went well during the first year. However, during the second year the O&M costs for the facility increased rapidly. The staff increased from two full-time employees to five. In addition, it was necessary to have outside contractors come in frequently to fix the plumbing, electricity, and other systems. A vendor was hired to do the gardening and another to clean up. It soon became necessary to bring in a specialist in the O&M of sports facilities to fix the shooting range, particularly the catapult mechanism for the clay pigeons.

The specialist that was contracted for this purpose was the Old-Line (OL) Company. Its performance was good and the service was reasonably prompt. However, since these activities were not scheduled but on an as-required basis, occasionally the facility was closed for several days until OL was available. At the end of the second year, the county formed a committee to study the O&M of the shooting range. The study concluded that leasing the facility to an O&M operator should be investigated. After some months of countering the objections of the county employees operating the facility, OL was asked for a quote.

OL's quote on a yearly basis was 25 percent less than what it cost the county to operate the facility. Accordingly, OL took over the facility at the end of the third year of its operation. Since then it has signed a series of fixed-price contracts. At renewal time the cost is adjusted for inflation and additional services. It has operated the facility now for seventeen years and has shown a very good profit each year. The facility is kept in good, serviceable condition, the grounds are neat, and downtimes are few and short. OL uses a program of preventive maintenance to avoid major breakdowns, and its safety record is the best in the country. No innovative services or features have been introduced since OL took over, although some additions to the building and public facilities have been made as the numbers of county and city police increased.

For the first fifteen years of operation, the shooting range was operated quietly and with no fanfare. Occasionally an individual would complain that no new services were being instituted or that the equipment was outdated, but for the most part the complaints were few and far apart. However, two years ago the complaints began to increase. Some members of the police force had used shooting ranges in other counties. Some of these ranges were more modern and had new cafeterias, better public facilities, and attractive patio equipment. These neighboring shooting ranges also sponsored other activities, such as social events, dinners, and shooting contests. Occasionally they rented the facility to the public, and the income from these events offset the operating costs. These reports were widely circulated to users of the shooting range and resulted in a great deal of dissatisfaction.

Enter the New Breed (NB) Company, which sees the facility as a very promising business opportunity. The NB manager claimed that the sole source (noncompetitive) contracting to OL is not in the best interests of the county and has not resulted in better service or lower costs. At first, the county officials, particularly those who were close friends of the OL owner, ignored NB's suggestion for a competition. However, because of inflation, the rising cost of operating the facility led to increased pressure from users for a competition. They wanted to see if a competition might result in innovative approaches that would improve the facility while lowering O&M costs to the county.

After dragging their feet for more than two years, the county administrators, all close friends of the OL owner, agree to a competition. The stage is set for NB to upset a sixteen-year incumbent. A Request for Proposal (RFP) is drawn up and a notice to interested bidders is posted. A history of the facility at this point is illustrated in Figure 3–1.

Three operators have requested copies of the RFP—OL, NB, and the High Technology (HT) Company. Each of the three competitors knows the other two. They have competed with one another on numerous occasions, so they know each other's strengths, weaknesses, and failures. In fact, there is little they don't know about each other and about the industry. To ensure fair competition, a neutral person is selected to head the source selection board. The source selection committee is equally divided between a progressive group that wants changes and a conservative group that wants things left as they are.

Having defined the operator, the customer, and the competitive setting, we are ready to look at the characteristics of the three competitors. Remember, we have structured these three competitors to have as many differences as possible. Thus we will have a large number of discriminators.

Let's start with the OL Company. Then we will look at the NB Company, the aggressive one that forced the competition. Finally, we will examine the dark horse candidate, the HT Company.

THE FIRST COMPETITOR: THE OLD-LINE COMPANY

The Old-Line (OL) Company, one of the first in its field, has been in business for forty years. It is a medium-size company,

FIGURE 3-1. HISTORY OF THE SHOOTING RANGE SHOWS OL AS THE INCUMBENT

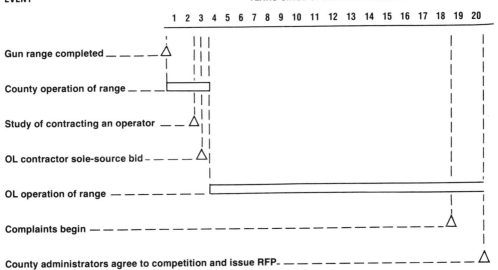

and its founder and manager, Mr. OL, in his early sixties, rules it with an iron hand. He is a Chicano who had no formal education beyond high school. Most of his employees, in their fifties or early sixties, have been with him for a long time; few have been with him less than ten years and many are thirty-year veterans. Many of them are also Chicanos. The OL people do good work and are very thorough. They don't cut any corners even when the customer would like them to.

OL is never the lowest bidder, and sometimes it is the highest. Lately, this has been cause for concern because the OL win/loss ratio has begun to taper off. At one time, OL had a win record of 80 to 90 percent. Now it wins only half of its bids.

In trying to find out what has gone wrong, the OL owner questioned some of the customers whose repeat business he has lost. They tell him that they switched to a new operator because of lower cost. Also, while the work was superior, the OL employees were too methodical and set in their ways. If a facility wasn't ready, they didn't allow it to open regardless of how many people were waiting to use it. The OL security guards were too strict and sometimes reprimanded users of the facility for small offenses. It appeared that the OL people thought more of the facilities than of the people using them.

The OL manager has determined that he will not sacrifice quality of workmanship. But he has determined that he will try to be more competitive in his bids. He will try to provide rationale in the future instead of just stating his bid, providing *how* and *why* in addition to *what*.

OL is well known, has a solid credit rating and an excellent safety record. Quality is its trademark. All its people are experienced in a wide range of sport facilities. The OL owner is a solid citizen who is well liked by people in the community and participates in many civic activities. He has been married for thirty-five years and has four grown children, all of whom attended local schools and now work in the community at other jobs. While he currently is in good health, he has a history of heart trouble.

The OL Company has a lot of old equipment that is still serviceable but isn't cost effective. Nevertheless, the owner has put off replacing the old equipment and instead continues to patch it up. He takes great pride in the smooth operating ability and low downtime of the old equipment. The company occupies an old building in an old, rundown part of the city. Although the building is kept in good repair, it is the only building in the area that is. Because of the location, however, the company and its employees have had trouble with vandalism. On occasion, employees have been robbed and even assaulted when they left the building after working late.

OL has trouble attracting new, young employees. The manager has had to hire new people as old-line employees retire, but young people, particularly young women, don't like the company's location and don't feel safe going to and from work. And they feel uncomfortable and out of place working with the older employees. Thus the turnover rate of new hires is high.

THE SECOND COMPETITOR: THE NEW BREED COMPANY

The New Breed (NB) Company, a recent entry into the field of recreational facilities O&M, is in its second year of operation. The company is financed by a sports company, which owns all of the stock. The manager, Ms. NB, has a stock option. She is in her early thirties and has an MBA degree. Her assistant manager is a young lawyer. She hires subcontractors for the O&M jobs she acquires and has only a small permanent staff. The staff, young and mostly white, specialize in organization and contracting. The NB manager is given a free hand by the parent sports company so long as she turns a profit each year.

Ms. NB is good at cutting corners and generally can cut the O&M of any job down to the minimum required to keep the facility operating. She is also good at renting the facilities and promoting dances, parties, and other money-raising operations. She subcontracts all of the O&M tasks. Sometimes she may have ten or more subcontractors working on one job. The nationalities of the subcontractors are mixed, with a high percentage of minority races. Some of her subcontractors are small, single-family businesses, particularly those who work as carpenters and gardeners. She prefers these kinds of subcontractors because they perform well and are conscientious about their work. Many of the well-established subcontractors are leery of accepting work from NB because sometimes it is late in paying. Frequently NB witholds payment over small matters or when it isn't totally satisfied with a subcontractor's performance. Some subcontractors suspect that NB does this to control its cash flow.

Many of NB's subcontractors hire teenagers and part-timers. They are paid minimum wage, and their performance is spotty. NB is very competitive about costs and almost always is the lowest or next to the lowest bidder. It writes airtight contracts with its subcontractors and customers, so it is never left holding the bag. Many subcontractors and a few customers have been hurt by these contracts, but NB has turned a profit on every one.

NB has experienced troubles in the O&M of those facilities that require a high skill level. In these cases, the NB manager feels uncomfortable because she is at the mercy of technical-specialist subcontractors, whom she cannot readily replace. Highly skilled subcontractors are few, but contracts with them are lucrative, so she hasn't turned her back on them.

NB generally gives the customers exactly what they contract for. The customers are sometimes disappointed at the minimum service but never at the price. NB wins about 60 percent of everything it bids on but receives less than 30 percent of repeat business. Most of its wins are on first-time business. Its second-time business comes from customers whose allocations to the recreational facilities are relatively small and inadequate. Repeat business beyond that comes from customers who operate marginal and second-rate facilities.

NB is well known, and it advertises widely. It has no plant or equipment. All of its labor and equipment is supplied by subcontractors. The company has only one office, located in a fashionable business district. It has only a fair credit rating because of its late payment policy.

The manager is a very hard worker and is in good health. She isn't well known in the community because she commutes, and she doesn't participate in civic activities. Her only concern is to turn a profit at the company, and the parent company looks upon her as a rising star. She is divorced and has no children.

The condition of the equipment used by NB's subcontractors ranges from very bad to good. It often isn't cost effective because most of the subcontractors are small concerns that can't afford the best equipment. Their equipment breaks down often, and this leads to a continuous scramble to meet deadlines, but the manager of the company wisely takes this into consideration and allows for contingency time in her schedule.

Although profits and the backlog are good, the manager is concerned about her inability to get repeat business and to operate satisfactorily facilities that require a high skill level. But she is convinced that her mode of operation is the best and that the flexibility and low overhead it offers give her a competitive cost edge. She is trying to make some changes and is considering adding one or two operating specialists to her staff to increase its expertise.

THE THIRD COMPETITOR:
THE HIGH TECHNOLOGY COMPANY

The High Technology (HT) Company has been in the business for five years. The company is an off-shoot of a company that builds golf courses and golf ranges. The manager, Mr. HT, is the son of the owner of the golf business. He is in his early thirties and has a civil engineering degree. His assistant manager is also an engineer. Mr. HT places great emphasis on the application of high technology to the business of O&M of sports facilities. He has eight years of experience in the O&M business.

Most of HT's employees are young whites with good technical educations. However, there are a few black and Chicano technicians. Many are engineering students, and all are high school graduates. The work force is small because the company relies on sophisticated machinery and skilled operators to do the O&M job. In the gun range business, HT uses modular catapults and target erectors plus automatic fault-finding machines for maintaining them. HT uses automated machinery for all of its O&M business, such as bowling alley pinsetters, repair equipment, screen and bleacher activation, and even cleaning and stoop-labor jobs. So long as there are no breakdowns in the O&M equipment, a larger staff is unnecessary. However, a high level of skill is required to keep the O&M equipment in working condition. The equipment is also expensive. The Mean Time Between Failures (MTBF) of most of the equipment, which is critical to efficiency, has been steadily improving.

When the machinery runs smoothly, HT performs O&M with almost no interference to users. The work is excellent and the time required for facility maintenance is short. However, when equipment fails, operations are disrupted. The facility must be shut down, sometimes for days, and customers and users complain loudly. Although this doesn't happen often, the parent company is concerned. Its owner has discussed this with his son, the HT manager. The father feels that a resident back-up manual force should be added to prevent shutdowns. The son, however, has high hopes that new technological breakthroughs, such as using modular replacement elements, will completely eliminate the problem. HT helped develop this equipment, and the manager is convinced that high technology is the answer.

HT is usually very cost competitive. It wins when the bid is based on an optimistic MTBF for its equipment. However, the company has not been profitable so far because the actual MTBF has been less than the figure used in estimating costs of winning proposals. The company has just broken even overall.

HT's win/loss ratio is less than 50 percent, based on the wide variation in the MTBF figures it uses in its proposals. When it goes with an optimistic figure, it usually wins; when it uses a conservative figure, it almost always loses. Every time its actual MTBF goes up, it bids low on the next job only to have some failure in equipment spoil its profits. In addition to some marginal ventures, it has experienced some big losses that have offset a few big wins. The potential to make large profits is there if the equipment functions with few breakdowns.

Customers like the services of the HT. When the equipment works, it is an ideal arrangement. But when the equipment fails, they find it frustrating dealing with the HT engineers. The engineers are always overly optimistic about the time required to fix the equipment. This has caused some customers embarrassment when they had to reschedule tournaments because equipment wasn't repaired on time. Some customers are becoming a little leery about HT's predictions that this situation will improve. This is a concern to the parent company and has put the HT manager under pressure, even though he is the son of the owner of the parent company.

The HT manager is married and has three children. He lives in the community and participates in some civic activities. He is in excellent health.

Because HT has invested in new, sophisticated equipment, much of it fully automated, its debt is high. In fact, if it weren't for the parent company, HT would have gone under on more than one occasion. HT occupies a new building in a modern industrial section of the city. It has no trouble attracting the educated people it needs to run its equipment. Turnover is moderate and about the level expected from young, well-educated, aggressive technical people.

THE REQUEST FOR PROPOSAL: AN OVERVIEW

An RFP has many parts and a lot of boiler plate, but we will list only those things that affect the determination of discriminators—the requirements, evaluation criteria, and the contract terms. We won't present a detailed Statement of Work (SOW) because we won't go beyond the white paper. The requirements of the RFP state what the customer wants in his solicitation. The evaluation criteria tell you how he will select the winner. The contract terms are the agreements between the two parties about how the job will be performed and what the payment terms will be.

Requirements

- Affirmative Action Program: Bidders must show plans for an affirmative action program for the hiring and training of minorities. They must have a plan to achieve a mix of employees working on this contract similar to the mix of races in the California county: 40 percent white, 25 percent black, and 35 percent Chicano.
- Equal Employment Compliance: Bidders must establish that they provide equal rights in employment and do not discriminate according to race, religion, sex, or color.
- Experience or Similar Contracts: Bidders must describe their experiences on similar contracts, as well as any special talents and capabilities that they feel should be considered in the evaluation.
- Sound Financial Standing: Bidders should provide material to establish that they can operate the program in a financially responsible manner over its duration.
- The O&M Approach: Bidders must propose an O&M approach that covers monitoring and controlling activities, janitorial and clean-up operations, maintenance and upkeep, security and policing. They should list any innovative techniques that might be employed and provide a schedule of maintenance events designed to keep the facilities attractive and operating efficiently. They must indicate expected MTBF of key equipment and plan for avoiding downtime.
- The Management Plan: Bidders should describe, at a minimum, personnel, any subcontractors and their responsibilities, management systems, and emergency procedures. They should also identify any O&M risks and tell how they will deal with them, listing contingency plans if applicable.

- Contract Plans: Bidders should suggest the type of contract; including fixed price, cost plus fixed fee, or cost plus incentive fee; liabilities and insurance coverage; and all contract terms. Bidders should list any innovative contract features that might improve services or produce revenue.
- Special Events Plans: Bidders should draw up a list of special events, including descriptions of contests, dances, picnics, and other events. Special events should describe funding plans and state policy for passing costs on to the users by charging admission or through other means.
- Fund-Raising Plans: Bidders should include a description of fund-raising plans, including events, fees charged, contract arrangements, and application of revenues to basic O&M special events if necessary.

Evaluation criteria (in order of importance)
1. Safety Plans: Safety obviously is of primary importance. Bidders must show the validity of programs to ensure safe operations and prevent accidents through the use of proven procedures.
2. O&M Approach and Plan: O&M includes providing essential services for operating and maintaining the gun range for the county police forces, keeping the facility open and operating, repairing equipment and facilities and getting them back on line, and providing security.
3. Innovative Approaches to Improve Services and Reduce Costs: Practicality of approach for generating outside revenue, making the facility more appealing to users, staging social events, and making periodic changes that keep the facility interesting to the user without affecting O&M performance should be included.
4. Innovative Contract and Operating Features: A plan for reducing risks and providing contract advantages to the county should be featured.
5. Record of Performance on similar contracts: The stability of company, including management, personnel, organization, and financial, should be documented.

Contract terms

The county wants to create the most competitive environment possible. Operators are therefore at liberty in formulating their contract terms. The county contemplates a contract on a calendar yearly basis with renewal options. Renewal costs will be adjusted for inflation and possible additional services required by the county. These costs will be negotiated thirty days prior to start of the calendar year.

Now we have everything we need to draw up discriminator lists for three competitors. Let's start with the OL Company (see Figure 3-2).

Notice that all of OL's strengths are relative to its competitors' weaknesses. Discriminator 16 is unusual in that it is both a strength and a weakness. It applies in this case because OL has such a long history as the incumbent (strength), but this is the very reason that the other companies are now challenging it (weakness). Discriminators 25 and 26 are similar. Rigid management practices produce consistent results (strengths), but it shows a lack of flexibility required for dealing with people (weakness). The same can be said for the stern enforcement policies of Discriminator 28.

This is a strong list of discriminators for the OL Company. If OL addresses all of them, it should have a very competitive proposal. But before we look at OL's competitive thesis, let's see how NB and HT fare with their list of discriminators. NB's discriminators are listed in Figure 3-3 and HT's in Figure 3-4. If you study these lists, you will find that NB and HT also have the potential for turning in very competitive proposals.

So what do we do with these lists? It is surprising that even though many companies regularly draw up good lists of discriminators, few have the patience and skill to capitalize on them in their proposals. The secret is to adopt a careful discriminator discipline in writing a competitive thesis. In the following theses, note how we carefully address all of the discriminators. Note how we feature the Aha!s, acknowledge and neutralize the Oh-Oh!s, and aggressively plan and exploit the Ghosts.

FIGURE 3-2. THE OLD-LINE COMPANY'S DISCRIMINATOR LIST
SHOWS O & M STRENGTH

DISCRIMINATORS	Aha!	Oh-Oh!	Ghost
	Feature Strengths	Neutralize Weaknesses	Feature Competitor's Weakness
1. Forty years of experience in the field	X		X
2. First company in the business	X		X
3. Founder/manager is high school graduate		X	
4. Operated and maintained facility for seventeen years	X		X
5. Proven record in the field	X		X
6. No complaints about service in seventeen years of operation	X		X
7. Reputation for keeping grounds neat	X		X
8. Downtimes are few and short	X		X
9. Program of preventive maintenance	X		X
10. Best safety record in county	X		X
11. No introduction of new or innovative services and programs		X	
12. No sponsoring other activities, social events, dinners and contests		X	
13. No cost-reduction schemes		X	
14. Some gun club members dissatisfied about lack of innovations		X	
15. No experience in renting facilities for profit		X	
16. Favored contractor image	X	X	
17. Friendship with county managers of facility and county administrators	X		
18. No education in modern management or equipment		X	
19. Minority manager/owner of business	X		X
20. Old work force		X	
21. Reputation for doing good, thorough work	X		X
22. Does not cut corners to minimize expenses		X	

FIGURE 3-2. (continued)

DISCRIMINATORS	Aha! Feature Strengths	Oh-Oh! Neutralize Weaknesses	Ghost Feature Competitor's Weakness
23. Reputation for being high bidder		X	
24. Workers set in ways and won't adapt to customer's wishes		X	
25. Rigid management practices	X	X	
26. Stern enforcement policies	X	X	
27. Insensitive to people using facilities, think more of facilities than people		X	
28. Solid credit rating	X		X
29. Well known	X		X
30. Quality trademark	X		X
31. Experience in a wide range of sport facilities	X		X
32. Owner solid citizen, a resident of community, and participates in many civic activities	X		X
33. Owner's children live in community	X		X
34. Loss of owner, who rules with iron hand and has a history of heart trouble, may affect operations		X	
35. Equipment is old and not cost effective		X	
36. Company knows its equipment and keeps it operating smoothly	X		X
37. Company located in old building in run-down area		X	
38. Company has trouble with vandalism		X	
39. Company has trouble attracting and keeping young employees		X	
40. Many employees near retirement		X	
41. Female employees don't like location, don't feel safe		X	
42. Turnover of new hires is high		X	
43. Pays bills and subcontractors on time.	X		X

FIGURE 3-3. THE NEW BREED COMPANY'S DISCRIMINATOR LIST
SHOWS BUSINESS STRENGTH

DISCRIMINATORS	Aha! Feature Strengths	Oh-Oh! Neutralize Weaknesses	Ghost Feature Competitor's Weakness
1. New company in the field of recreational facilities O&M		X	
2. Not locally owned		X	
3. Young manager with an M.B.A.	X		X
4. Assistant manager is a lawyer	X		X
5. Subcontracts most O&M jobs	X	X	
6. Small permanent staff	X	X	
7. Staff is young	X	X	X
8. Staff is mostly white		X	
9. Staff specializes in organization and contracting	X		X
10. Manager given free hand	X		
11. Turns a profit each year	X		X
12. Good at cutting corners	X		X
13. Can cut O&M to minimum required to keep facility open	X		X
14. Good at renting facilities and promoting fund-raising	X		X
15. High percentage of minorities among subs	X		X
16. Many subs don't like to work for NB		X	
17. Company sometimes late in paying subs		X	
18. Company withholds pay unless satisfied with performance of subs	X	X	
19. Company withholds payments over small matters		X	
20. Some suspect NB's slow payments to subs is to control cash flow		X	
21. NB subs hire teenagers and part-timers	X	X	

FIGURE 3-3. (continued)

DISCRIMINATORS	Aha! Feature Strengths	Oh-Oh! Neutralize Weaknesses	Ghost Feature Competitor's Weakness
22. Teenagers' performance is spotty		X	
23. Teenagers earn minimum wage		X	
24. Very competitive cost wise	X		X
25. Almost always lowest bidder	X		X
26. Writes airtight contracts		X	
27. Many subs and a few customers have been hurt in dealing with NB		X	
28. Company turns a profit on every contract	X		X
29. Company has O&M trouble with facilities requiring high skill level		X	
30. Manager is uncomfortable in handling skilled subs		X	
31. Customers sometimes disappointed by minimum service		X	
32. Customers never disappointed by price	X		
33. Company wins more than 60 percent of new bids	X		
34. Company wins less than 30 percent of repeat business		X	
35. Repeat business from companies who operate low-budget, marginal facilities		X	
36. Company well known	X		
37. Company advertises widely	X		X
38. No plant or equipment, only an office	X	X	
39. All labor and equipment supplied by subs	X	X	
40. Fair credit rating		X	
41. Office located in fashionable business district	X		X
42. Manager in good health	X		X

FIGURE 3-3. (continued)

DISCRIMINATORS	Aha! Feature Strengths	Oh-Oh! Neutralize Weaknesses	Ghost Feature Competitor's Weakness
43. Manager hard worker	X		
44. Manager isn't well known in community and doesn't participate in civic activities		X	
45. Manager does not live in community		X	
46. Manager divorced and has no children		X	
47. Equipment used (by subs) ranges from bad to good, not cost effective		X	
48. Equipment breaks down often		X	
49. History of scrambling to meet deadlines because of breakdowns		X	

FIGURE 3-4. THE HIGH TECHNOLOGY COMPANY'S DISCRIMINATOR LIST SHOWS TECHNOLOGICAL STRENGTH

DISCRIMINATORS	Aha! Feature Strengths	Oh-Oh! Neutralize Weaknesses	Ghost Feature Competitor's Weakness
1. Company five years old	X		
2. Division of company that operates golf courses	X		
3. Manager is son of the owner of the parent company	X		
4. Young manager with a civil engineering degree	X		X
5. Manager has eight years of experience in O&M business	X		
6. Assistant manager is an engineer	X	X	
7. Company technology-oriented	X		
8. Most employees are young whites with technical educations	X	X	

FIGURE 3-4. (*continued*)

DISCRIMINATORS	Aha! Feature Strengths	Oh-Oh! Neutralize Weaknesses	Ghost Feature Competitor's Weakness
9. Company has few minority technicians		X	
10. Many employees are engineering students	X		
11. All employees are high school graduates	X		X
12. Small work force	X		X
13. New, sophisticated machinery and skilled operators	X		
14. Efficient operation when machinery works	X		
15. New equipment with modular replacement elements to eliminate downtime	X		
16. Machinery requires high level of skill		X	
17. MTBF of most equipment not good		X	
18. Equipment expensive		X	
19. Maintenance time short	X		
20. Long shutdowns, often for days, when equipment fails		X	
21. Poor profit history		X	
22. Customers often frustrated dealing with overly optimistic engineers		X	
23. Some customers leery about HT's predictions of performance improvement		X	
24. HT manager under pressure to increase MTBF of equipment		X	
25. HT manager married with three children	X		
26. Manager lives in community and participates in some civic activities	X		
27. Manager in excellent health	X		X

FIGURE 3-4. (*continued*)

DISCRIMINATORS	Aha! Feature Strengths	Oh-Oh! Neutralize Weaknesses	Ghost Feature Competitor's Weakness
28. Company has big debt		X	
29. Depends upon parent company for survival		X	
30. Occupies good building with new and modern equipment	X		
31. No trouble attracting new people	X		
32. Moderate turnover in personnel	X		
33. Doesn't use subcontractors	X	X	

If you were the OL Company, here is what your competitive thesis might say:

THE OLD-LINE COMPANY'S COMPETITIVE THESIS

OUR APPROACH IS TROUBLE-FREE AND LOW-RISK BECAUSE WE WILL IMPLEMENT INNOVATIONS THAT WON'T AFFECT O&M QUALITY.

There never has been any question about our capability in performing the basic O&M tasks. That's more than any of our competitors can say. We've been in this business and community for forty years. You came to us for assistance some twenty years ago, and we've operated your facility in a trouble-free manner for the last seventeen years. Because of our preventive maintenance program, downtime has been essentially zero. There have been no lawsuits because we have a perfect safety record. The facility's grounds are impeccable. Our record with our other customers for forty years has been the same. When it comes to what has to be the heart of the matter—O&M performance—we are second to none.

We are aware of the complaints that brought about this competition. And we plan to take action to answer those complaints. We admit that we have been cautious in the introduction of innovative operations and changes. Innovations can be risky. We worried about incurring losses through lawsuits or overruns that would wipe out any gains. This would result in increased O&M costs to the county. We've never experienced any losses as a result of innovative schemes backfiring. We have never passed any losses on to you. We do know that many innovative schemes practiced by our competitors have backfired, and the losses were always passed on to the customer.

We won't pass losses on to you because we won't innovate in areas we haven't tested. Our innovations are cautious, but they will be risk-free. We propose to open the facility to the public periodically. The objective will be to generate funds to improve the facility. We will operate the facility for the public just as we do for you. O&M is our strong suit, so there won't be any risks. We will start on a monthly basis and increase the frequency toward a weekly basis or whatever the demand will support. This cautious approach will prevent losses and allow us to learn as we go. But most of all, we will be innovative in the area we excel in—O&M performance.

We will let you tell us how to spend the funds we generate. We will submit project ideas to you that we collect from the membership or generate ourselves. The ones you approve will be the ones that we implement. And before we implement them we will present an implementation plan to you. There will be no surprises. As in the past, you will always know where you stand with us. You will know in detail what we will be doing to improve your facility.

One of the major things we will be doing to improve our services is upgrading the sensitivity of our personnel to the users of your facilities. To achieve this, we have contracted the ABC company to conduct a series of public-relations classes for our guards. ABC is the undisputed leader in public relations. We will also be sponsoring a series of management-upgrade courses for our people. In addition, we are intensifying our campaign to hire young people, particularly young white people. As you know, we are the only minority-owned and operated company in this business. We don't have to have an affirmative action program.

We will consider any fund-raising ideas the county has. We will listen to what you want rather than present you what we think you want. If we don't have the expertise to conduct the extracurricular events you desire, we will subcontract these operations to qualified vendors. After all, that's what our competitors do for just about everything. But we pledge to you that we will never vend the heart of the operation, the actual O&M. We are determined that we will never sacrifice quality of workmanship. Our innovations will be restricted to fringe activities that are low risk and will not diminish O&M quality.

We are an integral part of this community. Our workers are mature and experienced. They require little supervision because of their long association with the company. We all live, work, and raise our families here, which means we are strongly committed to the community. Our plant is located in one of the oldest sections of the county. We have a solid credit rating and we meet all our commitments on time.

We are committed to providing the best service possible. Our equipment, which we own and service, clearly can perform this job. It has done so for seventeen years with very little downtime.

We want to continue the relationship we have built up over the last twenty years. It is one that we believe has been good for both of us. You have had the best, safest shooting range in the state, and we have made a fair and reasonable profit.

We think this competition is a good idea. Your RFP gives us the chance to try some operations that we have been interested in for some time. We wouldn't have thought these ideas appropriate unless you held this competition.

We think you will find our approach to be the right mix of preserving O&M quality and introducing low-risk innovations. With this approach, we look forward to another twenty years of business with you.

If you were the NB Company, you would take a completely different track. Your competitive thesis would look something like this:

THE NEW BREED COMPANY'S COMPETITIVE THESIS

ONLY WE CAN PROVIDE AFFORDABLE SERVICES BEYOND BASIC O&M BECAUSE WE ARE THE ONLY CONTRACTOR WITH FUND-RAISING AND COST-REDUCTION EXPERIENCE.

While we recognize that O&M performance is number one in your evaluation, we know that it is not the reason for this competition. Your current contractor has performed satisfactorily in that regard. We feel that everyone in this competition can do the basic O&M tasks satisfactorily.

The basis for this competition has to be affordable, innovative services above and beyond the basic O&M tasks. It's not enough just to keep the facility and equipment operating. The environment must be improved. Entertainment must be added. Contests and social events must be featured, and activities that generate outside funds must be put into operation so that these extras can be had at no additional cost to the county or its users. We are the only competitor with this expertise.

The biggest problem you will face in the future is inflation. Therefore, keeping your O&M cost down has to be your first priority. We are the only competitor who has the proven capability to drive O&M costs down and at the same time produce outside income. We are the only competitor who has experience in renting facilities and promoting fund-raising events. We can guarantee the future of your gun range through innovations that cut costs while improving social activities.

We are relatively new to the O&M business, but in our second year we tripled our number of contracts and volume of business. That's because we provide a new business approach to the O&M business. Every one of our customers is happy with the money we have saved him.

Our staff is small and efficient. We do not own plants or

O&M equipment. We perform our O&M business using only local subcontractors. Their racial mix naturally equals the racial mix in the county, so an affirmative action program is not required.

Our strongest suit is in O&M organization and subcontracting. Our manager, Ms. NB, is trained in business and has a M.B.A. from Stanford. Our assistant manager is a lawyer, so you can be sure that contracts with vendors and renters will be trouble-free. In fact, we have never been sued by a renter or vendor. That's more than our competitors, who have no legal experience, can say.

Like any new business, we had some problems getting started. Those are behind us now. We have always operated at a profit. We demand service from our subcontractors, and we see that they produce for you.

We are aware of the problems associated with extensive use of subcontractors. To avoid these problems on your contract, we will hire two specialists in the O&M of gun ranges. They are Mrs. Smarts and Mr. Wise, and between them they have forty years of experience. We are confident that with these additions we will be able to provide the innovations you want without any increase in cost. Our goal is to decrease costs, and we feel confident we can do this as we increase our familiarity with your facility.

The HT Company would take still another track. HT's competitive thesis might look like this:

THE HIGH TECHNOLOGY
COMPANY'S COMPETITIVE THESIS

WE ALONE HAVE THE TECHNOLOGY TO REDUCE YOUR BASIC O&M COSTS BY 50 PERCENT. OUR MAJOR SUBCONTRACTOR, THE INDUSTRY LEADER IN CONDUCTING SOCIAL AND SPECIAL EVENTS, WILL UPGRADE SERVICES WITHOUT RAISING PRICES.

We are well aware that quality O&M, improved services, and lower costs are the goals of this competition. Historically, the only way man has ever achieved these goals is through improvements in technology. We are the only competitor who has high-technology equipment and the skilled engineers to operate it. Both of our competitors use labor-intensive approaches because they have old, ineffective machinery. And everyone knows that the biggest single cost element in this business is labor. Without reducing labor hours, you can't reduce costs.

We have the latest O&M equipment available. This equipment has the potential for reducing O&M costs by 50 percent. We have worked with this high-technology equipment for five years. Only we among the competitors can realize this 50 percent reduction in cost.

In bringing this equipment to its ready state, we have established ourselves as the only high-technology contractor. This required a great deal of innovation. Through our persistence, we have steadily improved the Mean Time Between Failure (MTBF) of the equipment. Our competitors have never addressed this problem. And now, with the introduction of modular replacement elements, which we helped to develop, there will be essentially no equipment downtime. The 50-percent reduction in cost will be realized with no difficulty.

We are so confident of these cost savings that we have reduced our price for the basic O&M tasks by 50 percent. This will not only solve your cost problem, but it will assure you of high-quality O&M. The quality of our work has never been questioned.

We recognize that the requirements for innovation, to make the facility more appealing to users, is very important. We understand that staging social events and making periodic changes that keep things interesting without affecting O&M cost or quality is a primary objective. As a technology-oriented company, we appreciate the expertise necessary for those tasks. We have a plan for accomplishing changes and innovations. We recognize the need for outside expertise and question whether any good O&M-oriented organization could also be promotion oriented.

We will subcontract the social and special events side of the range to the DEF Company, the expert in the field. They have been in the business for twenty years and handle the social and fund-raising activities of twenty large firms. DEF's approach is to balance the cost of social events with the income from special events. We will not subcontract the O&M. This will remain in-house, and it will be performed by using the most cost-effective, highest-quality equipment available. We subcontract the fringe parts of the business only, and we do this with firms that have proven ability. They will carry out their jobs separately from the O&M activities, so there will be absolutely no chance that their operations will affect O&M performance and cost.

O&M costs are what brought this competition about. The only way to reduce these costs is through automation. We have that automation. With it we can reduce costs by 50 percent. You benefit from being the first to use this mature technology, and with it you will get complete expertise, and in promotion and social events as well.

Because each competitor addressed all of the discriminators, we have three very competitive theses. That's the start of three competitive proposals. Each competitor featured his strengths in relation to the others. Then he tried to neutralize his weaknesses first by admitting them and taking corrective action and then by refuting them. The competitors didn't avoid them. They took on the rivals and competed to the limit. From where we stand, the competition is about equal.

Which company would you select?

To complete your understanding of discriminators and develop skill in writing competitive theses, you should go through the same exercise. In the Appendix, we have developed three competitions. Each competition has three competitors. Pick one or all of these competitions and develop a list of discriminators as each of the competitors would see the competition. Then write a competitive thesis for each competitor. You will be startled by the number of discriminators you will come up with, and you will be even more surprised to see that you can establish a good competitive thesis for each of the competitors. These exercises will teach you how to neutralize your weaknesses and how to make the most of your strengths. By executing the exercises, you will be taking the first giant step in positioning to win.

4

Use Discriminators as Competitive Influencers

In Chapters 2 and 3, we showed how to use discriminators to position to win. Now we will formalize the process. Discriminators are the ammunition you have when you are about to enter the battle, and you use this ammunition to form competitive influencers. With these influencers you can mount a much more effective campaign because you are addressing the interests of your customer. At any time during the competition, you can measure your approach with your competitors' as seen through the eyes of the customer. If it isn't superior, then you have the chance to change, to formulate an approach that is superior. That is what competitive convergence is all about. Competitive convergence requires that you evolve the superior approaches that implement the benefits your customer seeks. If your approaches don't provide these benefits, you must modify them until they do. It is an iterative process, and you listen to your customer throughout the process.

You begin with what you have to offer. Then you go through the discriminator discipline to make sure that you understand all the aspects of what you are offering, especially in terms of your competition. But you also have to consider your customer's hopes, fears, and biases, particularly in terms of how the customer perceives you and your competition. To approach the marketplace with other than these two different views of reality—looking at what you actually have to offer and then looking at what your customer wants—is a sad mistake that many companies fail to recognize. Unless you understand and embrace the concept of competitive convergence, you will forever have a solution looking for a problem, or a problem looking for a solution. It happens often in the aerospace industry: the technical brilliance of what we have developed blinds us to its utter uselessness! Remember that competitive convergence means you are using the discriminator discipline to evolve a superior offering. The strengths in your proposal *converge* with your customer's requirements.

You can't put a value judgment on a discriminator until you objectively and dispassionately iterate it with the customer's hopes, fears, and biases. Only then can you determine how to use your ammunition to influence the outcome of the battle. And don't forget that *you* don't put the value judgment on the discriminators—the customer does. You can try to educate him to your way of thinking, but in the final analysis, it is the customer's value judgment that will make a discriminator work for you or against you. Obviously, then, you must come up with a process to sort out just how you will use the discriminators as customer influencers.

FEATURES, NEUTRALIZERS, COUNTERS, AND EXPLOITERS

When you go through the discriminator discipline, you soon find out that certain discriminators may be used in more than one way to influence the customer's thinking. For instance, one automobile manufacturer is currently featuring digital instrumentation and digital door locks as an important part of its advertising. If the customer sees that as a prestige item, then it becomes an Aha! discriminator that can be featured to draw a positive response. If the customer sees it as a maintenance headache, then it becomes an Oh-Oh! discriminator, one that a competitor could use to feature against you. If the customer believes that a dead battery could prevent the digital lock from working and make it impossible to get into the car, you have an Oh-Oh! that you had better neutralize. And if the digital instrumentation isn't just a gimmick but part of a broader technological thrust that perhaps includes the easy addition of a microprocessor, allowing you to read instantaneous gas consumption, this would become an Aha! to feature.

Obviously, there are a number of potentially different interpretations for every discriminator. Therefore, you have to select just how you will use each discriminator as a competitive influencer. We have formalized that discipline too by classifying our discriminators into four very useful categories: features, neutralizers, counters, and exploiters.

Features deal with the highlights of your approach. In your proposal, you feature your strengths plus your competitor's weaknesses. Features become your main selling points. Because many of your competitors will be featuring only their own strengths, you are making their job tougher by telling a customer "Why you?" and, "Why not the competitors?" Featuring your strengths and their weaknesses is the basic strategy in positioning to win.

Neutralizers deal with what the customer *thinks* are your weaknesses. In order to win, you have to neutralize your customer's concerns about those weaknesses. A weakness may be real or imagined. If the weakness is real, you have to correct it before you can neutralize it. If the weakness is imagined, then you must carefully refute it in your proposal. You claim it isn't true and then you substantiate that claim. Only the customer's perception of your weaknesses counts, so you must neutralize this perception, whether real or not. Neutralizers usually aren't as important as features. Sometimes outstanding features can overcome the lack of neutralizers. However, in a close competition the lack of neutralizers can be fatal.

Counters are directed against what your competitors claim as their strengths. Your task is to discredit and minimize those strengths. You state the reasons why your competitors' claims against your strength are suspect. Since your competitors' approaches are in answer to the customer's fears and concerns, or risks, you must discredit these too. It's a delicate game. Counters are much tougher than features or neutralizers. You know your features, but you can't always anticipate what your competitors might feature. A counter can backfire if you aren't careful. But where the risk is great, so is the payoff. If you are up to it, you can gain points with counters.

Exploiters deal with the customer's hopes, fears, and biases. In other words, you exploit your customer's emotions. That's the only way to say it. If the customer is concerned about risk, then you exploit that concern and in the process prove that your approach is low risk. You try to make your customer's concerns your concerns, the ones you already have answers for. Exploiters coupled with solid features make an unbeatable combination.

To get started, capture your discriminators in an Influencer Claims List (see Figure 4–1). Classify the discriminators according to Features, Neutralizers, Counters, and Exploiters. Your competitive theses should be similar to the ones in Chapter 3.

Your competitive thesis, usually one or two pages, addresses a particular discriminator. It could be a narration of how you will feature an outstanding strength, or it could explain how you will neutralize a weakness that the customer thinks you have. Perhaps the weakness is imaginary, or perhaps you had the weakness in the past but recently took corrective measures and eliminated it. Maybe it's just a matter of perception: the customer thinks it is a weakness because he has never heard your side of the story. Whatever it is, it is to your benefit to neutralize it. The only way to do this is to put it on paper, in a competitive thesis, to see what action you must take.

You may find out that your strengths aren't all that solid and that your weaknesses can't be explained away. The competitive thesis will alert you to any potential problems. If you can't write a thesis that competes, then you either have to change or quit. It might be best to withdraw and save your resources for the time when your competitive theses show you a potential winner. Then you can tune these theses with competitive convergence to the superior approach.

A SIMPLE EXAMPLE

Let's take a look at a simple set of high-technology discriminators. Imagine that you are answering a Request for Proposal (RFP) that asks for innovative but low-cost approaches. The customer recognizes that there are risks associated with innovations. Nevertheless, he is willing to go ahead, not only with innovative approaches, but with tailoring the system specifications to further reduce cost. Another thing the cus-

FIGURE 4-1. THE INFLUENCER CLAIMS LIST CLASSIFIES YOUR DISCRIMINATORS

CLASSIFICATION OF DISCRIMINATORS

	Features					Neutralizers											
	Aha!s	Your Competitors' Weaknesses				Oh-oh!s	Ghost Stories by Competitors				Counter of Competitor's Strengths				Exploit Customer's		
DISCRIMINATORS	Your Strengths	Competitor A	Competitor B	Competitor C	Competitor D	Your Weaknesses	Competitor A	Competitor B	Competitor C	Competitor D	Competitor A	Competitor B	Competitor C	Competitor D	Hopes	Fears	Biases
1.																	
2.																	
3.																	
4.																	
5.																	

tomer wants is the benefit of a good trade study. Point designs (wherein you have selected one design) are out. Furthermore, the customer requires that the proposed approaches have growth potential. He wants a breakthrough, a major step forward. This customer places great emphasis on technical integrity.

Let's assume that you fit the requirement of the RFP perfectly. You have been in tune with the customer for a long time, and you have done your homework and know exactly what he wants. Not only that, but your only competitor has failed to do his homework. Your list of discriminators might look like those in Figure 4-2. You will be featuring your strengths and your competitor's weaknesses, neutralizing your weaknesses, countering your competitor's strengths, and exploiting the customer's hopes, fears, and biases.

First of all, your approach is innovative and has large payoff potential. These are two benefits that you know the customer wants. Those discriminators should be featured in your proposal because you know that your competitor's approach does not include them. Thus you feature your strengths and your competitor's weakness simultaneously. It's obvious how you feature your strengths, but how do you feature your competitor's weakness? One way in this case is to say that you thought seriously about a conservative approach, but you remembered all the discussions you had with the customer's technical people. You point out that this led you to a bold, innovative approach. This approach raises all sorts of Ghosts. For one thing, it reminds the customer that his technical people were never contacted by the other guy. And by putting all the emphasis on your bold approach, the customer perceives the other guy's approach to be conservative, something the customer doesn't want.

You know that your competitor has a more costly approach and that your approach will cost less. That's what the customer wants. So again you feature your strength relative to your competitor's weakness. You do this by pointing out that dated technology is more expensive. That's why you use the latest technology. This again causes the customer to wonder

FIGURE 4-2. YOUR INFLUENCERS TELL HOW TO USE DISCRIMINATORS

CLASSIFICATION OF DISCRIMINATORS

DISCRIMINATORS	Features		Neutralizers		Counter Competitor's Strengths	Exploit Customer's		
	Your Strengths (Ahas!)	Competitor's Weaknesses	Your Weaknesses (Oh-Ohs!)	Competitor's Ghost Stories		Hopes	Fears	Biases
1. Your innovative approach has large pay-off potential, while your competitor's conservative approach has limited pay-off potential.	X	X				X		
2. Your approach may cost less, while your competitor's approach is well documented but has little cost-reduction potential.	X	X				X		
3. Your approach is risky, while your competitor's approach has built-in safeguards.			X	X			X	
4. You overtailored the specifications on the XYZ Program and lost performance. This gives you a high-risk image.			X	X			X	
5. Your competitor has a "point design" image. This RFP calls for trade studies and stresses holding all options open as long as possible.		X						X
6. You have data that indicate your competitor has overstated the performance of his design.					X		X	
7. Your customer is suspicious of contractors who overstate design claims.							X	
8. Your customer is very ambitious and hopes to make a major breakthrough with this program.						X		

about the other guy's approach. And that's exactly what you want him to do.

Now you have to deal with some weaknesses. Your innovative approach, with all that pay-off and low-cost potential, surely will be perceived as very risky (Discriminator 3). Your competitor's simple approach with its built-in safeguards appears to have no risks. Your competitor is therefore going to feature that strength and make hay with your risky approach.

You had better spend much of your proposal effort and maybe a good part of your discretionary research money in addressing risks. You have to convince the customer that the risks are tolerable. He wants a breakthrough, but he has to think that he can have his cake and eat it too. It's a tough job, but remember that the customer wants to believe you. If you show him a validation plan that can reduce risk, if you convince him that you are working on the problem, and if you give him a warm feeling that he is safe with you, then he will be inclined to select you. But if you ignore this shortcoming, and if your competitor exploits the customer's fears and concerns about failure, you may lose even though you have what the customer wants. If so, you will be unhappy because you lost the business, and the customer will be unhappy because he didn't get what he wanted. Ultimately, the winning competitor will be unhappy too because he won't be able to satisfy the customer. Everyone will be miserable. So do your job right and make everybody happy. Win by addressing all the discriminators.

IS THERE A GHOST IN YOUR CLOSET?

We aren't through yet. There's another hole you have to dig your way out of. Your competitor and the customer know about the ghost in your closet (Discriminator 4). They know that in the XYZ program you overtailored and lost performance. That past performance casts a shadow on you; it presents you as an irresponsible contractor. But tailoring is exactly what the customer wants you to do. So again you have to neutralize a weakness and explain away a recent shortcoming. Probably the best way to do this is to walk the customer through that recent tailoring process and show him all the things you learned. You might not have performed perfectly at tailoring, but you certainly aren't a novice. And who is the novice?—your competitor! You have learned your lessons. You know how far to go and what not to do. If the customer selects you, he won't have a contractor who has to get smart on the customer's dollars and time.

The object in addressing that Oh-Oh! discriminator is to turn the lemon into lemonade. You do that by looking your weakness right in the eye. Tell the customer why it won't apply to this program. Present proof that the weakness has been corrected. And while you are at it, plant the thought that because of that experience the customer is better off going with you. Out of that a Ghost is born: "Without that experience, the competitor will cost you time and money."

Having neutralized your weaknesses and turned them into strengths through the use of a Ghost, you now feature your competitor's weakness (Discriminator 5). Only this time you place the emphasis on your competitor's weakness relative to you, rather than the other way around. That's a bold step, and you do it only when you are very sure of yourself and only when it concerns a requirement with a lot of customer emphasis. In this case, the discriminator is that the competitor has a "point design" image. He closes out all his options and presents one design—take it or leave it. It's a discriminator because a point design is exactly what the customer doesn't want. It's also a discriminator because you have a "trade study" image. You always check how every design and performance variation affects the whole. Everyone knows you always hold your options open as long as possible. Your customers, including the prospective one, know that they always have the opportunity to control the final selection. They know they will be allowed to examine all the alternatives in the process.

You could have featured this strength relative to the competitor's weakness. But because you are so secure in the knowledge that no one is better at trade studies than you, you decide to emphasize the competitor's weakness relative to your vast strength.

Just to make this example interesting, suppose that you come across some customer-generated data that contradict some of the claims your competitor makes (Discriminator 6). You think you have won this competition, but you don't want to take any chances. This is one contract you really want. So you use this data to counter your competitor's strength—to discredit him completely. In doing so, you play upon your customer's fears of being misinformed (Discriminator 7). You close by exploiting his hopes for a breakthrough (Discriminator 8), and remind him that only your bold approach holds promise here.

Of course, this is a simple, one-sided case. It's obvious that if you did everything right you would simply overpower the competition. But you can also imagine that, even when the cards are stacked totally in your favor, you can still lose if you don't identify and address all the influencers. That should show you the power of discriminators as influencers. When used properly, they assure that the superior approach will win. They can also reveal your inferior approaches and drive you toward a superior approach by forcing you to drop or neutralize your weaknesses and adopt better approaches.

In positioning to win, it is important to hit the competition with your strengths (the Ahas!), then hit them with their weaknesses by using Ghosts. While you are doing this you have to defend yourself against your own weaknesses (your Oh-Oh!s) and neutralize them with logic. And if you see an opportunity and feel confident, you can just go for broke and take on your competitor's strengths with a counter.

5

Feature Your Strengths and Your Competitor's Weaknesses

Now that you have disciplined yourself to put together a discriminator list, and to sort out the Aha!s, the Ghosts, and the Oh-Oh!s, you are ready to go to work and put your proposal together.

Features are the highlights of your proposal. They are pivotal in presenting the answer to "Why should the customer choose you?" Feature your unique strengths (the Aha! discriminators) and your competitor's unique weaknesses (the Ghost discriminators). Describe and emphasize your strengths and concerns. Convince the customer that your strengths benefit him. Convince him that your fears and concerns are his fears and concerns, and then hand him the solution. Expose and magnify your competitor's weaknesses. Convince the customer that these offset the benefits of the competitor's approaches. Features are argumentative because, more than anything else in the discriminator discipline, they have the potential to establish you as a winner. But you have to substantiate them.

There are a lot of lesser, garden-variety claims (Ho-Hums) that comprise a large part of what you are offering to your customer. For the sake of completeness, you will have to treat these areas, but only in passing. For example, remember the car manufacturer in Chapter 4 who featured a digital push-button door lock and digital instrumentation for the speedometer? They were the major thrust in his advertising, his Aha! discriminators. Even though they were trivial features in the overall requirement of the car, they could be perceived—and perhaps desired—as differences from the competitors' cars. The undistinguished motors, transmissions, and suspensions that are at the heart of any automobile's conceptual design were merely Ho-Hummed aside. The inference is that "we're all the same in those areas, so let's concentrate on where we are different and why you'll like us for those differences."

Features can be strengths, such as an outstanding management team, a fundamentally low-risk approach, a unique pioneering effort that leads the way, superb styling, serviceability, low price, high price but the prestige leader, or a truly balanced design. They can also lean heavily on what was a unique going-in strength regardless of design or cost or styling, such as the best record with this customer, the strongest financial standing, or the most available machine time. Your proposal also features your fears and concerns. If your approaches solve these fears and concerns or have the potential to do that, you will want the customer to accept them as his own. But they have to be the right fears and concerns and, by definition, that means the customer's fears and concerns. You have to substantiate them and make them legitimate.

Features are also your competitor's weaknesses. For instance, if you are selling cars and your competitor's cars are smaller and lighter than yours, you will feature your competitor's reduced ruggedness and poor safety record. You can tabulate some data and even show a few photographs of wrecks. Along with that, you neutralize the concern about reduced gas mileage by showing only a small percentage decrease between your safe car and his unsafe car. You also counter your competitor's comfort claims by showing how little padding there is on the seats and how flimsy the springs are under the seat.

You bring out your competitor's weaknesses by comparing them with your strengths. When you do that, you score both ways. Let's look at a few high-technology examples of how you can feature your strengths and your competitor's weakness simultaneously.

A FEW HIGH-TECHNOLOGY EXAMPLES

One example that we used in our previous book, *Creating Superior Proposals,* is a photograph from an aerospace company's proposal. This photograph shows management accepting a performance improvement award. The title of the ad says, "We are the *only* contractor in any field to receive this award seven times." Obviously that is a strength feature for that company, but it also features a weakness for the competition. The potential customer who sees the ad has to ask, "Why didn't the competitors win it seven times?" Then it occurs to him to ask, "Has the competition *ever* won the award?" The evaluator looks through the competitors' proposals to see if they ever did win the award. If he finds no mention of the award, he will probably conclude that the competitors never have won it. "Now why is that?" he asks. Perhaps their performance has never improved! The subtlety of the ad is the word *only* in the title. This signified to the potential customer that winning the award was unique to the company that featured it. And it's something the potential customer should keep in mind when he selects his contractor.

Another piece of art from a proposal shows how to feature a competitor's weakness versus your strength. It shows a capsule for a missile that was damaged when it was loaded aboard a submarine. The title says, "Our Capsule Provides Handling Protection." Now obviously the purpose of the photograph isn't to show that the capsule gets all banged up when the missile is loaded on the submarine. Capsules cost money too. If the capsule damage was all there was to it, pointing it out in the proposal wouldn't be wise. But the damage was featured in order to alert the evaluator to the question of what happens to the competitor's missile when it is loaded on the submarine—because it is unencapsulated. Here again strengths and weaknesses are featured.

Let's take a look at another high-technology example before moving on to some medium- and no-technology examples. A photograph shows a missile being recovered by parachute; another photograph shows the same type of missile that had been recovered four times. Under the first photograph is the title, "We have proven the XYZ missile recovery system numerous times." Under the photograph of the missile with four recoveries is the title, "One of our more experienced XYZ missiles." This is a balanced strength/weakness feature. The proposal that these photographs appeared in featured them only because the competition did not have a proven recovery system at that time. That proposal was instrumental in winning a contract.

A FEW LOWER-TECHNOLOGY EXAMPLES

Featuring strengths and weaknesses also applies to lower technology subjects. In a medium-technology example, for instance, you might feature how your fuel-injected automobile engine burns just regular gasoline without requiring a catalytic converter in the exhaust gas system (which is expensive, tough to maintain, and probably will be easily contaminated) like the one that the other fellow has to use. The idea behind all of this, of course, is to get the evaluator to go and check the weakness of the competitor in an area where you are strong. Specifically you want the evaluator to see how a particular competitor addresses an apparent weakness (an Oh-Oh!) in his proposal. If he has an answer for it, you haven't lost anything. But if he doesn't, or is lazy and hasn't treated that Oh-Oh!, he will lose points in that area.

Weaknesses can be featured in the going-in position of your competitors as well. A background weakness, for instance, might be the competitor's lack of experience in the subject matter. You can feature this nicely by overemphasizing your own extensive background (your Aha! discriminator strength). This will cause the evaluator to look for a similar treatment by the competitor. Or you can just say bluntly you have ten years' experience in the field and your competitor has none. If you really want to lay it on, you can point out all the troubles you had getting started. You could even itemize the failures that anyone would experience in breaking into the field. Of course, you had an easier time than most because you are more capable! So the other fellow is in even more trouble than you were many years ago, before you learned something and got your act together.

Cessna advertising refers to the world's most popular aircraft because it happens to dominate a particular segment of the general aviation marketplace. A car manufacturer indicates that he "wrote the book on four-wheel drive," still drawing on the emotional commitments of men who drove a Jeep in the Big War. And some folks have even managed to feature their Aha! discriminator so well that it has become part of our everyday jargon: "It's the Cadillac of the line."

Features can be found even in the harshest environment if you are up to evolving a superior approach. Consider this proposition: how about finding a feature for a product that is dangerous to your health if you use it as intended? And by law you have to state that the product is dangerous in your proposition. Now that is a real challenge. Imagine that you had to undertake such an assignment. How would you go about it? If you were advertising cigarettes, you would have that problem every time. But just suppose you have been positioning to win from the start, first by determining what kind of cigarette would benefit your die-hard smokers the most, and then by changing from your high-tar cigarette of yesterday to your new lowest-of-the-low-tar cigarette of today. How do you make the most of what you have to offer? How do you convince the customers to buy your product because it offers the most benefits to them (i.e., damages them the least)? You would probably come up with an ad that looks something like the one in Figure 5-1.

As Figure 5-1 shows, even in the toughest environment you can find a feature that the customer will perceive as superior—the best of the worst in this case. The featured Aha! discriminator suggests that if you have to smoke, smoke Lowest Tar Delights because they aren't quite as bad for you as the competing brands. Or, put another way, "You won't damage your health quite as much or as fast if you smoke Lowest Tar Delights."

In this case the company looked at a demand for a product that literally damages the health of the user. It looked at the product through the eyes of the user and was still able to see benefits in a new low-tar brand, relative to the existing competition. The user wants to smoke and he knows there are risks, but he would like to minimize the risks. The company even substantiates the claim in the ad. It offers solid proof that its cigarette has less tar than the competing brands. This is a perfect feature in that it simultaneously reveals the seller's strengths, the customer's concern, and the competitor's weakness relative to that concern. The company knows that concern is real. Even the required (Oh-Oh!) warning brings it out. In this case, the seller takes advantage of the warning Ho-Hum! (everybody is the same), and the Oh-Oh! (smoking is dangerous to your health), and it ends up with a combination Aha!/Ghost discriminator (we are the least hazardous), which it features in the ad.

Strength features sometimes are difficult to find. But if you are willing to look at it from the customer's standpoint, you can always create one. Consider a recent ad for a company that has the same rates as its competitors. That could add up to a lot of garden-variety (Ho-Hum!) claims, without some extraordinary effort at creating a strength feature. But the company created one. The ad says, "Come directly to us and save money." The argumentative headline might be: "Because we eliminate the middle man [feature], you save hundreds of dollars on a loan to finance your pool [benefit]."

Eliminating the middle man is not a really strong feature

FIGURE 5-1. A PROFESSIONAL JOB FEATURING YOUR
STRENGTH AND YOUR COMPETITORS'
WEAKNESSES

Warning: The Surgeon-General Has Determined That Cigarette Smoking is Dangerous to Your Health.

100's smokers:
Guess who makes these high-tar brands of cigarettes?
How can you reduce tar without reducing taste?

With ours:

Lowest Tar Delights
The Lowest Available Without Loss of Taste

because it doesn't simultaneously expose and magnify the competitor's weakness. For all we know, the competitors might offer the same service. But the strength claim is clear. And to get the point across, the ad shows an attractive lady dunking the bad old middle man. It suggests that if you buy a swimming pool, attractive people will flock to it. Finance it with this company and one day you might see a beautiful blonde in it. And when you do, you will have a few hundred dollars in your pocket, saved by dealing directly with no-middle-man. That and the young lady add up to two more perceived benefits.

Consider the poor guy who is trying to sell margarine and looking for a strength feature. Margarine is just margarine to many, but not to one company. It wrapped up its margarine in a squeeze bottle and found a strength feature: "It won't slide off the cob." For the person who loves corn on the cob but gets terribly frustrated every time the butter or margarine slides off, it is a big plus. It may seem to be only a seasonal ad, but it might sell margarine.

One toothpaste maker chatted about his Irium, and another fellow had a White Tornado in his cleaning product. These are manufactured Aha! discriminators, and they often sell products very effectively. Remember the ad for instant coffee that is "mellowed" with chicory? The company claimed that it was "the end of bitter coffee taste." There really wasn't much to it, just a photograph of the coffee jar with the title on it. The label gave the company's name, defined the contents as instant coffee, and stated that the contents were mellowed with chicory. Of course this was accompanied by a national TV ad that implied all sorts of good things about having chicory in your coffee. To some people, these combined ads implied that adding chicory to coffee makes it taste better. To a great deal of the folks who read the ad, it implies that any coffee without chicory *must* be bitter. In any case, you have a nice featured Aha!/Ghost discriminator. The forehand stroke implies that this coffee is very mellow. The backhand stroke makes it clear that all other coffee is bitter. One of our secretaries said that she never realized that coffee had any bitter taste. But when she saw the ad, she tried a jar of coffee with chicory. And so did a lot of other people. Because that company looked for a superior approach, and kept at it until they created a superior discriminator that they could feature, they possibly bit off a nice piece of the market.

The ad is far from perfect, of course. It doesn't supply any substantiation for the claimed Aha!/Ghost discriminator. Maybe the tickler is enough to get a significant number of folks to give the product a try. Maybe they will find coffee is bitter and stick with the mellowed-out brand. Maybe they'll find they prefer coffee's bitter taste. The company is hoping that if you try it, you'll like it, especially if you have been biased to believe the alternative is bitter. But remember, if the product doesn't substantiate the claim, the success will be fleeting at most, and it could even backfire. Ultimately, only the superior product succeeds.

Most of us don't have too much trouble with features because it is almost second nature to feature our strengths relative to the other fellow's weaknesses. But we should add a little twist to show how to get the most out of our features. In reality, a feature is simply a way of implementing a benefit, and it's the benefit that gives you the leverage. What you perceive as a feature might result in a benefit for your customer. So remember, always tie the benefit in with the implementing feature.

Only when you begin to understand the leverage you get from the benefit rather than from the feature will you begin to see that there are two ways of thinking about everything. For instance, one view of exercise is sweat and exhaustion. Another is a beautiful body. It depends on your perspective. Another example is buying gasoline for our cars. But what we really are buying is the benefit of being able to transport ourselves from place to place. Or take this example: Three and a half million people bought quarter-inch drills last year. Probably no one really wanted quarter-inch drills. They bought them to make quarter-inch holes. But that wasn't what they wanted either. They wanted the benefit that came from the electric light that resulted from the wire that went through the hole, or the benefit that came from the water in the pipe that went through the hole. And that's why it is always necessary to tie the feature in with a benefit.

6

Neutralize Your Weaknesses

Neutralizers correct or eliminate in the eyes of your customer any real or imaginary weaknesses (Oh-Oh! discriminators) that he attributes to you. There are many sides to a proposition. You put your best foot forward with Aha! discriminators. You know that you cannot make an effective proposal without claiming that your approach has advantages for the customer. But how about any weaknesses, drawbacks, and shortcomings that your customer thinks you have? Of course, it doesn't matter whether or not they are real. All that matters is that the customer thinks you have them. Perceived weaknesses are Ghosts that your competitors can use against you, and these Ghosts can be just as damaging as real problems in your approach (your Oh-Oh! discriminators). Ghosts are even more dangerous when they are brought up by your potential customers.

What happens if you don't address these real (Oh-Oh!) or

imagined (Ghost) weaknesses, drawbacks, and shortcomings? Will you lose points in the customer's evaluation? Will your chances of winning be reduced? Look at it this way: if your customers have concerns about you or your proposals, these concerns are bound to influence their judgments. Until you remove them, they remain factors in the competition. Even if they are only subconscious concerns, they still hurt your chances of winning. If you make a commitment to win, to go all out, then you have to neutralize your customers' fears and biases about you and your proposal. Your customers can't be completely objective about your proposed approaches until you alleviate the real or imagined negative feelings they have about you.

Obviously everyone has weaknesses. Your customers know about many of your weaknesses. They also know about your past failures. In addition, they may have concerns about certain aspects of your approaches. Your competitors, if they do their job right, will make your customers aware of all of the questionable areas of your approaches, as well as any experience or capabilities that you may lack. In the process, they will fabricate a few Ghosts, too. These Ghosts may have no real basis, but you will have to refute them if you are to ensure a win.

Common sense tells you that if you ignore your weaknesses, whether real or perceived, you will hurt your chances of winning. In today's highly competitive market, you can't afford to ignore weaknesses, shortcomings, or drawbacks any more than you can fail to highlight all of your strengths. You must correct the real weaknesses (Oh-Oh!s) so that you can deny them, and you have to bring the imaginary weaknesses (Ghosts) out in the open and dispel them as meaningless concerns. If you ignore your weaknesses, you enter the competition with handicaps, and you can't afford to do that. Even the big boys get hurt when they do.

You lose points by default when you ignore weaknesses and fail to dispel Ghosts. If you ignore them, your customers will have to assume that your supposed weaknesses are real; otherwise, they reason, you would dispel them. Ignoring your weaknesses is also an insult to your customers. Thus you must isolate your weaknesses and evaluate, refute, or deny all of your major Oh-Oh!s and Ghosts. The minor ones that you can't refute or deny, you will have to minimize.

Start by identifying your Oh-Oh! discriminators. Be sure that you address every one, particularly those that are perceived by your customers. A customer may have pointed out some weaknesses already. Others you address because you fear that your competitors may feature them as Ghosts in their proposal. The only weaknesses you can afford to ignore are the insignificant ones—the ones that you are sure your customers won't find out about or otherwise will overlook. But even that is risky, so you have to be extremely confident—and right!—to take this chance and still win.

Once you have identified your weaknesses, you must then neutralize them. Be methodical. Draw up a list of weaknesses, number them, and find a neutralizer for each one. You may discover that you can't neutralize some of your weaknesses because they are not just Ghosts, but real Oh-Oh!s. In those cases, you have to bow out of the competition, take corrective action, or take the chance that they aren't crucial.

The best way to understand how to use neutralizers is to study a few examples based on actual cases. The examples include how to neutralize both real and imaginary weaknesses.

NEUTRALIZING A REAL WEAKNESS

Imagine that you are bidding for a production subcontract from a large aircraft company. The subcontract is for the manufacture of the wing of the airplane that has been developed by the prime aircraft contractor. You have an excellent reputation for producing aircraft structures. In fact, you are outstanding. Your aircraft-structures project engineer also has an excellent reputation according to the prime contractor. But this prime contractor isn't impressed with your corporate management. Your project people have talked with the prime contractor about joint efforts in the past. They convinced him to do business with your company on two previous aircraft programs. But in each case, at the last moment, your corporate headquarters backed down and you had to leave the prime contractor at the altar. In both cases, the contractor had to scramble to find another subcontractor to do the job. The subcontractor didn't do a good job, and the prime contractor holds you partly responsible for that lack of performance. So you have a well-perceived going-in weakness.

YOUR GOING-IN WEAKNESS: The image of your corporate management is low in the eyes of the prime contractor. The customer doesn't trust your corporate management. If you don't correct this situation, you might as well not bid. The weakness is real, not imaginary. This is no Ghost but a bona fide Oh-Oh! You must take specific action before you can neutralize this going-in weakness.

What do you have to work with? Well, for one thing, the prime contractor knows that you are the best in the industry. He also thinks highly of your project engineer. These two strengths provide you with a lot of leverage. You must use this leverage in your neutralizer.

THE NEUTRALIZER: Actually, there is only one way to neutralize this weakness. You must meet it head on and make it the main thrust of your proposal. First, you arrange for one-on-ones between your corporate managers and the customer's corporate managers. You do this before you even start to write the proposal. You failed to win in the past because your corporate management didn't commit itself to the business arrangement at the beginning. Management stood off to the side until the last moment and then stepped in and said, "We don't like it." And that killed it! If you can't get your corporate management to go along with this, don't bid. The prime contractor has had enough of those last minute pullouts. This time he is going to make sure that he isn't left with a poor substitute.

If you can convince your corporate management to structure the business arrangement from the start, you will have overcome this problem. You know before you start to write the proposal that the weakness has been neutralized. Now all you have to do is follow through and verify what you have already agreed on. You can include your corporate management's letters of commitment in your proposal. And to sweeten the pot, you assign your aircraft-structure project engineer—the one the customer admires so much—as the subcontract program director for his wing.

The most important thing that you have to do is to be candid at the beginning of the proposal and state, for example: "We have had an unmistakable pattern of courtship with you on past programs right up to the moment of truth, and then we have let you down. We know that has tarnished our image, and it is understandable and justified. We know the major question in your mind is, 'Why should we go through this whole exercise again?' Well, that's a legitimate position that we understand because it is similar to the same unhappy feelings we've had each time we got to the altar with you in the past, and our corporate management stopped us from going ahead with the marriage. This time we tackled the corporate problem first. This time we zeroed in on what has bothered them in the past. Then we eliminated the problem and got a policy decision for full support. We made sure that management got involved early, that they discussed their concerns with your executive management, and that we had a firm meeting of the minds on policy decisions."

Address your weaknesses honestly and openly. Be candid. In your proposal, state the real feelings that exist in the customer complex. Only when the customer's hopes, fears, and biases are out in the open and realistically answered can your customer objectively consider all the excellent Aha! discriminators that you have going for you.

NEUTRALIZING AN IMAGINARY WEAKNESS

Imagine that you are a nonprofit social club. For twenty-two years you have operated a shooting range on county property. The range is open to the public. You charge your members a small usage fee and the public a larger usage fee. You charge county and city personnel, sheriffs, and policemen a slightly lower fee. Periodically you schedule free shooting clinics for the public and for county personnel. You have a perfect safety record, and you have spent $250,000 to improve the property, landscaping, adding buildings, and upgrading plumbing and lighting.

A commercial contractor who operates a nearby shooting range objects that you have never had any competition. Therefore, you can't be providing the best service. A monoply never does. He says that you overcharge the public. Why should the public have to pay a higher fee than your members do? He says that you have abused your privilege and are taking advantage of the public in order to keep your profits high. In addition, he says that you haven't done anything to improve the range in years.

The commercial contractor wants the shooting range operation put up for bid. The truth is that he wants to close you down because your rates are lower than his, and this is hurting him. He will even buy in for the first year or so to get you out of the business. Then he plans to increase his rates yearly until he is back on a profit basis. He figures that by eliminating you and making the county his captive customer, he will be able to make a bigger profit.

YOUR GOING-IN WEAKNESSES: Your weaknesses are imaginary Ghosts, but they are still formidable. Here is a businessman asking for a chance to compete. What could be more American, more fair? He says that you have a monopoly and that monopolies are always bad, aren't they? You are overcharging the public! That's enough to make everybody mad at you. All this time everyone thought you were a good bunch of people, a nice social club. But you have never had any competition. You have taken advantage of the public without providing good service in return.

Even though none of these accusations is true, each one nevertheless is extremely hard to neutralize. If you can't put these accusations to rest, if you can't expose these Ghosts and dispel them with neutralizers, then you can't win.

What do you have going for you? Well, for one thing, you are now charging the public less than the other contractor's rates at his facility. You must make that come across loud and clear. You aren't in this business for the money; you are nonprofit. And look at all the free clinics you put on. When did your competitor last do that? He would have to charge a fee, wouldn't he? So he hasn't scheduled any clinics.

Isn't the main concern to provide a safe shooting range? And in twenty-two years, you have a perfect safety record. You have the data to prove it too. Compare it with the other contractor's record. You already have him beat on price. If you can also beat him on safety, you will have him on the run. But don't stop there. Don't forget to emphasize that you put $250,000 in improving the property—and at no cost to the county. Make a generous estimate of the number of hours that your club members have donated to the improvements. If you have some old photographs of the property, you can show before-and-after shots to enhance your position even more.

Now that you have taken care of those Ghosts that might have been scaring the public, address the really scary ones, the ones addressed to the county—the customer. The contractor has implied that you have been bilking the county. Go back through your old files and collect all the complimentary letters from the police, sheriffs, and firemen, the letters that praise your free clinics as being the best in the state. Stack your proposal with this evidence. You say, in effect, "This Ghost isn't real. I've done right by the county. Look at the evidence." And then you present the evidence, which is so extensive that the reader finally gives up and says, "What is this other contractor talking about? These guys have been performing beautifully!"

But you aren't through yet. Don't be satisfied only with the neutralizer. Now you must practice the sharpest defense of all: Go on the offensive! You do this by conjuring up your own Ghost, and you make it a scary one. You point out that no commercial contractor can make a profit by bidding lower than you. You tell what your operation would cost if you were a profit organization and had to pay your club members, who now donate their time. You prove that even on the most optimistic basis a commercial contractor couldn't make a profit if he charged what you do. Say it isn't so. Then ask the question, "Why would any contractor want to bid the job at a loss?" You don't even have to provide the answer, but do it anyway. Point out that once you are out of business, the contractor can raise his rates. And where would the county find itself then? You would be out of the picture, and so would those free clinics, the unbeatable safety record, and those low rates.

Now that you have banished all the Ghosts, you can put forth your proposition for continued operation of the shooting range. If you have done your job right up to this point, it should be easy. Your competitive thesis will say:

> WE CAN BEST SERVE YOUR INTEREST AS LEASEE OF THE
> SHOOTING CLUB BECAUSE WE HAVE OPERATED IT FOR
> TWENTY-TWO YEARS IN A TROUBLE-FREE, LOW-COST, SAFE,
> AND RESPONSIVE MANNER.

Your thesis implies that you will continue to operate it this way in the future. And your customer will think twice before he abandons you for your competitor.

NEUTRALIZING REAL AND IMAGINARY WEAKNESSES SIMULTANEOUSLY

Our first two examples dealt with a real (Oh-Oh!) weakness and an imaginary (Ghost) weakness. Rarely are weaknesses that black and white, however. Usually they are mixed—some real, some imaginary, and some a little of both. Let's take a look at a few typical examples.

What do you do if the customer tells one of your marketing people that he doesn't know why you are bidding, that you haven't done this kind of work in the past? There's an easy response to this. You give him data on your experience well before proposal time. You do this through one-on-one contacts. Don't just talk about your experience. Show him pictures of the products. Better yet, let him come see and operate your real hardware. Show him your color-coded mockups. Show him movies of your products performing. Give him tables that list your similar efforts and the dollars and time spent on those efforts. Detail the results, and show him the results before the question of a proposal comes up and the door closes. Then show them to him again in your proposal. By then he expects them, and you simply will be verifying all those things you showed him before he asked questions.

What do you do if you had a tough go with the customer on a related contract? Eventually the contract came out all right. In fact, at the conclusion you actually got back within cost and met the final schedule. But along the way there were some harsh words spoken and many frustrations in addition to a few threats by the customer. How do you address this weakness?

This is more of a Ghost than a real weakness. It is an emotional issue. Although you were dealing with a tough bunch of problems the first time around, you and the customer solved the problems together. This is the main theme of your neutralizer: you and the customer know how to work together. And eventually that led to the two of you meeting the final schedule and cost line. Not only that, but you gained all that technical expertise along the way. If the customer starts all over with someone else, he not only has to learn to work with him, but the other guy has to gain that same experience that you already have. They will have just as hard a time gaining it as you did the first time around. Emphasizing this point to the customer should take care of this Ghost.

You have to handle both of these situations skillfully and candidly. And its's not an easy job. The customer may not like you after you neutralize that Oh-Oh! or kill the Ghost any better than he did before. But getting him to like you isn't the objective. Getting him to select you because your hard-earned experience offers him the most benefits is the real objective.

Here's another example of a neutralizer. What do you do if the customer points out what he regards as a weakness in your approach? He says he doesn't like the location you have selected for your test program. How do you neutralize that weakness? This is both the easiest and the hardest thing to do. First you sit down and try to look at the weakness through his eyes. Why does he feel this way?

If you can't figure out why, don't bid. You don't know enough about the competition to change the customer's mind or to evolve the winning approach. But if you think you know why he doesn't like the test location you selected, you have to make a tough decision. Select another location, one that you know he wants, or try to convince him that you are right in your selection. The latter course is scattered with dead losers and a few brilliant, alive winners. If you decide to convince him that you are right, which means that he is *wrong*, you will have to muster all the skill and polish you possess. More often than not, it will require *more* skill and polish than you possess. So keep in mind that it won't do you any good to be right if you are the loser. You can't help anyone in that role.

The safest course of action is to change your approach to accommodate the customer. You know what he wants, so now all you have to do is try to see things his way. Show him that with his help you are flexible and can compromise. Show him that you can meet him more than halfway. The message here is that not all weaknesses can or should be explained away. Some should be corrected. The important thing is to identify the weakness and then classify it as real or imaginary. If it's real, you have to take corrective action before you can refute it. And that corrective action may mean changing your approach instead of performing tests or analyses to substantiate your original claims.

If you do decide to stick with your approach and go against the customer's hopes, fears, and biases, then give it everything you've got. Don't pussyfoot. Tell the customer that you know he has a real bias, and that he probably would much prefer to see you going his way. After all, that's what your competitors are doing. Get his thoughts out in the open by acknowledging them. Then tell him what benefits you can offer him by adopting his approach. Now plant a Ghost in the middle of all those benefits. Tell him that you know you could probably win if you ignored that Ghost just as your competitors are doing, but you have to be responsible. It is not just a matter of integrity, but a matter of both you and your customer looking bad when the Ghost surfaces. So you, and you alone, have had the courage to go the other way. It is a matter of turning a Ghost or maybe even an Oh-Oh! into an Aha!

Handling an Oh-Oh!—the other guy's Ghost story about you—usually can be accomplished effectively by turning what at first seems to be a weakness into a strength. Ronald Reagan intuitively uses discriminators and Ghost story/Oh-Ohs! to his own benefit. One of his favorite tactics in his political speeches is to refer to his more-than-balanced budget when he was governor of California. One pitch before a Western rural audience went something like this:

> At the end of the year we realized that we had done the impossible, more than balanced the budget, and come up with a surplus. So I called my advisors together and asked them all what we should do with the surplus. Every one of them had something they wanted to spend it on. So I asked them all why we shouldn't just turn the money back to the poor overburdened taxpayer? And they said, "Governor, nobody has ever done that before." And so I said to them all, "Well, no state has ever had an actor for Governor before either." (Thunderous applause.)

He very effectively turned the other guy's Ghost story about him into his own Aha!

HOW SOME OTHER GUYS USE NEUTRALIZERS

Neutralizers are used extensively every day in marketing. Rather than presenting all the merits of a product, companies will often create a Ghost that their competitors will be forced to neutralize. Never underestimate the damage that a Ghost can do, even if it's an imaginary one. Take the example of the American Express television commercials, those "don't-leave-home-without-them" ads. American Express implied that people who lose travelers' checks may not be able to get a refund on their checks if they were bought from the competition.

Perhaps the competition ignored the ads and underestimated the power of the Ghost. Perhaps they thought the public wouldn't react to the Ghost. But the public did, and it expected someone to dispel the Ghost. When no one provided a neutralizer, the public started to believe that the Ghost was real. The public expects to hear all sides of the story. If you don't make the effort to neutralize all adverse claims, the public will assume that the claims are true and the problem is real. If your customers think you have a weakness, you do have one until you convince them otherwise. You must neutralize the customer's concerns or lose the argument by default. And that's just what American Express' competitors found out. The Ghost hurt them and they lost business. They realized that the Ghost had created a real problem, and they had to neutralize it in order to compete.

One competitor took out full-page advertisements in papers such as the *New York Times*, the *Washington Post*, and *The Wall Street Journal* to advise: "Don't leave home without all the facts." It told the public that it would refund its money, and do it quickly, on all lost travelers' checks, just like American Express would. In fact, it even sounded indignant that American Express would even hint that only it would refund money for lost travelers' checks. Well, American Express modified its ad and the competitor polished his, and peace returned to the business of selling travelers' checks. But to this day, to some degree, the competitor will pay for not having neutralized that Ghost more promptly.

You can never afford to ignore a weakness, whether real or imaginary. Any mistake that you make is visible to the public and to your customers. You must take action to neutralize weaknesses or suffer the consequences. Remember the Firestone 500, the radial tire that had major performance problems? After a number of accidents related to the Firestone 500, the government got into the act and forced Firestone to recall the tire. There was a lot of publicity, all of it unfavorable. And that spawned more fears and biases that Firestone makes poor products.

Firestone didn't ignore this weakness for very long. It knew this was a threat to its future. It was a real weakness that had to be neutralized if Firestone was to stay in business. So it hired movie star Jimmy Stewart, a bona fide Straight Arrow, a true Good Guy, and launched a big TV advertising campaign for a new radial tire, the Firestone 721. It had all of the good features of the 500, but it had none of the weaknesses. Its safety and performance was guaranteed and backed up with a warranty. Well, the public didn't bite all at once, but slowly it came around. Firestone had a long way to go, but it got to work and tried to correct the problems and neutralize its bad image. If Firestone hadn't dealt with that weakness, it could have found itself out of business. It makes no difference what the product is—high technology, low technology, or no-technology. You have to deal with any weakness, and you have to take steps to neutralize it quickly.

McDonnell-Douglas Aircraft found that out when an American Airlines' DC-10 crashed near Chicago in the summer of 1979. It was a tragic accident, and many people were killed. For days, the stories of the crash dominated the front pages of the newspapers. The crash also was the main story and feature item on TV news. Everyone talked about the DC-10 crash, and out of all of this came a weakness that compromised the future of the DC-10 and McDonnell-Douglas. Many stories were circulated that hinted the DC-10 was unsafe, and many people became convinced.

The press didn't help McDonnell-Douglas either. There were stories about design deficiencies and other fundamental aircraft problems. Cartoonists picked it up too. One showed aircraft executives saying the DC-10 was sound, while in the background an engine fell off as a mechanic tightened a nut.

Even the airlines contributed to the problem: Those who didn't own DC-10s openly advertised the fact.

Never had such an established, reputable contractor taken such a beating. McDonnell-Douglas never fought back. It never launched an all-out campaign to neutralize the weakness that resulted from the crash. It claimed that the Chicago DC-10 crash was the result of maintenance procedures that American Airlines used, and this was supported by the government's investigation. But the DC-10 never did get a convincing bill of health. Perhaps the company was afraid it would injure its relations with its customers or with the government. Perhaps there were other reasons that stemmed from the lawsuits surrounding the crash. Whatever the reason, many people feel that the DC-10 was never vindicated.

How much in the way of future sales of DC-10s did McDonnell-Douglas lose? We will never know. But no one will dispute that it hurt the company a great deal. And some will always wonder why an all-out effort wasn't mounted to refute the fears and concerns that resulted from the crash. One might have expected full-page ads, sophisticated, well-thought-out ads designed to restore the public's faith in the aircraft. To many, it looked like a missed opportunity. Except for a few character statements by Pete Conrad, the silence was ominous. Even the airlines were silent. There are reasons, of course, and no doubt history will sort it out.

Most companies don't ignore weaknesses and Ghosts. Some aggressively address every possible customer concern. We see some excellent neutralizers in advertisements. Take the case of Volkswagen, a leading small car manufacturer. It refuted its apparent weakness of its Rabbit's lack of space. Many people thought that this little car, like all little cars, would be uncomfortable and crowded. But the company neutralized this concern by showing a very big basketball player climbing into the car with space to spare. Not only did the company neutralize this Ghost/Oh-Oh! but it went so far as to turn an apparent weakness into a strength.

The company claimed that the car had more headroom than a popular big car—the plushest of the plush. And it claimed an advantage over every imported car in its class. The only substantiation it provided for these claims was showing the basketball player getting out of the car. But that was obviously enough. After all, that basketball player is a pretty big guy!

Avis brilliantly turned being second into "We try harder." And Honeywell talked about being the "other" computer company. Goodrich poked fun at not being the guy with the blimp, and it kept its name (and perhaps its tires) in the public's eye. And the Bell Telephone folks remind us that "the System's the solution," and that it's not what the telephone looks like, but what's inside it that counts. All of these companies started with a fundamental understanding of the Ghost/Oh-Oh! Then they creatively neutralized it.

Just in case you missed a subtlety about Ghost/Oh-Oh!s and the importance of developing a neutralizer, let's reiterate: Ghosts don't have to be *true*; they only have to be *believed* by your customers. If they are believed by your customers, or, perhaps more important, if there is any reason to believe that they *could* be believed, they have to be identified, acknowledged, held up to the light of day, and dispelled. You don't do this by adopting an attitude of "the customer is dumb; it just isn't so." Instead, you have to listen to the customer. Acknowledge his hopes, fears, and biases. Then neutralize them.

7

Counter Your Competitor's Strengths

Whenever you enter a competition, you must be prepared to present more than just your side of the story. Otherwise you will be competing only partway. Featuring your strengths is one of the most important aspects in positioning to win. If you have no strengths to feature, you aren't a viable competitor. To compete, you must have a sound going-in approach. And to determine how sound your approach is, you must look at the other side of the coin—the claims that are being made by your competitor. You should begin by analyzing your competitor's claims to determine how valid your approaches are. This is an essential step in evolving the superior approach. Furthermore, this analysis allows you to compete more effectively on another front: You then can counter these claims.

Figure 7-1 shows how you can classify and evaluate your competitor's claims so that you can determine what actions you will have to take against them. Competitor's claims fall into two categories: (1) those that are similar to your own, the common, garden-variety claims, and (2) those that are unique

FIGURE 7-1. COUNTER YOUR COMPETITOR'S CLAIMS TO MINIMIZE HIS STRENGTHS

COMPETITOR'S CLAIM	Common Claim	Unique Claim	Conceded Claim	Overstated Claim	ACTION AGAINST CLAIM (COUNTER/GHOST)
All the components of our bottling machine are completely proven.		X		X	Not true: The feed system is in development, and it's a high-risk item. Moreover, it is well known in the industry that they are having trouble with it. We need a strong counter. Jim Jones by the 5th of May.
Our innovative control system is not only completely automated, it is also capable of continuous fault isolation.		X	X		Many electronic control boards are required and these are hard to come by, hence expensive. We need a ghost story to that effect. Mary Brown by the 5th of May.
We can have the unit fully validated two weeks early.	X		X		So can we. Lee White by 3rd of May.
We have many satisfied customers.	X		X		So do we. Lee White.
Our manager is experienced.	X		X		So is ours. Lee White.

to your competitor. In evaluating a competitor's claim you either concede it as true or attack it as untrue. Obviously, you will concede garden-variety claims. They are not the discriminators in the competition. Unique claims are the ones that are a major concern because they will be used by your competitor as Aha! discriminators.

If you think that you may lose the competition, you may have found the reason why in your competitor's unique claims. So you will have to try to shift your customer's perception of these into the overstated, untrue category if you can. If you can't, you will have to make sure that you have enough offsetting strengths to win. When you find common or unique competitor's claims that are either overstated or untrue, you have the opportunity to compete more effectively. Indeed, you owe it to your prospective customer to expose or counter your competitor's overstated or untrue claims.

It is naive to turn your back and hope that a good fairy will come along and reveal an overstated or untrue claim to the customer. If you are truly going to compete, it's up to you to reveal your competitor's hollow claims. If the competitor says his bottling machine is completely proven, but you know that the feed system is not, expose that fact. In your proposal, say that you considered the same feed mechanism but turned it down because it had never been proven. And then reveal the results of your analysis in painstaking detail. If your competitor has left his feed-system claim unprotected, you can discredit him, and not just with the feed system. When you undermine one claim, the customer will begin to wonder about all of the competitor's claims.

You want to bring out all of the questionable aspects of the competitor's claims even when they relate to his unquestionable strengths. If the competitor says his control system is completely automated and capable of not only controlling the operation but also of doing continuous fault isolation—and you have to concede this—you still look for negative aspects that can influence the evaluation of that control system. Even though the claim may be 100-percent true, there may be other factors, such as the availability, reliability, or cost of the electronic systems that make up the control system, factors that cancel or at least compromise the advantages of the system itself. These you subtly reveal with Ghosts.

Again, you might say that you considered an automated control system with fault isolation features, but your analysis showed that the number of electronic subsystems required were increased an order of magnitude. Develop this point and substantiate it. Then drop the bomb by saying that the number of electronic subsystems in itself isn't bad, but what about the availability of high-quality systems? And you agree with the customer that risk avoidance is the number one priority. Therefore, you opted for the proven mechanical system that everyone knows works. But you made it even more efficient and less risky by adding your own features. Then tell how your features will benefit the customer.

Don't think that this tactic is underhanded and questionable. You can use it only when your claim is valid. You will hurt yourself if you raise obviously invalid counter-arguments. But the world is rarely black or white. A good unanswered Ghost can surely change the customer's perception of the competition's Aha! discriminator. If you act in good faith and at least present the other side of his argument, you won't get hurt. If you and your competitors compete to the hilt in this manner, the validated superior approach will be selected.

Counters are theses directed at the competitor's overstated or inaccurate Aha! discriminators. Of all of the influencers, the counter is the riskiest and the most difficult to carry off. It is risky because it takes the competitor's strengths head on. You are in essence attempting to prove that the competitor's claims are inflated or wrong. You are trying to keep him honest. If you succeed, you make it impossible for the competitor to win, for without Aha!s he can't establish benefits to the customer.

Before going further, let's take a careful look at the differences between the bold counter and the more conventional feature and neutralizer.

COUNTER YOUR
COMPETITOR'S
STRENGTHS

It's obvious that if you are going to win you have to feature your strong points (Aha! discriminators) in relation to your competitor's weak points (Ghost discriminators). Winners have always used their strengths to attack the losers' weaknesses. If you don't have those strengths and can't find the competitor's weakness, it will be very difficult, or even impossible, to win. And while you are in the process of clobbering the competition, you had better be able to protect against your own weaknesses by neutralizing your Oh-Oh! discriminators. Otherwise you might get clobbered while you are looking for that little chink in the competitor's armor.

We have just described the typical competitive scenario: one competitor attempting to exploit his strengths against another competitor's weaknesses. The goal—to win the battle. The classic example is the boxer competing against the brawler. The boxer attempts to score points with technique and quickness while exploiting the brawler's lack of style and speed. The brawler, on the other hand, moves in steadily, attempting to end it with one explosive punch. The one who gets the most out of his Aha!s while covering up his Oh-Oh!s will be the winner.

But occasionally we see that explosive show in which someone comes directly at his opponent's strengths. He attacks them head on and destroys not only the strengths, but the offensive thrust. He disarms the opponent and in the process destroys him. We see it almost every Sunday in the fall when one football team stops another team's supposedly unstoppable running game. The opponent fumbles the ball, drops punts, and falls down in his own end zone. The winner never mounts an offense at all. He doesn't have to because his defense crushes the opponent's strength. Or how about the puncher with the iron jaw who gets knocked out with the first punch? Or the runner with the sprint who is outsprinted in the final stretch?

These are examples of countering the competitor's strength. Perhaps in football, boxing, and running there is little finesse and a total lack of planning. Most of the time it just happens. But in business competition the counter is a calculated step. When it works, it can be even more dramatic than the most exciting football game. You are meeting the competition on his field, selecting his weapons, and trying to beat him at his own game. That's a big order, and not too many succeed at it. Yet the leverage is so great and the payoff so good that you dare not overlook the counter.

The payoff of a successful counter is tremendous. You succeed in discrediting your competitor. The risk is tremendous, too, because a counter, unlike a Ghost, claims the competitor's approach is invalid. If you are wrong, or more important, if the customer perceives you as wrong, the counter backfires. The prospective customer will adopt a critical view of you and your Aha! discriminators. He will think that you tried to fool him, and he will dig hard to find mistakes in your approaches. The customer would like to think you objectively made trade studies and looked at all possibilities. In selecting your approach you should have eliminated the competitor's approaches because he was either faulty (Oh-Oh!/Ghost) or you had a better approach (Aha!). But if your counter backfires, you will actually make the competitor's approach look even better.

A FEW EXAMPLES

The best way to get a handle on counters is to look at some examples.

Example 1: Your Competitor Is the Best in the Business

Imagine that you are in the decorating business and a large clothing firm has asked you and a competitor to submit a proposal on redoing its sales room. The customer wants you to patch the walls, put in new molding, and paint the room. He also wants you to select the color and type of paint for the walls. The competition will be based on craftsmanship, aesthetics, quality of the patchwork and molding, and color and quality of the paint.

Your competitor is the best in the business. He has the best plaster people and the best molding craftspeople. He also has in stock high-quality paint that he bought at a reasonable price before the price inflated to its present prohibitively high level. You strongly suspect that your competitor will propose using that paint and cost it out at a reasonable price, below the current market value, just to ensure a win. In fact, his salespeople talk openly about this.

Your plaster and molding people are good, but they are by no means as good as your competitor's. But because your people are less experienced, you don't have to pay them as much as the competitor must pay his. Therefore, you have the potential for being lower in price if you propose a paint that cost no more than the competitor's high-quality paint.

Given this information, draw up a list of influencers for your proposal. Your list will probably include the following:

1. Your strength will be your low cost.
2. Your weakness will be the lower quality of your paint and the lesser capabilities of your workers.
3. Your competitor's strength will be his higher-quality paint and his outstanding craftspeople.
4. His weakness will be a higher price. How much higher depends on how far down you feel you can drop in paint quality without discrediting yourself.

From these proposal influencers, your competitive thesis will be: **Adequate Quality for Lowest Cost.**

Your competitor's competitive thesis will be: **Best Quality for Affordable Cost.**

From the competitive theses, it appears that you will be waging an uphill battle, particularly if you and your competitor pursue the competition in the conventional manner of featuring each of your strengths and the other's weaknesses while neutralizing each of your own weaknesses. The deciding factor is price versus quality. You will refute the claim that you are weak in quality by saying yours is adequate; your competitor will refute the claim that he is weak in price by saying his is affordable. The outcome in this competition is in doubt. It could go either way.

You would like a surer path to winning. So before you go off the deep end, you investigate the bold approach—countering your competitor's strength. On the face of it, it still looks like a losing battle. Your investigation reveals that without a doubt the competitor's paint is the best quality and far superior to what you can afford to buy for a similar price today. The competitor's paint goes on easier, spreads smoother, never flakes, keeps its shine, and lasts forever. Furthermore, you verify that your competitor's craftspeople are indeed as good as he claims they are. At first glance, the competitor's strengths appear to be rock solid.

But what about the color of your competitor's paint— RED! Is that the right color? Check it out and do some homework. All of a sudden you have found a counter. Red is the wrong color for a sales room! You have data from a government study that show the color red inhibits sales. People buy more when they are surrounded by cooler colors. Pastels are the best. And you know that you can buy quality pastel paint at a reasonable price.

You now have an option. You can abandon the conventional feature/neutralizer approach for the bolder counter approach. If you can pull off the counter approach, you can win the competition. You will have discredited your competitor's approach. The customer will select you before he ever gets to the point of examining the feature and neutralizer influencers. It's a bold move, but it's better than the alternative, a conventional-win approach. You have good counter influencers that your competitor doesn't know about. You catch him completely by surprise. So you change your competitive thesis to: **Because we thoroughly researched your requirements, instead of using an inappropriate paint, we offer a low-cost decorating approach that actually will increase your sales!**

Wow! This counter has everything. It's loaded with discriminators, Ghosts, and Aha!s It starts out with three Ghosts that are aimed at discrediting the competitor. By saying that you researched the customer's requirements, you plant the Ghost that the customer didn't. You then imply, again through Ghosts, that the competitor is pushing his available stock onto the customer. Not only that, but he will use a color of paint that actually inhibits sales. Considering that the competitor is going to feature that red paint for all it's worth—and you have made sure it isn't worth anything—you actually have your competitor working for you. He is cutting his own throat. When he proudly says that his warehouse is full of the stuff, he's actually verifying your competitive thesis. And since he never addresses the suitability of his red paint—because he never thought of checking it out—he comes across as trying to pull the wool over the eyes of the customer. Now, having completely discredited the competitor's approach, you calm the shocked customer by telling him everything is okay. The fact of the matter is that you can give him a low-cost alternative. In addition, it will actually increase his sales.

Then you substantiate your claims. You parade out the government study that shows the color red inhibits sales and that pastels are conducive to sales. Obviously you win. You win because you countered the competitor's approach, stopped it dead in its tracks. Then you roll out your approach. When divided by zero, your approach is infinitely better than your competitor's.

Example 2: You Are the Best in the Business

Let's use the same okay/low-cost approach versus the best/ affordable-cost approach in another example.

Imagine that you are in the missile business and you have the best missile at affordable cost. Your competitor has the adequate missile at a lower cost. At least that's what he claims. And he has a good approach considering that your customer is a tightwad.

You know you have the best missile. Not only is it the best, but it's the most modern in design. The other guy's design is sloppy and not nearly so efficient. It bugs you that you have to compete with this guy on a conventional features/ neutralizers basis. Besides that, you can't figure out why his inefficient design can be lower in cost than your efficient, well-designed missile. Then it dawns on you that maybe this guy doesn't have a lower-cost missile. Maybe his going-in approach is a low-cost come-on and nothing more. Maybe his missile costs just as much or more than yours does. It's worth a try, so you check it out.

You start out by counting the parts on your missile and your competitor's. After all, you both have displays and mock-ups all over the country. It's easy to figure out the subsystems that make up the whole. And if you don't know all the details of the subsystems, your engineering and systems people can figure out what it takes to make them work. When all else fails, you can always call the vendors who supply the pieces. One way or another, you add it all up and, surprise of surprises, your efficient missile actually has fewer parts than the competitor's supposedly less expensive missile.

Now you swing into action full force. You look at each system one by one. You perform an economic analysis of each and every piece. You figure out machine time, assembly time, checkout time, and test time. As you do this, you begin to see a solid story of deception unfolding. The other guys' missile is actually *more* expensive than yours. So now you have the best of all possible worlds: you can win both ways. First, you pull out the props from under the competitor by countering his strengths. Once you have discredited his claim of having a lower-cost missile, you parade out your strengths. And since there never has been any contest as to who had the best performance, you win, hands down.

Example 3: You and Your Competitor Are Equal
So far we have used examples of a service and a high-technology item. Now let's look at an ordinary item, one from a real-world advertisement.

The cheapie, also ran razor-blade maker takes on the established leader in the razor-blade field by attempting to counter the leader's quality claim. He does it by setting up a test in which several men are shaved with the two competing blades. Then they are asked if there is any difference between the shaves they got from the two blades. Naturally they say, "No difference." In fact, they actually *sing* it. That's supposed to be a counter! Then they follow up the counter by featuring their low, low cost. They sum this up by singing, "Big difference!" No difference when it comes to quality, but a big difference when it comes to cost.

Actually this is a weak counter. There is no evidence establishing that the cheapie's quality is any better than that of the established leader's. You get a fleeting glance of a few smiling guys rubbing their faces, then some music and singing. From this performance, you're supposed to believe that the cheapie is better. Pretty thin. But at least it gets some new customers who periodically check it out. They may go back to the established leader after a brief try with the cheapie. But, you know, that cheapie blade isn't all that bad, and it does cost less!

Now go back and look at the counter that was used by Firestone in Chapter 1, the one where it looked the leader's car battery offer right in the eye and said it was second best. By now you should have the idea. Whether or not you are aggressive enough to use counters, you should at least do some preliminary groundwork and check them out. You may find an easy path to a win!

8

Exploit Your Customer's Hopes, Fears, and Biases

No matter how sophisticated a market is, there is an emotional side to every competition and to every sales effort. Logic has little to do with emotions. In fact, the emotional aspects of the competition are sometimes contrary to logic, but they are every bit as important. So while you address the logical side of the competition by featuring your strengths and your competitor's weaknesses, by countering your competitor's strengths and neutralizing your own weaknesses, you also address the emotional side of the competition by exploiting your customer's hopes, fears, and biases.

Exploiters are theses that include claims and substantiation of how your approaches address the emotional aspects of the competition. They also include Ghost stories, which you use to point up the deficiencies in your competitor's approaches. On the one hand, you appeal to the customer's Straight Arrow logic by showing how your approach will dispel his concerns. On the other hand, you appeal to his Little Boy hopes, play on his fears, and address his biases in order to show him why he should select you rather than a competitor. If you do this effectively, he will begin to think he'll have problems if he goes with anyone but you.

Your customers know their business better than you or anyone else, so their opinions and prejudices, based on past experiences, are well worth considering. Their fears and concerns result from past failures and problems as well as concerns about the future. You can't exploit these worries without considering them and incorporating them into your approaches. This is simply another way of evolving a superior approach, one that offers the customer the benefit he seeks. Every customer wants to be relieved of his worries and concerns. Every customer wants to feel that he is in good hands, that the people he is dealing with are concerned with his best interests.

You should never underestimate the strength of an emotional bias. The emotional aspects of all competitions are extremely important; indeed, they are probably overriding. If your strengths don't reassure your customer, you are in trouble. And if what you perceive as your competitor's weaknesses are of no concern to the customer, you have missed the boat. Weaknesses don't exist unless they are perceived to be real by the customer or the competitor. Your feelings don't count. Understanding that is essential in responding to your customer as well as in countering your competitor.

Whenever you neutralize your weaknesses, you have to do it in response to what your customer feels. You may have to spend a great deal of effort in neutralizing what to you is a minor concern. It may even be meaningless to you. But somehow you must relate your approach to that concern. If you do this well, your approach will still appeal to your customer even though he may be nagged by that concern. Likewise, when you counter your competitor's strength, you do so relative to the customer's hopes, fears, and biases. If you can show that your competitor's features do not respond to these emotions, you have come a long way toward countering those features.

In the aerospace industry, a proposal meets some very complex customers, and if it didn't exploit the hopes, fears, and biases of these customers, it wouldn't be able to deal with the other complexities either. More than one major program has been sold because a proposal contained a fundamental understanding of the interservice rivalries and career objectives of certain strong personalities. The strategy behind a proposal may boil down to fundamental motivations, such as, "General, do you want to keep pace with Charlie in your career? Then let's get this new show on the road or he is going to be fielding that competing weapon system before you do." Or, "Admiral, if you fiddle around much longer deciding on whether to go ahead on this program, the Air Force will force its solution down your throat." This may seem like an unhealthy way to build an inventory, but it has been the basis for a new weapons system more than once.

Everyone has noticed how at certain times this country discovers a major flaw in its defense. We had a missile gap, a second-best position in space, a megatonnage gap. We discovered a new threat and we were concerned that we had no response. Exploiters were at work. Soon we had new requirements, new funded studies, and shortly thereafter a rush to build hardware.

Exploiters are candid. It used to be that taking the competition on in head-to-head battle was a no-no. But not anymore. If you swing from the hip, your exploiter can be a more deadly weapon than your most outstanding feature. Remember, your customer's hopes, fears, and biases are real ones and thus the only ones that matter.

HOW EXPLOITERS WORK

The copy of the advertisement in Figure 8-1 implies that subcompacts are not particularly safe. It doesn't substantiate that claim. That is left up to the vivid imagination of the reader, and in this case it is more effective than spelling it out. The ad shows a monstrous truck bearing down on a little subcompact trying to enter the traffic lane. Everyone has been in that situation at one time or another, either as a driver or passenger. That giant truck is always a menacing sight, and the thought of it flattening you always flashes through your mind.

If this were your ad, you shouldn't stop with the photograph and the unsubstantiated accident-statistics claim. Add some text to it. Point out that you put a much higher premium on safety than you do on saving gasoline. If you were a timid subcompact competitor, you would complain that that was a low blow! But it's a very effective line. Your ad could go on to tell how strong your big car is and how your big strong car not

FIGURE 8-1. BIG CAR'S EXPLOITER OF DRIVER'S FEARS

IS IT WORTH RISKING YOUR LIFE FOR 45 MILES PER GALLON?

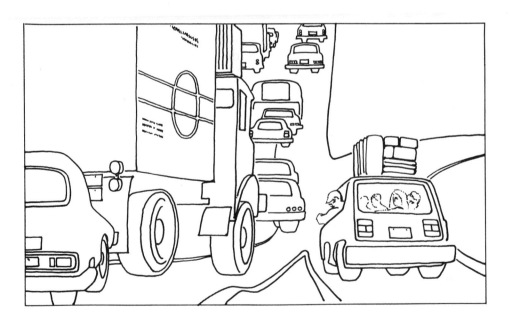

She's Dying and No One Knows It

CALL NOW:

The "HELP ME" System

only saves gas but also can save lives. Now, when the customer goes to see the subcompact dealer, he will ask him
questions about safety. He may still like the subcompact, but
he might go and take a look at that big car too.

Some companies use *only* exploiters to sell their products.
Often they never even bother with features, counters, and
neutralizers. Instead, they just appeal to the emotions of the
customer, to his hopes and fears. Look at Figure 8-2. This
advertisement plays on the fear of potential disaster for that
crippled loved one who just might not be able to get to the
phone in time: "Your loved one is dying and no one knows
it." What a Ghost! Death itself! And if you don't do something
about it, your loved one just might be the poor woman in the
ad! But you can relieve yourself of that concern with the
"Help Me" system. What a relief! Now if you aren't too

shocked at the cost, everything will be okay. You will be buying peace of mind, actually the same peace of mind that you had before you read the ad. And your loved one will have another electronic gadget for protection. The questions of whether or not your loved one will know how to use the system or whether help will get there in time go unanswered. But you have done everything you can to protect that loved one from disaster.

Notice that the ad tells you nothing about the features of the "Help Me" system. You don't know how big it is, how it works, how much it costs, or whether it's reliable. How long will it operate between failures? What is the difference in fatalities for people owning the "Help Me" system over those who didn't have one? Maybe the company has good answers to all these questions. When you go to look at the system, ask the salesperson.

Don't be afraid to use exploiters. Exploiting customer concerns is almost the sole basis of marketing in certain fields. Without exploiting concerns, the insurance business might fold. For the most part, insurance companies don't bother with features: they just go after your fears and concerns. Look at Figure 8-3 for an example of how they do it: "Don't risk your family's future." "Oh no," you say, "I didn't know that I *was* risking its future." But by the time you have read the ad, you realize that without buying insurance you really *are* gambling with your family's future. So, just like with the "Help Me" system, you put your mind at ease and buy the insurance. Putting your mind at ease might be worth every penny, too. However, you don't know any of the details of the insurance plans. You don't know how good the company is. Nothing in the ad has been substantiated. It presents no record of accomplishments. The ad does nothing but scare the hell out of you so that you'll buy the company's insurance.

EXPLOIT THE CUSTOMER'S HOPES

Exploiters work on more than just fears. They also deal with hopes. Some appeal to desires for good feelings, like those for

FIGURE 8-3. LIFE INSURANCE COMPANIES EXPLOIT THE
FEAR OF FUTURE FAMILY SECURITY

111

EXPLOIT THE
CUSTOMER'S
HOPES

Don't gamble

Get protection

XYZ
LIFE INSURANCE COMPANY

recreation and adventure, and they do so on a high plane.
There are some very good examples of ad campaigns that play
to the whole gamut of customers' hopes. For example, exploiters are always used in travel ads. And the messages are
beautifully simple. The country, the city, or the island is the
implementing feature. The picture in the ad shows the tran-
quillity or the excitement you will experience when you ar-

rive. All you have to see is the name of the place—Aruba, Mexico, Paris, the Orient. Just glance at the name and the picture and you get the message. Then if you are thinking of taking a trip, you are ready to listen to more.

Some advertisements simply relate the place to some beautiful activity: "Sail in the Caribbean!" "Explore the mysteries of the Orient!" What you get here is more of that same message. Each message appeals to a sense of adventure. Each is a variation on a simple theme. The feature is still the place. After all, there is only one Mexico and only one Paris. The activity is the exploiter.

Exploiters can be subtle too. Suppose you are putting together an ad for the luxurious bathroom fixtures that your company, XYZ, makes. Your message is, "Buy XYZ fixtures if you want a luxurious bathroom." You might present the benefit as an obviously happy, healthy, squeaky-clean young woman. The features would be the designs and know-how of XYZ. You illustrate these features as the key pieces of art in your ad. Use photographs, not drawings, because they provide believable substantiation. If these designs are appealing to potential customers, you have your exploiter. But don't stop there. Make your message "luxury." Say it over and over—luxury, luxury, luxury! In between, use words like dazzle, graceful, delicate, beautiful, flattering, fashionable, fine, famous. Get the message? These are exploiters at work.

Exploiters also can be dynamic. If you were selling water skis, your ad might show a water skier making a fantastic turn. The benefit would be performance; the feature would be your high-quality ski because it permits skiers to perform so well. If you do it right, your equipment will be seen as essential to anyone who wants to ski like the guy in the ad. The photo substantiates your claim of superior performance.

EXPLOIT THE CUSTOMER'S EMOTIONS

Let's finish our discussion of exploiters by pointing out how they appeal to sensations such as taste or sight. Actually, the key to the exploiter is the tie between benefit and feature. The message might be one of simple satisfaction. A photo of a smiling girl with a cold drink presents satisfied taste as the benefit; the can of soft drink is the implementing feature. It says, "Cheer up, Drink up." If you are hot or thirsty, satisfying that thirst may be your number-one desire at the moment. Likewise, a smiling grandmother talking to her grandchild on the phone presents the phone as the implementing feature and happiness as the benefit.

Now what does all of this have to do with proposals? Everything! It opens up a completely new world of competitive tools. If you have been staggering along without considering your customer's hopes, you haven't been making the most of what you have to offer. You may be losing just because you haven't considered all of the factors in the competition.

Look at the influencers we presented in previous chapters. They are loaded with emotion as well as logic. For instance, look at Figure 4-2 in Chapter 4. Each of the influencers in Figure 4-2 is a combination of an exploiter and some other influencer, either a feature, neutralizer, or counter. For instance, when you talk about your innovative approach having a big pay-off potential, something you know the customer is interested in, you are simultaneously presenting a strength feature while playing on the customer's hopes for a breakthrough. That is the value of the exploiter concept.

If there is no exploiter in a feature, neutralizer, or counter, you might as well give up. You are wasting your time and valuable space in your proposal by cluttering it up with meaningless influencers. Influencers are meaningless unless they appeal to the customer's emotions. So that opens up yet another challenge in proposal development and marketing. You have the opportunity to expand the customer's perceptions of influencers by exploiting his hopes, fears, and biases during the competition. You don't have to accept the rules of the game when you go into the competition. At this point, the rules are far upstream of the Request For Proposal. But you can affect the evaluation criteria, if you are in early enough, by influencing the customer's perceptions. You must be disciplined in doing this, however, and keep the real benefits to the customer foremost in your mind.

This is what we mean when we say that in positioning to win it is just as important, and maybe more so, to substantiate your benefits as your features. If you do a good job of this and communicate with the customer at every step, you will be playing to a modified set of perceptions, different from those the competitors are addressing. You will be addressing current perceptions, the ones you brought about, while the competitors will be addressing those now-outdated going-in perceptions. That opens up a whole new world of marketing potential for you. If you are disciplined in your approach, you are positioning to win.

Before you leave the Figure 4-2, run through all of the influencers and note the hopes, fears, and biases that go with each of the strengths and weaknesses. When we talk about costs, we touch on strong emotions. Risks bring out strong fears as well as biases. Past performance affects the customer's perceptions of you; therefore, you have to deal with them in detail, and you have to neutralize them so that they won't bias the evaluators against you. Unfavorable images bring out biases that may be decisive if exploited to the hilt. Overstating claims of strengths certainly brings on strong biases. And finally, the ambitions of the customer must be recognized and considered in your approaches.

When you use exploiters, you have to be right; otherwise you can get hurt. The best thing that can happen to you in such a case is that you just waste dollars and get nothing in return. The worst is that you bring about your own defeat.

9

Evolve the Superior Approach with Competitive Convergence

Remember, every competition begins by discriminating—by identifying and classifying the influencers in the competition. First, you list all of your strengths and weaknesses as well as your competitor's as perceived by the customer. You then put these discriminators to work by:

- Featuring your unique strengths and your competitor's unique weaknesses
- Neutralizing and refuting your weaknesses
- Countering your competitor's strengths
- Paying special attention to your customer's hopes, fears, and biases and exploiting them with approaches designed to satisfy and accommodate them

Obviously this approach is designed to make the most of what you have to offer. It forces you to identify the strengths and

116

EVOLVE THE
SUPERIOR
APPROACH WITH
COMPETITIVE
CONVERGENCE

weaknesses of your going-in approaches relative to your competitor's approaches. You know what to feature, what to neutralize, and what to counter. But this approach does something else too, something that isn't quite so obvious but is even more important than making the most of what you have to offer. It forces you to evolve a superior approach, to change your going-in approach to one that is clearly better than your competitor's.

Evolving a superior approach requires discipline. And inherent in this discipline is a crystal-clear comparison of how you stack up to your competitor. It provides absolute visibility of the relative value of your approach. If your approach isn't superior, it will be obvious. And once it's obvious, you have to do something about it. Knowing that your approach is inferior is the first step to evolving a superior approach. In fact, it is the foundation of competitive convergence.

We defined competitive convergence earlier, but let's give it a review. Competitive convergence is the process of evolving your going-in approach to the approach that is superior to your competitors' approaches. It involves determining the customer's perspectives and substituting them for your own, and it requires that you examine all of your claims to see if they can be substantiated. If you can't substantiate your claims, you will have to find different ones that you can support. Maybe—probably—you will have to modify your design or approach so that your claims become bulletproof and your design fulfills the desires of your customer. This is the continuous evolution toward an eventual winner.

In this chapter, we will detail how you can substantiate your claims. First, we will look at the fundamentals upon which competitive convergence is based. Second, we will drive the process home with a simple but highly revealing example. Third, we will follow that up with some discussion of real-world examples of competitive convergence. And finally, we will discuss how all this will affect your future marketing efforts.

The fundamental key to providing a winning approach is to give your customers what benefits them, not just what you think they should have. This requires that you be objective and look at the proposal through the eyes of your customer. Keep in mind that at this point your customer has little idea of what you have to offer. So, except in rare cases, you will have to evolve your perceived going-in approaches to those that will coincide with your customer's. To develop features that implement winning benefits, you have to follow a disciplined procedure that permits you to select unique approaches. In selecting winning features, you have to establish and maintain interchanges with your customer at all levels. And for those interchanges to be effective, you must never close your mind to your customer's requirements.

Turn off your filters and put your personal preferences aside. This is particularly difficult for technically oriented people and for organizations that offer a product or service that dominates the marketplace. If you have developed a product or service that comes close to fitting your customer's needs, you may begin to obscure his real requirements. To the objective third party, there will be obvious differences between in-house concepts of the product or service and the customer's needs. If you have developed in-house concepts, you may see only those factors that satisfy the requirements. Don't be blind to shortcomings. Listen to your customer and respond to his needs.

Why do you have to select the approaches that benefit your customers? Look at it this way. You and your competitors may be trying to sell the same things to a particular customer. Each of your approaches will be different. All the approaches probably have some good, valid benefits, but the customer will usually select only one. The customer wants the best—the best for the customer. And from the customer's standpoint, the best is the one with the approaches that implement the most benefits for him.

118

EVOLVE THE
SUPERIOR
APPROACH WITH
COMPETITIVE
CONVERGENCE

Another fundamental that you should recognize is that your customer knows his business better than you do. It is the height of marketing arrogance—or brilliance—to believe that you know more about his business than he does. Most of the time, what benefits the customer and what he wants are one and the same. In rare instances you can scoop the market and move from tenth place to first place in one fell swoop by convincing the customer that what he wants and what he needs are two different things. But you had better be careful because it usually leads to disaster.

The truth is that no matter how well you know your customer you simply don't have all of his background and experience, so you won't be able to make a judgment about what he needs. Every customer is different. What appeals to one may turn off another. If you don't watch out, you will be applying a composite view of your customers to each one individually. And there goes the personal touch that is so

FIGURE 9-1. TO SUCCEED, GIVE YOUR CUSTOMERS WHAT THEY NEED.

essential to success. So why waste your energy trying to determine what is best for your customer when all you have to do is listen to the ultimate expert, the customer himself? Almost without exception, he will be more than eager to tell you what he needs. He will want to talk about the knotty problems he faces today, and he will tell you his concerns about the future and what solutions he seeks. Without too much prodding, he will usually unload himself gladly, particularly if he senses that he is talking with someone who is sincerely trying to understand what he needs.

One thing that you should never do is to try to push your hobby shops (untested ideas) on your customer. Don't get out of step with the customer. If you are going to try to turn him around, you had better take a very careful, dispassionate look at what you are doing, then go all out to substantiate your position. Better yet, educate the customer first and try to bring him around to your way of thinking before he calls the question. In other words, evolve superior approaches that implement the benefits your customer seeks. Evolving the superior approach is different from trying to convince your customer to select your off-the-shelf approaches, or, even worse, to give him alternate proposals for something he didn't ask for. It's the difference between winners and losers. On the one hand, you are in tune with your customer, swimming with the tide, running downhill. On the other hand, you are trying to change his mind, swimming upstream, climbing uphill. It wouldn't be so bad if you had no competition. In that case, of course you could do whatever you liked, and sooner or later you would get there. But when your competitor gives the customer what he wants, you most often will be second best if you handicap yourself by trying to sell him what you *think* he needs.

You start by clearly stating how your initial approaches implement benefits to your customer. That forces you to think of what your customer needs rather than what you want to sell him. Right off the bat you have to start evolving your going-in approaches until you have found the approaches that satisfy his needs. You will end up going nowhere until your approaches really do match his needs. Otherwise it's like trying

120

EVOLVE THE
SUPERIOR
APPROACH WITH
COMPETITIVE
CONVERGENCE

to put a square block in a round hole. You will find yourself struggling to make sense, and then logic will take over and you will begin to develop the right approaches. This is the foundation of competitive convergence.

You can accelerate this process by headlining your claims. Doing this will bring out the differences between where you are and where you should be. Using argumentative headlines, which we will discuss in Chapter 10, clearly identifies the discrepancies between your approaches and the approaches that your customer seeks. You simply cannot hide those differences when you try to state succinctly how your approaches implement benefits to him. The differences are obvious. Then without realizing it you begin to evolve, to change, to make things right. One by one, you fix the discrepancies, repair the differences, shore up your weak points, and emphasize your strong features. And as you do, it becomes easier to identify the differences between your custom approaches, those tailored to each particular customer, and the competitors' off-the-shelf, make-fit approaches. You can hardly go wrong with these custom approaches. They are, after all, exactly what the customer thinks are right for him. And when it comes to the customer he is always right.

What do you do when there is a difference between what you think benefits the customer and what the customer wants? First, you had better make sure that the difference is real and not just a figment of your imagination. You had better make sure that it's not just another attempt to pass on to the customer your hobby-shop approach in place of the approach he would like to see. Generally you are on the wrong track if what you think benefits the customer matches your off-the-shelf, going-in approach. And remember, in responding to a Request for Proposal, what the customer says he wants and what he needs are quite probably the same thing. If you don't treat them as the same thing, the customer will think you are nonresponsive.

We have talked a lot about how to get leverage from discriminators. We have told how to respond to the discriminators that are peculiar to you, your customer, or the competitor.

We said in Chapter 2 that a requisite for a discriminator is uniqueness. Discriminators provoke competitive convergence. If your discriminators don't favor you, look for ones that do. That's just another way of saying that you must evolve the approach that implements the most benefits to the customer.

Once you come up with the superior approach, you establish a winning position by addressing all the discriminators in your proposal. Do this first with competitive theses to see how well you can articulate your strengths and weaknesses. Your competitive thesis, usually one or two pages, addresses a particular discriminator. It could be a narration of how you will feature an outstanding strength or your competitor's weakness. It could explain how you will neutralize a weakness that the customer thinks you have. Use your competitive theses when you write the argumentative headlines at the start of each chapter of your proposal and in the lead-in paragraphs of each chapter. Of course, the most powerful influencers go into the argumentative headlines, and these set the stage for the material that follows—the substantiation of what you claimed in those headlines and lead-in paragraphs.

Be totally honest. Your customer probably knows (or at least thinks he knows) ten times more about you than your average employee. He knows all about your past failures, particularly if he was involved in one of them. Answer all his questions. Answer not only the questions he asks, but the ones you think he would like to ask. Oversubstantiate your claims. If there are ten ways to prove your point, include them all. The customer might not understand one or two of them, so you should leave nothing to chance. But the most important thing of all is to substantiate every claim you make. If you can't prove it, don't claim it.

A SIMPLE EXAMPLE

The best way to illustrate how to evolve the superior approach by competitive convergence is with a simple example of an

122

EVOLVE THE
SUPERIOR
APPROACH WITH
COMPETITIVE
CONVERGENCE

elementary competition. Here the evolutionary process is very clear. We will go through the same mock competition a number of times, but we will change the attitude of one of the competitors each time. The first time around, the competitor will offer what he has off the shelf. In the succeeding scenarios he will become more and more competitive. He will start to practice what we have been preaching until he becomes a master of the competitive convergence discipline and knows how to establish a winning position (see Figure 9-2). The subject matter is purposely simple so that none of the stages will get lost in technology. It isn't our purpose to create a clever technical operation; we want only to illustrate competitive convergence.

Imagine that the competition starts with a Request for Proposal (RFP). Crusty Mr. Baron needs some new furnishings: tables, chairs, drapes, and so forth. In the past he has always called up his old friend Mr. Red, but this time he decides to hold a competition. He is pretty sure he will still go with Mr. Red because he always has in the past. Besides, the Baron likes the color red. But he needs to make money. Times are hard lately, and he wants to find a way to improve his sagging sales. Mr. Baron thinks that new furnishings are a good first step in that direction.

The bidders in the competition are completely different. The biggest difference is that Mr. Red is the incumbent. He already has the business from Mr. Baron. If he does everything right, he can't lose. Mr. Blue is the challenger. But for him to win, Mr. Red has to blow it somewhere along the way. In a push, it will be Mr. Red, and that's a real handicap for Mr. Blue. This will be a major proposal influencer. All Mr. Red has to do is refer to all those years of good service and Mr. Baron will react favorably. Mr. Blue can't talk about the past at all because he has never worked for Mr. Baron.

But there are other influencers in this competition, and some may be big enough to elevate Mr. Blue from the also-ran to the winner. Whereas the first influencer deals with the difference between the two competitors (Mr. Red has a lot going for him; Mr. Blue has very little), the second influencer

FIGURE 9-2. EVOLVE UNTIL YOUR COMPETITIVE EVALUATION INDICATES THAT YOUR APPROACH IS SUPERIOR.

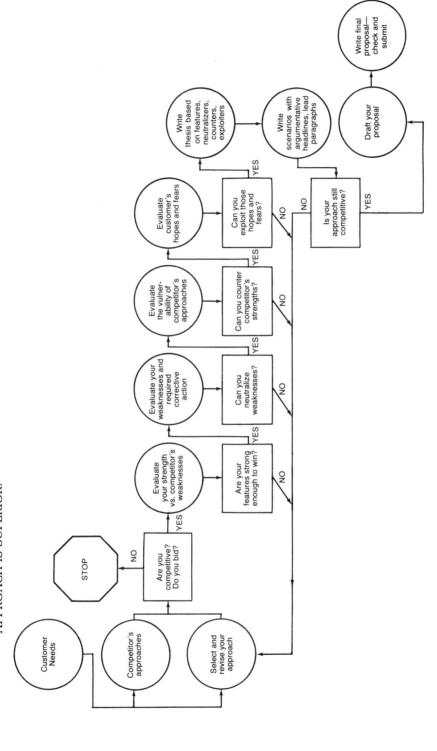

124

EVOLVE THE
SUPERIOR
APPROACH WITH
COMPETITIVE
CONVERGENCE

deals with the differences in attitudes of the competitors. Mr. Red will always bid red, no matter what. Mr. Blue, however, is flexible. He would like Mr. Baron to select blue, but he is willing to change if it would make him the winner. Mr. Blue may not know this now, but his flexibility is his ticket to win if he can figure out how to take advantage of it. Mr. Baron likes red, but he also likes profits. If a different color will help boost his sagging sales, he probably will go for it, especially if Mr. Blue is convincing.

The third influencers are those that offer benefits to Mr. Baron the customer. The discriminators in the competition are obvious:

Mr. Red
1. Mr. Red is established. He has had a long, satisfactory relationship with Mr. Baron.
2. Mr. Red is inflexible. He offers red or nothing.
3. Mr. Red offers a lower initial cost.

Mr. Blue
1. Mr. Blue is the newcomer.
2. Mr. Blue is flexible.
3. Mr. Blue offers better service.

All of the discriminators represent potential for Mr. Blue. If he does his homework, he can turn them into major factors. If they become major factors, it will have to be because of Mr. Blue, since we know that Mr. Red won't change. He is going to bid red no matter what. There are two discriminators that Mr. Blue must address in order to succeed:
1. Red has lower initial cost.
2. Blue has better service.

However, the biggest potential influencers that Mr. Blue must deal with are:
1. The good past history that Mr. Red has with Mr. Baron
2. The potential of Mr. Blue to evolve a different, superior approach.

Let's see what happens as we go through a number of scenarios. Each scenario starts with Mr. Blue discovering that he has a big hurdle to overcome in the competition. He finds out that Mr. Baron has done business with Mr. Red for the last twenty years. And since Mr. Baron has a red building, it looks like he likes the color red—for everything. So how does Mr. Blue react to all of this?

Scenario 1: This could be called the Half-Hearted Thrust. It obviously is a tough road to a win for Mr. Blue, and in this scenario he just isn't up to the test. He wants to bid, but he takes the easiest way possible: He bids blue. It's business as usual in the proposal, and without a discriminator that elevates him into a winning position, it is a loss all the way. After reading Mr. Blue's proposal with its color blue and its high initial cost, Mr. Baron wonders why he went to all this trouble to hold a competition in the first place. If Mr. Blue expects to get another shot at his business, he is going to have to wait a long time.

Scenario 2: Mr. Blue does some homework. He doesn't just sit down and bid. He does a little checking up and finds out what most of us have known all along: Most people don't like a steady diet of red. And that goes for Mr. Baron's customers too. In fact, none of them has red furnishings or a red building. But Mr. Blue doesn't follow up. It's a blown opportunity. He presents the facts and hopes Mr. Baron will change his mind. That is a fatal mistake. He assumes that Mr. Baron is just waiting to figure out all of the features of his approach and how they will benefit him. Mr. Blue still loses, but he put a bug in Mr. Baron's ear. The old man is sharp and he will start to think about this. The odds are that the next time he makes a procurement he will hold a competition again, and, if it is any comfort, Mr. Blue will be on the bidder's list.

Scenario 3: Mr. Blue follows up his checking. He knows that none of Mr. Baron's customers has red furnishings. He asks why and things start to happen. His research turns up the fact

126

EVOLVE THE
SUPERIOR
APPROACH WITH
COMPETITIVE
CONVERGENCE

that, according to a leading government study (an Aha!), mixed colors help sales. Mr. Baron would do much better if he did not have red furnishings in a red building. Mr. Blue again doesn't follow through, although he writes a good proposal, one that proves to Mr. Baron that mixed colors are the best. But he doesn't prove that *blue* furnishings in a red building are the best. His proposal discredits Mr. Red's approach, but he doesn't establish that his approach, blue, is the best.

Mr. Baron doesn't know what to do in this scenario. He knows that he is wrong to stay with red. He suspects that it isn't good business and it might even be a factor in his declining sales. But what *is* the right color to go in his red building? Most likely he will delay buying until he figures out this answer. Mr. Blue almost walked off with all the marbles, but he still didn't convince Mr. Baron that he had a better approach. If he had just gone one step further, he might have won.

Scenario 4: The big difference in this, the winning scenario, is that Mr. Blue addresses all the discriminators. He knows his service is better than Mr. Red's. He also knows that he can't match Mr. Red's low initial cost. So he checks up and does trade studies on the relative merits of service and initial cost. He finds one survey that proves his strong suit, service, is more important to a customer than low initial cost. He is now in a position to take Mr. Red's strong suit head on in his proposal and to discredit it with a counter.

Mr. Blue goes further and conducts his own survey. He asks Mr. Baron's biggest customer what colors he prefers for his furnishings. Lo and behold, the big customer hates red. Aha! So Mr. Blue researches the effects of color on sales and, at long last, finds that white furnishings in a red building are best for sales. Another Aha!

Mr. Blue is now in a very strong position. He can take on all of Mr. Red's strengths and counter them with his own strengths. He can make strong benefit claims and substantiate them with hard (Aha!) data. But first he must evolve the superior approach. He has to change from blue to white furnishings. That's no problem in this scenario because Mr. Blue—now Mr. White—is dedicated to winning.

He doesn't stop just here. He goes on to write a hard-hitting proposal that leaves nothing to chance. His white furnishings implement benefits to Mr. Baron, and he substantiates his claims with hard data. He shows the results of his survey of Mr. Baron's biggest customer. In bold print, he tells Mr. Baron that his biggest customer hates red.

His substantiation is overpowering, and he wins. Mr. Baron needed a lot of substantiation to dump Mr. Red in favor of Mr. White, alias Mr. Blue. Mr. White provided him with substantiated benefits and showed him how his sales would improve in the process.

What would have happened if the survey had revealed that initial low cost was the most important? Mr. Blue would know that his priorities were wrong and he would have no choice but to restructure his approach: emphasize low initial cost at the expense of service. But Mr. Blue is dedicated to winning. He will change his approach to provide benefits to the customer, even if it means adapting his competitor's approach. At least he ends up in a push, on that point, instead of an outright loss.

SOME REAL-WORLD EXAMPLES

Our simple example is not that far from the real world, but let's now consider a scenario adapted from an actual competition.

The Almost-Lost-It Win

Company A was engaged in a competition with one competitor for a flight-demonstration test program. Each company proposed an airplane that carried sensors to measure temperature and turbulence, whose suitabilities were to be evaluated in a series of demonstrations. Company A's plane was vastly superior to the competitor's. It was bigger, had more payload volume, better performance, a whole host of extra features,

128

EVOLVE THE
SUPERIOR
APPROACH WITH
COMPETITIVE
CONVERGENCE

and best of all it had been tested in an environment similar to the requested application, rough weather at high altitudes. With very few alterations it was ready to go.

Company B's plane was a cheapie that required a lot of jury rigging just to fit the mission. Its internal payload volume for the sensors was so small that some sensors had to be mounted externally to get the job done. Everything was marginal. It just barely met the required performance standards. It had no extra features and it had never been used in the proposed environment.

Company A's going-in approach looked fantastic. It looked so good that the company wondered why the other guy was competing at all. But the competitor showed no signs of withdrawing, so, even though it brought cries of anguish, Company A's beautiful going-in approach was subjected to a competitive convergence operation just to make sure that nothing had been overlooked. The operation revealed some very serious flaws. Once Company A looked hard at its wonderful demonstrator, it found a potential disaster glitch. When the company backed off and looked at its approach through the eyes of the customer, it saw a gold-plated demonstrator far more expensive than the competitor's. And when it looked at the competitor's approach through those same dispassionate eyes, it saw a low-priced, adequate demonstrator. Company A realized that unless it converged to a more competitive approach it would lose the bidding.

It was a difficult convergence because no one wanted to change anything on that beautiful demonstrator. It provided a whole host of Aha!s that were hard to walk away from. For awhile they thought that they actually had to degrade their demonstrator to become more competitive. And then the factory people dropped a bomb. They announced what should have already been obvious—that to degrade the demonstrator would cost still more money. So they were stuck with it.

If they couldn't reduce their price by modifying their demonstrator, they had to examine other areas for improvement. And that's when they began to score. They quickly realized that they could use the bigger payload volume of their demonstrator to perform more tests per demonstration. This cut down the number of demonstrations and thus saved a lot of dollars. Furthermore, they found even more ways to increase the amount of data gathered per demonstration by taking advantage of all of their demonstrator's extra features. These innovations in themselves were enough to put Company A back in the competitive range. But they didn't stop there. They kept looking and innovating and found ways to cut down on the refurbishment time between demonstrations and to take advantage of all the added performance capabilities of their demonstrator. And while they were at it, they featured all of the shortcomings of the competitive demonstrator and exploited the customer's hopes, fears, and biases for a successful demonstration program. Once the process got started, it snowballed and the costs tumbled. Company A won.

Remember, even when you think you're ahead, you should play the competitive convergence game. You may find, as did Company A, that from the customer's standpoint your approach may have one or more major flaws. You have a chance to correct this if you expose them. There are all sorts of ways to innovate. Many of us restrict our innovative thinking to our engineering and hardware. We should also consider testing, management, tooling, support and all other activities applicable to the effort. There is a world of ways to innovate, but for the most part we just scratch the surface.

The Impossible Win

Company C decided to go after a study in a field they were trying to develop. They had some good people in this area and had spent a moderate amount of discretionary funds developing expertise in associated disciplines. Still, they had captured no contracts and had only a passing acquaintance with the customer's functional people. They had many competitors that had been under contract with the customer on very advanced, risky studies. These contracts had lasted on and off for a decade. The objectives of these advanced studies had never been achieved. Indeed, there had been many failures,

130

EVOLVE THE
SUPERIOR
APPROACH WITH
COMPETITIVE
CONVERGENCE

which caused great disappointment to the customer. Nevertheless, the customer persisted. He wasn't looking for low-risk, modest payoff solutions. He wanted a breakthrough, a bold giant step forward. Failures irritated him but didn't deter him.

All the signs said that Company C had no business trying to step into a competition that had been going on for ten years. But it broke all the rules and gave it a try. It should have failed, and it would have except for an outstanding application of competitive convergence.

At the start, it looked for a "why us?" discriminator. Naturally there wasn't much to go on. The other guys had more experience and seemingly more capabilities, even with the failures. Company C had no innovative approach that could elevate it from the back of the pack to the winner. About all it could say was that it was the new kid on the block, and because it had no track record, it didn't have any marks against it. Pretty thin? Actually, so far as winning discriminators go, it's the bottom of the barrel. But being the new kid on the block does have its advantages. A newcomer with a new idea is always a good combination. But first Company C had to find that new idea.

Company C searched hard. Every week it generated a new approach. It began with: "We do good work or, at least, we haven't done any bad work for you." Then it evolved to the "champion" approach. A champion is assigned to every approach that seems viable. The idea is that as the champions fight it out, the best approach emerges. However, it didn't take long to realize that that wasn't the case. Instead of the strongest approach emerging, the strongest champion emerged. So, still searching for the right discriminator, the champion gave way to a strong trade-off approach, where each performance feature is traded for another. And then the long search paid off abruptly. The trade studies revealed a new, theoretical approach that was formulated by some young Ph.D. in the laboratories. This was just the kind of approach the customer might be interested in.

A visiting consultant, a college professor, noted that the

theory had fantastic payoff potential. And a marketing analyst noted that it was the kind of approach the customer was looking for—the bold step forward. So what appeared to be a tame trade-off study revealed a dynamic discriminator with the potential to propel Company C from an also-ran to a winner.

It didn't take long for Company C to firm up that approach and build its competitive thrust around it. It shifted from no bad points to the champion to the trade study and finally to the bold, innovative, theoretical approach with great potential and risk. And because its competitors, after many failures, were toning down their approaches, Company C, and only Company C presented the kind of a bold, risky approach that the customer was seeking. Who won? Company C!

What is important to remember here is that if Company C had proposed its going-in approach, or the second or third approach, it would have lost. The only reason it won is that it never stopped searching for the superior approach. And it never forgot that it was only the customer's perception of what was superior that counted. That allowed Company C to converge on a winning approach.

COMPETITIVE CONVERGENCE AS A WAY OF LIFE

Evolving the superior approach by competitive convergence is a disciplined frame of mind, an attitude, actually a way of life among those who consistently win. It is a dynamic balance between what the customer wants and what you are capable of giving him. You match his needs and counter his hopes, fears, and biases with your capabilities. And the more you iterate those ever changing balances, the more you'll have a chance at competitive convergence.

Failure to keep up with these changing balances can be seen in the American automobile industry. Both the Europeans and the Japanese did a far superior job of striking this balance, and the price the American industry paid was a dramatic loss in the marketplace. Factors such as government

132

EVOLVE THE
SUPERIOR
APPROACH WITH
COMPETITIVE
CONVERGENCE

regulation, fickleness on the part of the buyer, and a sudden increase in energy costs were easily predictable by the dispassionate analyst. The American marketing function tried to shape the marketplace instead of the product. When customers exercised their choice, those manufacturers who couldn't or wouldn't respond to the discipline of competitive convergence suffered, and they suffered badly.

The move toward condominiums is a fine example of competitive convergence with the realities of increasing land costs, the desire for more leisure time and less time spent on private home maintenance, and the pragmatic advantage of tax shelter through ownership rather than rental. Similarly, the dramatic rise in the number of aircraft sold for General Aviation, the growth in the sophisticated avionics market to supply these aircraft, and the increasing trend for larger and faster General Aviation aircraft is another good example of competitive convergence. Here it was occasioned by economics, which drove the major airlines to service only city-pairs with long-range, high-density markets. The enormous growth in the service industry is yet another example of competitive convergence. The industry supplies what the consumer needs in this bewilderingly sophisticated, highly specialized world.

Competitive convergence is a disciplined process that can be used to attack the marketplace in every phase: It can be used when you are investing in technology perhaps years before it will pay off in a specific product; when you are examining the nature of the customer's needs, as well as his hopes, fears, and biases; when you are examining your own capabilities and your own hopes, fears, and biases; and of course when you are preparing for a formal competition. Obviously, there is no way you can go through the discipline of competitive convergence unless you begin the process early.

Figure 9-3 illustrates the iterative process that occurs throughout the formal proposal strategy. In major Department of Defense programs, in which whole new weapon systems are evolved, the period from the beginning actions to the end may extend over four or six years and involve many tens of millions of dollars. Unlike our simplistic Mr. Baron scenario, where Mr. Blue took some elementary actions in evolving his win through competitive convergence, competitions often take some unexpected turns with very little warning.

Consider the discipline of a pilot who must fly his aircraft under instrument conditions. You live and die in instrument flying because you do or don't keep your options open and have the discipline of knowing when and how to execute those options. The pilot never begins his final landing approach until he knows exactly when he will have reached his minimums. He understands that he may indeed not break out in time for a safe landing, and he must know what his missed approach go-around procedure is even as he is preparing to land. To the very same extent that the instrument pilot knows that he may have to abort his landing at precisely the time he is setting himself up to make that landing, those who believe in the discipline of competitive convergence must recognize

FIGURE 9-3. TO WIN, YOU HAVE TO GET IN EARLY AND STAY LATE.

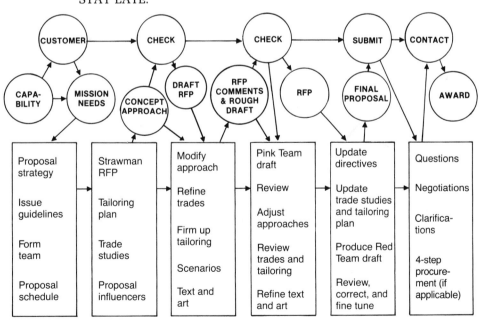

there are times when they must abandon what they have been doing because things have changed.

One big thing a pilot has to fight is his ego. It's an incredible feat to bring a plane through turbulence and wind, rain, snow, and ice down to the threshold to plop it on the runway. And it's difficult to admit at some point in the approach that you may not be lined up with the runway or that the weather has changed for the worse. Even when you're lined up, you may not be able to see far enough ahead to get it safely flared out on the runway once you are there. And there are always three other guys in the pattern, one a Pan Am 747 from London with a twenty-thousand-hour pilot, parking several hundred people up there while you are floundering around trying to get your tiny plane down. The moral of the story is that you had better make the competitive convergence discipline a part of your life or you will probably end up as a statistic.

When you're down to minimums and either haven't got the runway in sight or maybe just aren't mentally ready to get it on the runway, to hell with the 747 and your pride! Bring your nose up, put the throttle to the wall, and tell the tower that you are executing a missed approach. When you have the gear, flaps, altitude, and airspeed back where they belong, maybe then you will call the tower and tell the controller to forget about you and get the Pan Am flight down. Meanwhile you can get your act together for another try. There are old pilots and bold pilots, but no old, bold pilots!

In every competition you have to be ready to abort what you are doing. Every day gives you another opportunity to ask yourself if you should still be in the competition, and in every competition you have to be ready to submerge the company ego in favor of the realities of the marketplace. Where you've been, what you've accomplished in the past, how much money you have spent to date, or how foolish you will look if you quit now have no bearing on the question of whether you should continue in the same direction, whether you should alter that direction, or whether you should bring the whole thing to a halt because you can't get there from here.

When you have reached your minimums and nothing is

going right, you are headed for a crash if you don't abort. You should be prepared to withdraw from the competition or make a no-bid decision at any time. If you don't know what the name of the game is, don't play it. Or as soon as you know what the game is, if it isn't your game, fold.

FIGURE 9-4. BEFORE YOU COMMIT YOURSELF, MAKE SURE YOU KNOW THE NAME OF THE GAME.

10

Argumentative Headlines and Competitive Theses— Get What Matters Up Front for Maximum Effect

Argumentative headlines are essential in a superior approach because they tell the customer, "Why you? Why your approach?" Your headlines tell how your approaches implement benefits to the customer, and as you try to figure out how they do, you will begin to evolve a superior proposal.

An argumentative headline is the lead-in to your competitive thesis. It tells how your most important feature provides the most important benefit to the customer. The competitive thesis merely continues your opening thought, presenting a paragraph or paragraphs that deal with lesser features and benefits. You follow your argumentative headline with a paragraph that addresses all of the major influencers. Then you can continue with several paragraphs that address the influencers that you think deserve special attention.

Argumentative headlines force you to be specific. Often you will need only a "because preamble" to what otherwise would be empty breast-beating. Argumentative headlines tie in benefits to features, provide immediate substantiation of your claims, get immediately to the point at hand, and avoid the deadly getting ready that is typical of proposal writers who don't know how to get started because they don't know what it is they have to say.

The ad that says, "Ask the man who owns one," demands your attention because it suggests that the claimant feels very sure that he has a satisfied customer. But you can never be quite sure what it is that you can be sure of when they tell you, "You can be sure if it's Westinghouse." "Buy now, pay later" launched a whole new economic theory, and we happily responded by mortgaging ourselves to the hilt while the piper merrily played on. In the long run, though, the argumentative headline is an opener to get your attention. You have to follow up with substantiation to make it pay off.

Let's look at an example of a controversial argumentative headline—"Buy now, pay later." The approach is obvious: You get to own this wonderful thing now; tomorrow you can figure out how to pay for it. But where is the benefit? Supposedly it is tied up in the words *now* and *later*. You get it now, but don't have to pay for it until later. That isn't necessarily a benefit. You will have to pay for it eventually and if you don't pay up immediately and in full upon receiving your bill, you will have to pay interest on the deferred balance. The small convenience benefit to those who pay their bills promptly can become a major liability to those who pay the bill over a long period of time. They pay the interest and thus reduce their buying power. The collection agencies have long lists of people who found out that this implied benefit was little benefit at all. So "Buy now, pay later" is a good argumentative headline, even if it is misleading, because it is an exploiter. The company sells its products because it appeals to our desires. But it gets people into early economic difficulties. Its proponents can't substantiate that the implied benefit is *always* a benefit to the buyer. The only person who may benefit is the seller, and in the long run this imbalance is bad for everyone. If the seller took on the job of showing benefits to the buyer, he would probably prove that for most people the claimed benefit is more of a liability than an asset. The point here? Argumentative headlines do have a way of forcing the question.

SUBSTANTIATE YOUR FEATURES AND BENEFITS

When you write your argumentative headlines, you must substantiate the features as well as the benefits that you claim. If you claim that "Walking is the best form of exercise," you have to substantiate the feature, "walking," and the benefit, "the best form of exercise." The feature is obvious. You don't have to substantiate that walking is a form of exercise. But some may not recognize exercise as a benefit, much less that walking is the best form of it. So, first of all, you have to substantiate that exercise is good for everyone. If you can show data that proves it helps your appetite, makes you sleep better, promotes good looks, and improves your sex life, then you can win over most people to the fact that exercise is good for them. But now you have an even bigger task, and that is to prove that walking is the best form of exercise. To substantiate that claim would take a book in itself. Imagine the statistical health data and medical opinions you would have to bring forth. And you would probably be only partially successful in winning people over. Not many joggers and swimmers are likely to change their minds, even if you could point to a mountain of good data in favor of walking.

Let's take a high-technology example:

THE ACME GYRO PACKAGE IS THE BEST SINGLE SOLUTION FOR UNDERWATER, SURFACE, OR AIR LAUNCH.

Where is the implementing feature? Obviously it is missing. All the bidder says is, "I think my gyro package is best for the intended missions." Of course he thinks his product is the best. But the customer in turn could say, "No kidding, I knew you would say that. So what? All the bidders should claim that. Otherwise we don't want to hear from them."

To be effective, the headline must feature some specific claims that separate the bidder's approach from the competitor's. It has to be a real difference and one that is unique to the bidder, something the bidder can substantiate. If you were writing an effective headline for Acme, you might say:

> BECAUSE OUR GYRO PACKAGE IS OFF THE SHELF AND AL-READY QUALIFIED FOR UNDERWATER, SURFACE, AND AIR LAUNCH, ITS RELIABILITY, SERVICE LIFE, AND COSTS ALL BETTER YOUR SPECIFIED GOALS.

Now these are specific claims! You feature an off-the-shelf, already qualified package. You claim that these features benefit the customer with reliability, service life, and cost that are superior even to his own requirements. If these claims are unique to you, then you have some powerful claims, particularly if these benefits are what the customer seeks the most. If you've done your job right and looked at the competition through the eyes of the customer, you have a superior approach. But remember that you have the superior approach only if you can substantiate your claims.

The leverage in the discipline of substantive marketing is very powerful. Of course, real leverage comes with *substantiation*. In addition, there are unique features, benefits, claims, and perceptions. These all add up to discriminators. If you substantiate your claims, substantiate how your approach features benefits according to the customer's perceptions, you are positioning to win. And if you are specific, you will avoid the "arrogance" trap. Let's examine a case where we transform an arrogant claim into a challenging claim just by being specific. First, look at the arrogant claim:

> MY XYZ APPROACH IS THE BEST DOLLAR VALUE FOR YOU.

This headline is a chest thumper all the way. It says "believe me" without giving you any reason why your customer should. And what is "best value?" Without a lot of digging, he may never know. And even if he does dig through what follows, he won't know what you are talking about until he gets all the way through and analyzes everything you wrote to see what might be classified as a dollar value. Then it's up to him again to figure out what's best. Obviously he isn't going to keep this game up long if there are other proposals to examine. Instead, he will look for those sellers who went right to the heart of the matter, sellers who made it crystal clear and supplied the answers to "why me and my approaches."

Now let's turn the arrogant claim into a specific claim that shifts it to a challenging argumentative headline:

MY XYZ APPROACH GIVES YOU 25 PERCENT MORE PERFOR-
MANCE FOR 10 PERCENT LESS COST.

Why isn't this claim arrogant? Because the claimer lays it on the line and validates his claim to anyone who wishes to challenge his headline. We are no longer dealing with the vague "best dollar value" claim, but with a specific claim of 25 percent more performance and 10 percent less cost. The buyer can look for substantiation of these real and definite claims, and if he doesn't find that substantiation, the claimant is in deep trouble. You can and should be argumentative if you are specific, but you shouldn't be arrogant, particularly if you can't back up your claims.

MAKE YOUR CLAIMS SPECIFIC

Look at the world of difference between the following claims:

I'M THE BEST.
I CAN RUN THE MILE IN 10 SECONDS LESS THAN ANYONE
ELSE.
I CAN RUN THE MILE IN 10 SECONDS LESS THAN ANYONE ELSE
WHILE CARRYING A 20 POUND WEIGHT.

The attitude to these specific claims changes from cynicism to active interest. "Can the guy really deliver?" becomes the attitude. If he does deliver, he is acclaimed the best in that specific area. When that leads to a sell or a win or a contract, you have won through substantive marketing.

Let's consider another bad headline:

OUR BANGER GUN MEETS THE SPECIFIC REQUIREMENTS OF
THE LAUNCH VEHICLES.

All that is said here is that you meet the specification of the procurement. A sarcastic customer could say, "No kidding, we thought you would be unresponsive!" Or, "So what? Everyone else will be responsive too. If they aren't, we will disqualify them." You have to show your features are unique and then implement the benefits that are important to the customer.

Try again. You could say:

OUR BANGER GUN'S HYPER-FEED SYSTEM, COUPLED WITH ITS
FRIGGER COOLING SYSTEM, PRODUCES A SUSTAINED FIRING
RATE THAT BETTERS YOUR THRESHOLD BY 30 PERCENT. IT
CAN BE FITTED ON ALL THE LAUNCH VEHICLES USING ONLY A
FIELD CONVERSION KIT.

Here you have three features: the hyper-feed system, the frigger cooling system, and a field conversion kit. You claim the first two features give you a 30-percent higher sustained firing rate. The third feature allows the field troops to install the system with only a field conversion kit. Now you have to substantiate both the features and the benefits claimed.

Let's take one more example of a bad headline:

WE CONDUCTED EXTENSIVE TRADE STUDIES TO ARRIVE AT
THE OPTIMUM MIX.

What does *extensive* mean? Why not give the number of trade studies? And what does *optimum* mean? Optimum, maximum, and minimum are cop-out terms. They tell the evaluator that you have no hard data to substantiate a real claim. So you cop out and say you can give some optimum (undefined) mix. Optimum is perfect, isn't it? Maximum means infinite or something approaching it. And minimum means zero. These are not very realistic terms for a quantitatively oriented world. In describing the mix, relate it to the customer's requirements, his threshold and goals. Furthermore, make the claim argumentative. In making a claim, give the reader the challenge to read further for substantiation. If the reader is a friend, provide him with proof. If he is an enemy, make him uncertain, neutralize him at least. In the extreme, you might even change his mind.

A FEW EXAMPLES

Let's look at some good examples of "no-technology" argumentative headlines. How can two cigarette salespersons use argumentative headlines in selling their product to a wholesale buyer? Assume that Seller A has the lowest tar cigarette but the highest cost. Seller B has a low-cost cigarette but one with a high-tar content.

Seller A's argumentative headline might read:

BECAUSE WE USE THE PATENTED SCRUBBER FILTER, OUR CIGARETTES' TAR CONTENT IS 50 PERCENT LESS THAN OUR COMPETITOR'S. SURE, IT COSTS A LITTLE MORE, BUT YOUR HEALTH IS WORTH IT.

That's a good argumentative headline. It features the scrubber filter, which provides the benefit of 50 percent less tar. The claim features this strength at the same time that it features the competitor's main weakness, a high-tar cigarette. Then the claim neutralizes Seller A's biggest weakness, the high cost, by pointing out that the buyer's health is worth this cost. Neat, huh? You don't have to read further to see that Seller B might as well roll over and play dead. But Seller B also knows how to compete.

Seller B's argumentative headline might read:

OUR CIGARETTE IS THE MOST SATISFYING BY FAR. BECAUSE WE DON'T SCRUB OUT ALL OF THE TASTE WITH FILTERS, YOU

DON'T SMOKE AS MUCH FOR SATISFACTION. YOU SAVE
MONEY TWO WAYS: YOU SMOKE LESS AND OUR CIGARETTES
COST LESS.

143

A FEW
EXAMPLES

Seller B knows that people don't smoke for their health. They smoke for satisfaction. Therefore, he features unfiltered good taste as his main strength. And while he is at it, he takes a crack at the highly filtered, tasteless cigarette of his competitors. He uses a Ghost here to imply there is no taste in Seller A's cigarettes. The wholesale buyer has to be concerned. He knows he isn't selling a health product! Seller B's headline then goes on to feature his low-cost discriminator: "You Save Money Two Ways." All in all, it is a very competitive headline. Seller B features his strength and his competitor's weaknesses. He neutralizes the health Ghost that the competitor will obviously raise. He counters the strength of the competitor's filter. He exploits the hopes, fears, and biases of the customer. And he does all this in three sentences that contain fewer than forty words! Now if he can substantiate most of those claims, he will be very competitive, even if his cigarette has the highest tar.

Before we leave this example, let's play the game one step further. Suppose Seller A anticipates the approach that Seller B might take. What might Seller A do to counter it? For one thing, he might add another sentence to his argumentative headline. It might go something like this:

OUR SURVEY SHOWS THAT PEOPLE WHO SMOKE FILTERED
CIGARETTES SMOKE LESS.

That undoes the neutralizer that Seller B put in his headline to counter the health problem. Seller A might then try to put the nail in the coffin by adding:

EACH YEAR MORE PEOPLE SMOKE FILTERED CIGARETTES.

Seller B comes back with:

HOW MUCH YOU SMOKE IS UP TO YOU.
OUR SALES HAVE INCREASED EACH YEAR AS MORE PEOPLE

RECOGNIZE OUR SUPERIOR TASTE. THEY GET MORE SATISFAC-
TION FOR LESS.

Who wins? Probably the seller who competes the hardest and produces the most substantiating data. If they both go the limit, the buyer will probably split the order and let the public figure out who's best. It's tough to look away from a seller who employs competitive convergence!

Let's look at some examples of good high-technology argumentative headlines:

EXERCISING THE ADVANCED OPTION OF THE SLICK DE-
STROYER NOW WILL REDUCE THE COST TO THE GOVERNMENT
BY MORE THAN $100 MILLION.

This headline has both a feature and a benefit. It is straight to the point, and it deserves to be in bold print at the beginning of your proposal. The implementing feature is the action you want the government to take—exercising the advanced option of the Slick destroyer now. The benefit is a claimed $100 million savings. The relationship between the approach and the benefits is clear. It is an argumentative claim. Even your strongest advocate has to wonder if this is true. He will read your proposal to make sure you can back up that claim, but that makes him a better advocate of the proposal because he knows the substantiation that goes with the claim.

But what about the government evaluator who is negative? The claim is argumentative, but he dare not take it on before reading your proposal. After all, he doesn't want to look bad anymore than you do. He is just insecure enough to check it out. That's your opportunity to neutralize or cancel an enemy. If you do it right, you might even win him over to your side. It all depends on the strength of your substantiation.

If you offer no substantiation, you have a disaster on your hands. Your supporters are in a vulnerable position until they figure out some way to get off your bandwagon. Your enemy's cup runneth over. Do they have you now? You bet they do! They don their most professional manner and play critic to the hilt. They actually use your nonsubstantiated claims to shout you down. They counter what you intended as a strength feature with your lack of substantiation. It is the worst of situations. You have not only lost this bid, but you have compromised your chances on future bids.

Here is another example of a good high-technology argumentative headline:

OUR ZEBRA MISSILE, WITH ITS $200 MILLION DATA BASE,
MEETS OR BETTERS ALL SURVIVABILITY REQUIREMENTS OF
YOUR LION MISSION SPECIFICATION.

Here again the headline has both a feature and a benefit. It is succinct and straight to the point. And because of that it deserves to headline the chapter on this subject, and in bold print. It is the most important message to your reader in the survivability chapter. Certainly it is argumentative: you claim a benefit of bettering all of the survivability requirements. The requestor laid out what he thought was a tough set of requirements and you tell him that you can do better than that in every instance. That has to startle him and challenge him to question you.

You told him the benefits were based on a $200 million data base. That is your implementing feature. All he has to do is check that out. He can't walk away from it without questioning it. If you are right, if you have the substantiating data for those claims, then you have a strength feature that just might blow all of the competitors out of the water before going any further. But, again, substantiation is the key to it all. Without substantiation your opponents can counter your strengths by simply pointing out your lack of substantiation. The burden of proof is on you. You can't claim anything without proving it. If you don't prove it, it works against you.

Let's look at another good example:

BECAUSE OF THREE YEARS OF ZEBRA MISSILE TESTING,
CONSISTING OF FIFTY FLIGHTS, THE LION TEST PROGRAM IS
ALREADY 40 PERCENT COMPLETE.

Here again you have a clear, easy-to-understand benefit and an implementing feature. The benefit is a test program that is 40 percent completed before you even start. That has to make the customer want to check you out. He can't walk away from that claim. He may even put a team on that chapter of your proposal to look for holes in your claim. To help that team out, you tell them the major implementing feature they should check out—Zebra missile test program results from fifty free flights. They know exactly what to do and what to look for. If you have substantiated these claims, you are on your way to a win!

Remember, always to be specific. You can always improve the quality of your argumentative headlines by being more specific. Look at Figure 10-1, which illustrates how to strengthen your headlines with specifics. Note how the quality of your headline is improved as you add specifics first to the feature and then to the benefit. The last headline will make the customer more interested in investigating your product, and that's the first step in selling him. He has to find out if

FIGURE 10-1. ADD SPECIFICS TO STRENGTHEN ARGUMENTATIVE HEADLINES.

FEATURES ◄─────┬─────► BENEFITS

Recommendations for improvement

Design recommendations for improvement

10 design recommendations for improvement

10 easy design recommendations for improvement

10 easy design recommendations for cost-reduction improvement

10 easy design recommendations for 50-percent cost-reduction improvement

FEATURES ◄─────┴─────► BENEFITS

those ten recommendations really are easy and inexpensive. And he wants to see if that claim of 50-percent improvement is really true. If you substantiate, you have sold him.

Remember that argumentative headlines, like lead-in paragraphs, have the added value of forcing you to the superior approach. But having a competitive approach isn't the only thing that's required to succeed. You have to compete with it and make the most out of it to win.

A SERVICE EXAMPLE

Assume that two contractors are bidding on a county job to dig ditches for foundations for new buildings. Company A is a big high-technology contractor from out of town. It has the best equipment in the state: with this equipment it can dig more ditches per hour than anyone else. Company A doesn't require much labor either. It can do the job with just a few people and its wonderful machines.

Company B is a local company that is well known in the county. It doesn't have much equipment, but what it has is good. Usually Company B uses low-cost labor to make up for its lack of equipment. That and its good relationships with local customers keep it busy.

Let's examine how the winner uses competitive convergence. First, look at Company A's competitive thesis:

Our modern equipment assures you of the best performance in the least amount of time. Our costs are competitive because the time we spend on the job is 50 percent less than what our competitors would spend.

That's a tough one to beat, but the local boy, Company B, takes a crack at it. Its first attempt leaves something to be desired:

My equipment plus local labor is adequate to do the job. Because the cost of local labor is low, my costs are competitive.

There isn't much to shout about in that competitive thesis. It sounds more like a hope and a prayer rather than a claim that can be substantiated. But Company B hasn't survived all these years without learning how to make the most out of what it's got. The company looks the job over carefully and finds out that the ditches don't have to be dug in a short time. It could stretch out the digging somewhat, and would offset the lack of high-performance machinery. So Company B combines that with its knowledge of local facts to produce a stronger competitive thesis:

We have selected an approach that is tailored to the county's building program. It provides adequate equipment to dig the ditches as they are needed. As such, our approach is geared to the building program, not to digging ditches fast. It saves money and uses lots of labor. That helps our local unemployment problem. By taking people off the street and putting them to work, it cuts down on the crime rate and saves even more money. Our approach is geared to our local problems, not optimized for the sake of ditch-digging technology.

This competitive thesis is filled with Aha!s and Ghosts, and it takes care of all the Oh-Oh!s. Company B is making things difficult for the out-of-town moguls too. But just to make the competition more interesting, let's assume that Company B's operating engineer, after reviewing the claims, informs management that it doesn't have enough equipment after all to match the county's demand schedule. Close but not quite close enough. That throws Company B for a moment, but it quickly realizes that it can rent equipment from a local agency. And wouldn't you know it, the head of the agency is a nephew of someone on the County Board of Supervisors. So Company B modifies its competitive thesis with an insert. After the second sentence, it adds:

We augment our equipment with J. Evans rentals. Between our two local outfits, we have everything that's needed to meet your schedule.

When it's all over, a confused Company A executive tries to explain to his corporate people why they lost the contract to the local yokel. If they asked the local yokel, though, they would be startled to know that it was just good, sound business that beat them. Company B looked at all the competitive influencers and used them to evolve the superior approach. It overlooked nothing. Even though Company B proposed nothing that was outstanding in itself, when it was all put together, it spelled winner!

ARGUMENTATIVE HEADLINES AS LEAD-INS

Now let's consider an example that uses argumentative headlines as the lead-in to competitive theses. Remember the competition in Chapter 2 between the fiberglass (FG) rowboat and the aluminum (AL) rowboat? Go back to Chapter 2 and take a hard look at the two lists of discriminators and imagine what the argumentative headline for the FG competitor might be. Now compare yours with this one.

Broaden Your Market with the Attractive, Colorful and Rugged FG Rowboat

This headline emphasizes the ability of the FG boat to broaden the market as the benefit. The implementing features are the attractive, colorful, and rugged FG boat. Now read the following competitive thesis. You will find that it addresses all of the discriminators listed in Chapter 2. Note that the Oh-Oh! is saved until the end, but it is addressed in an equally clear and positive style.

> *FG rowboats offer new dimensions in style as well as attractive shapes. There are no seams to leak. It isn't necessary to assemble pieces with unsightly rivets. FG boats are molded in one piece. The color is blended in and a glossy finish applied. If you should puncture the hull, you can easily patch it. FG boats are cool to the touch. You can move around in them without the noise of a metal boat. That they are somewhat heavier is no drawback. Rollers and lifters are available. You can't build an equally styled AL boat for any price. So broaden your customer base with our FG boat.*

It appears that the FG rowboat is a sure winner. But before we call the race, let's look at what the AL rowboat competitor might say. It's easy to guess what his discriminators will be. Certainly he will build on his strength—low cost. In fact, he will really dig in there:

Increase Your Sales with the
Lower-Cost, Lightweight AL Boat

AL rowboats outsell FG rowboats ten to one. Why? They cost less and weigh less. And in the mass-production rowboat market, the record clearly shows that cost and weight are the only meaningful differences. In the last five years, three stores have shifted from FG to AL rowboats. The heavier, more costly FG rowboat just doesn't sell. People who use rowboats don't go for style or colors or finish. They want a low-cost, rugged, lightweight boat. They will put up with small drawbacks if they have these features. Our record shows that we can serve your high volume interests best with our rugged, long-lasting, easy-to-repair AL rowboat.

Notice that he features both his strength (low cost) and his competitor's weakness (weight). His competitive thesis is also a strong one. If the customer is interested in selling a lot of boats, the AL rowboat is the way to go.

What can the poor old maker of FG rowboats do? The AL boat builder will kill him every time in the small-boat market unless he does something. So he practices competitive convergence and evolves a superior approach. He recognizes that he will never win on cost, but he also knows that he can turn out a boat that the AL maker can never come close to. He goes after that part of the market where he is clearly superior, and he rewrites his competitive thesis:

Use the Stylish FG Boat to
Augment Your AL Boat Sales

The FG boat offers you the style and attractiveness to reach a new and affluent class of customers. Added to your stock of the cheaper, less flexible AL boats, FG boats will broaden your line to include a prestige boat and increase your sales and profits.

Here he shifts his emphasis to augmenting the customer's sales. The benefit is an increase in sales for the customer. He not only makes money with AL boats but also with FG boats. And that is exactly what has happened in the real-world marketplace between these two boats.

11

The Proposal
Challenge:
Positioning
Your Proposal
to Win

So far we have treated the fundamentals of positioning to win and developed various approaches and disciplines. In Chapter 1 we introduced a fundamental philosophy: the discriminator discipline and competitive convergence. In Chapter 2 we introduced and detailed the most basic competitive tool of all, the discriminator itself which is the starting point for all serious competitors. Then in Chapter 3 we demonstrated the leverage the discriminator discipline provides. But compiling a list of discriminators is only the beginning of the battle. You then have to know how to use them in positioning to win. So in Chapter 4 we introduced influencers.

We discussed the four types of influencers—features, neutralizers, counters, and exploiters—in Chapters 5 through 8, respectively, and we loaded these chapters with examples to show how to make use of them in your proposals. Then we topped off the treatment of positioning-to-win fundamentals with two important chapters: Chapter 9, on using competitive convergence to evolve the superior approach, and Chapter 10, on argumentative headlines and competitive theses, approaches for getting what matters up front for maximum effect.

Now we are ready for the specifics of positioning proposals to win, and we'll start, appropriately enough, with the proposal challenge and why proposals are so difficult. We follow this with a detailed analysis of why we win or lose, examining the specific reasons as we wind our way through the process of proposal development. This chapter ends with guidelines showing how to meet these proposal challenges. In Chapter 12 we will continue this line of thought by looking at the bid/no-bid decision, the point where right at the start most proposals go astray.

WHAT'S SO DIFFICULT ABOUT PROPOSALS?

Proposals involve many people and many activities. From the list in Figure 11-1, it is easy to see that many people are involved in every step. Solid lines indicate primary responsibility. Dashed lines indicate support roles. Every step requires a coordinated activity.

Proposals are difficult to write because they have to be such a careful blend of bravado and modesty, brevity and depth, and innovation and conservatism. Executive summaries are difficult because you must write something perfect about something that is imperfect. Management proposals are almost always unsatisfactory because they tend to lack innovative punch. Technical proposals vary in difficulty, depending on how many problems your approach contains. Cost proposals are always important. It is hard to win unless your validated costs are the lowest.

In fact, we have rarely worked on a proposal where we felt

FIGURE 11-1. A PROPOSAL DEVELOPMENT FLOW CHART PROVIDES A ROAD MAP TO TASKS AND RESPONSIBILITIES.

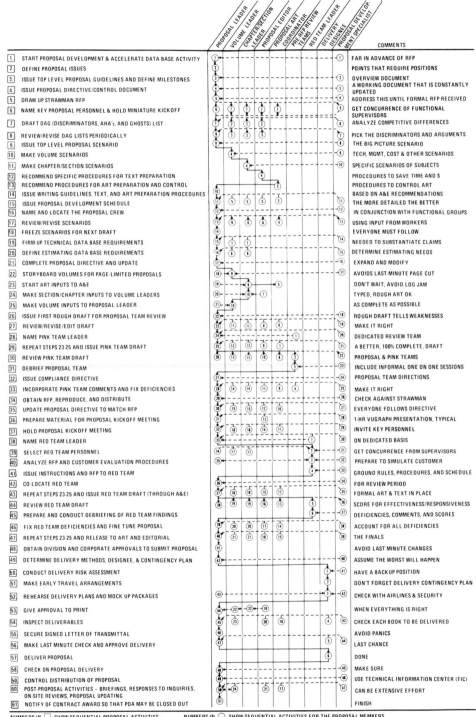

NUMBERS IN ☐ SHOW SEQUENTIAL PROPOSAL ACTIVITIES   NUMBERS IN ◯ SHOW SEQUENTIAL ACTIVITIES FOR THE PROPOSAL MEMBERS

From Creating Superior Proposals, by J. M. Beveridge and E. J. Velton, © 1978.

the full potential of the company, its people, the proposed programs, and the technical approaches were completely captured and communicated to the evaluator. We question whether most winners ever succeed in communicating fifty percent of the competitive potential. Remember, you realize your competitive potential only when you capture and utilize the discriminators of the competition in your proposal, presentation, brochure, or advertisement in a manner that influences the evaluators in your favor. Losers obviously never come close to their competitive potential. That means a lot of business is left on the table for someone else to pick up, forfeited because bidders either couldn't get their act together and drive out that superior approach or couldn't and didn't make the most of the imperfect approach that they did drive out.

Proposals are tough, and they contain much more information and require more planning and discipline than the familiar subject report that some try to pass off as a proposal. Obviously, the subject matter is the most important part of any report or proposal, but a proposal contains more than just a discussion of the approach's characteristics.

A proposal has more substantiation requirements than a simple subject report. In a subject report we substantiate the claims of the approaches we are featuring with analysis, tests, or reference data. For instance, you claim that your operational and maintenance approach will reduce employee turnover, and you substantiate that claim with the records from similar jobs. You claim that your delta-wing fighter will go so fast and fly so high, and you substantiate those claims with analyses of wind tunnel and propulsion unit tests. You claim that your gadget will dig holes so fast based on demonstrations. Or you claim that you can process so many pieces of equipment based on the results of reference data.

But this is only one of three steps involved in positioning a proposal to win. The second step deals with determining the benefits the customer seeks. The last step, and perhaps the most important, attempts to match the characteristics of these substantiated features with the useful benefits sought by your

156

THE PROPOSAL
CHALLENGE:
POSITIONING
YOUR PROPOSAL
TO WIN

customer. If they don't match, you know you are on the wrong track, and can change your approach before it's too late. Any one-third of the effort without its other two-thirds is a job only partially done: it's called a loss.

Most proposals never get beyond substantiating the characteristics of the approach. Try as you may, you will probably never get an equal emphasis on benefits. If you do and you find out that the performance features don't produce benefits, you will have a difficult time getting the team to change from its going-in approach to an approach that is superior in the eyes of the customer. That's why proposals are so difficult. You not only have to demonstrate that these fabulous features bring very real and desirable benefits, but you have to make sure that these marvelous benefits are exactly what the customer perceives that he needs.

Benefits deserve more attention than features. And benefits aren't benefits at all unless the customer perceives them as such. So you must ask yourself these questions: Are you just as attentive to your studies of the customer's needs as you are of the design features of your product? Are your studies objective or are they only backing-in efforts? Can you substantiate features and benefits and then substantiate that these are indeed exactly the benefits that the customer perceives are right for him? We call this substantive marketing, and it takes a great deal of discipline to do it well. If at any time perceived benefits to the customer don't match your features, you should modify your approach. We call this competitive convergence, and it also takes a great deal of effort and discipline.

WHY WE WIN OR LOSE

It's true that you can't win them all. But few of us seem to know what to do to win the majority of our bids. We all seem to make the same mistakes over and over. Assuming that you are a capable contractor going after a viable business opportunity, let's examine the specific reasons for winning or losing.

WHEN WE START AFFECTS HOW WELL WE DO: Let's start at the beginning. The way to ensure a win is to conduct most of the proposal upstream in Leverage Country. You should spend roughly 60 percent of your resources prior to the time the RFP is released, 30 percent from release time to the proposal submittal date, and 10 percent on follow up. Unfortunately, the majority of proposals don't have an upstream phase! If yours doesn't, you will always begin in a losing position. The most common mistake in proposal development is to hold off until the RFP is in. That way you will be backing in all the way. You may think you will be saving money this way, but probably you won't be. And even if you were to save 50 percent, you would probably be turning out two losing proposals for the price of one winner.

COMMUNICATION IS EVERYTHING: One of the single most important factors in a win is how you address the customer's perceptions. In this regard, you win when you do the following:

- Talk to the customer. You don't work in a vacuum, so check everything out and keep an open mind from start to finish.
- Give the customer the ammunition he needs to say no to the other fellow at the same time he is saying yes to you. Feature the other fellow's weaknesses as well as your own strengths. And if you can, counter his strengths too.
- Get the message up front in bold type. State it clearly and succinctly so that no one can miss it. You can do this only with a superior approach. That's one of the primary advantages of the message approach; you can't highlight a message that you don't have! A bad approach is exposed just as fast as a good one. Then you have the option of changing and improving your approach or not bidding.
- Tell the customer what the significant differences are between your design and your competitor's. Point out the benefits of your approaches. Feature, neutralize, counter, and exploit all of the significant discriminators. Leave nothing to chance.
- Treat comparisons as inherent parts of the process. Trade studies are an integral part of the search for the superior

158

THE PROPOSAL
CHALLENGE:
POSITIONING
YOUR PROPOSAL
TO WIN

approach. Never select a point design without comparing it to all of the viable alternatives, paying particular attention to the competitor's approaches if you know what they are. If you have a good marketing department, you should know all of the competitor's approaches.

You lose when:

- You talk to each other but not to the customer. If you arrive at your final approaches without including the customer, he will be in for a surprise when he opens your proposal. And most likely you will be in for a surprise when you lose, because in the eyes of the customer your approaches were inferior to your competitor's. Why shouldn't the customer see them as inferior? No one checked them out with the customer, and he is as capable of not-invented-here as you are. He is the fellow with the money, so you lose!

- You ignore the customer's problems of selecting a winner. You merely present the data and let him do all of your marketing. If you bet on his being very perceptive and totally unbiased and feel that it is his job to do the comparisons, you will be surprised when he tells you that he has more pressing things to do, like getting the competitor under contract.

- You lose your messages in the proposal and try to obscure them in order to hide their inadequacies. The evaluator has to ask: Where is the message? *What* is the message? Does the bidder have any idea what he is offering?

- You water down the proposal, thus removing the teeth from your arguments. How many times have you heard the consistent loser say that his customer doesn't want him to flag all the features and benefits? According to this loser, the customer would rather dig it out all by himself. Nonsense! Talk to the customer. The customer is as busy as you are, and he isn't about to do your work for you.

- You leave everything to chance. Watch out when the proposal leader says he didn't bother to look at alternatives to his approaches, that he feels his approach is the only way to go. You can't possibly know if you are better until you examine all the alternatives. So get on with it or get ready for your Dear John letter.

HOW YOU START AFFECTS HOW YOU END: A good start gets everyone off on the right foot. It sets the pace throughout the proposal. It's one thing to get off to a good, positive start, where everyone understands what he is getting into and that the commitment from top to bottom is to win. It's quite another matter when you drift into a proposal without having a good idea of what it takes to win. The first meeting of the Sales Board sets the pace. You win when:

- The Sales Board's decision to bid is a sound, unemotional yes based on an upstream state of readiness, a willingness to sacrifice required resources, and an innovative going-in approach with great potential. This kind of approach puts the proposal team on notice that it is accountable for winning. It also demonstrates that management is in the act and is responsible and committed.

- The Sales Board funds the proposal with a realistic set of resources. You can't blindly establish the amount of money you will spend on a proposal. The RFP tells you what you have to do to be responsive. If that's too much, and if the business doesn't warrant that kind of expenditure, don't bid.

- The Sales Board funds a first-class proposal, double column, art and text in place, produced by professional publication people. That's just another way of saying, "Wrap up that superior proposal in a package that compliments the contents." Cosmetics are important. Put two copies of the same proposal side by side, one crudely done and the other first class—not showy or gold plated, just first class. Who do you think will win?

You lose when:
- The Sales Board indulges in meaningless exercises that result in a "wish-list" decision to bid when you aren't upstream, aren't the incumbent, and don't have a major

160

THE PROPOSAL
CHALLENGE:
POSITIONING
YOUR PROPOSAL
TO WIN

discriminator to unseat the incumbent. General managers often have a nasty habit of stating that you should be in the field, but they never sit in on the Sales Board to see if you have a winning approach.

■ The Sales Board ignores RFP requirements and underfunds the proposal: "That's all the money we've got. Cut corners and make it go." This attitude defies common sense and good business practices. You won't do yourself any good if you turn in a partially responsive, marginal proposal. Don't bid if you're underfunded, undermanned, and can't commit.

■ The proposal leader uses his day-to-day report writers for art and editorial tasks instead of using graphic illustrators and publication professionals. Don't try to save money by eliminating the middle man. It won't work. In the end you will probably have an inferior proposal. Go with the professionals.

THE LEADER IS ALL IMPORTANT: The right leader can make almost any system work. He or she can get even the most difficult people to work together. The leader must be at the heart of the process. A pure administrator just won't do. You win when:

■ You have one leader throughout the proposal: pre-RFP, proposal, and follow-up. Select that leader early and carefully, and commit the leader for the duration of the proposal. The leader is a strong manager and organizer as well as an innovator. Remember that the majority of innovators are not good proposal leaders. We all know that good leaders are scarce, and technical people are no exception to this rule. Select the leader carefully. He or she will be the biggest factor in projecting management into the proposal.

■ The program manager and proposal leader are the same person. If this is so, you will have positive, bold, and innovative leadership. If they aren't one and the same, you will get the middle-of-the-road treatment. The proposal leader is always concerned about how the program manager will react to his or her policies. The proposal leader/ program manager knows that he will have to implement the promises in the proposal. Therefore, he will work the proposal harder and make it more complete and substantiated. That's the description of a winning proposal.

- Management picks the best person to lead the program proposal. This shows total commitment, and that's what wins.
- The leader is open and takes advantage of the expertise of the corporation. He's a strong leader and a very good listener. He looks for talent and attracts the best people.

You lose when:
- Management changes leaders and key personnel often during the proposal development process. When you take the innovative leader off the proposal to take care of some other important job first, that means the proposal was less important to you. And, that's less than a total commitment.
- The leader has only a specialty background with no management expertise. There is no other way to say it; about 90 percent of your best technical people have absolutely no business leading a proposal. And you should be very picky about the remaining 10 percent.
- The proposal leader knows he isn't going to be the program manager. He is tentative, always wondering how the real program manager will react to his earlier decision. He is not fully committed because there is no risk/reward payoff. So he takes the middle of the road—a nice comfortable path to a loss.
- Management names the program manager at the last moment, just prior to submittal. This shows a noncommittal attitude. It means the proposal was leaderless during its formulation. And more important, the customer never met the fellow that he is being asked to bet on. You can't possibly expect to win under these conditions.
- Management picks whoever is available to lead the proposal. This is a classic mistake, and it is usually made by

162

THE PROPOSAL
CHALLENGE:
POSITIONING
YOUR PROPOSAL
TO WIN

incompetent managements who have no comprehension of how difficult it is to win.

■ The leader insists on doing things his way, neglecting proven practices and techniques. He reinvents everything and goes over and around the functional barons. He plays it close to the vest, operating as though it were his proposal, not the company's proposal. And amazingly enough, on small study contracts he has a good win record. But he loses when it counts, when the program grows to the point where many departments and standardized practices become a must.

YOU CAN'T WIN WITHOUT FEATURES: This is as important as starting early and choosing the right leader. If your influencers don't consist mostly of your strength features and innovative approaches, you will have a tough time being competitive. You win if you do the following:

■ Start with innovative approaches that have the potential to evolve to the overall superior approach. These are your going-in approaches, from which you will evolve the superior approach. A faint heart never won a fair lady, and plain vanilla approaches cannot be perceived by the customer as different from anyone else's approach.

■ The team checks out your approach with the customer before the RFP. At every opportunity you should schedule one-on-ones with the customer. Before the door is shut, make sure that the customer is knowledgeable about all aspects of your approach. Don't let him find any surprises in your proposal. Explain the difficult points to him in person and in advance.

■ The team incorporates the customer's perceptions into your conceptions. Listen to the customer. If you do your job right, at some point the customer will begin to think of your approach as *his* approach.

■ Evolve approaches whose features implement benefits to the customer. This is the key. The customer isn't buying quarter-inch drills; he's buying quarter-inch holes. A winning approach must have customer benefits.

- The proposal leader and management orchestrate pre-RFP technical one-on-ones. Anything less than this will produce an ordinary, no-win approach. The leader must be active and totally involved in the process. It is a tough job to delegate and still keep up with all the details, but that's what winning proposal leaders do regularly.

You lose when:
- You don't have an innovative approach. No matter how much money you spend, your approach won't win unless it has innovation behind it. Cosmetics won't do anything for a poor proposal. The customer must perceive a difference. You must have a discriminator to move into first place.
- The customer sees your approaches for the first time when he opens the proposal. You didn't presell him, and he had no input in the approach.
- The team stays with the going-in approach. If you refuse to change or modify your going-in approach, if you fail to listen to the customer, and if you close your technical mind and defend your ideas at the expense of the customer's, you will be a loser every time. Remember, there is no fact; there is only the customer's perception of fact. Don't forget who the customer is and what the objective of the proposal is.
- You make no customer contacts before the RFP, or you did but then you ignored the customer's comments. If you aren't in touch with the customer, you won't recognize the depth of his bias, the degree of his commitment to a particular thought, or his hopes and fears that weren't expressed in the RFP.

ALWAYS START WITH DISCRIMINATORS: No matter what you have done wrong up to the start of the proposal effort—and particularly if you have done a lot of things wrong—you can't afford to go any further until you look at the discriminators. If you lack an innovative approach, seeking discriminators will at least point you in the direction of maximizing what little

164

THE PROPOSAL
CHALLENGE:
POSITIONING
YOUR PROPOSAL
TO WIN

you do have to offer. Discriminators are always the seeds of a win. You win when:

- The team maintains a list of discriminators in the competition throughout the effort. You can't tell how your approach implements the most benefits to the customer if you don't compare it to the alternatives available to him. You may have to do as much unselling as selling. Always be aware of the customer's alternatives.

- The team addresses your strengths relative to the competitor's weaknesses. To do so, you must have some knowledge of your competitor's approaches. If you don't know what they are, make the comparison relative to what you perceive are viable alternatives. Chances are, you will address most of the competitor's features if your trade studies are comprehensive. If the competitor doesn't do likewise, he is in trouble.

- The leader orchestrates your response with competitive theses (white papers) that address major discriminators. This is the best way to test your influencers. If they come over well in white papers, you will be able to articulate them well in your proposal. But you musn't forget to search for and identify claims because you have to substantiate each claim. Otherwise they may be invalid. Use competitive theses to check it all out and find out what you have to do to evolve the winning approach.

- You capture, document, and protect all of the discriminators—the Aha!s and Ghosts—that you so carefully dug out. Articulate these to the customer up front and then also sprinkle them throughout the proposal. There is nothing wrong with making comparisons; this is the essence of competitive action.

You lose when:

- Your team fails to address the competitive discriminators and ignores the competition. The team ignores the strengths and weaknesses of all the competitors, including yourself. It is a subject report all the way. You don't treat the alternatives to show why you are superior.

- You state your approach without telling how it implements benefits to the customer. If a competitor tells how his approach implements benefits and you don't, you could lose even with a superior approach. And to a true competitor, that's inexcusable.
- You let your discriminators drift away in the inner workings and hidden mechanisms of your company labyrinth. You make a passive, safe presentation but never show a discriminator. You throw your Aha!s on the waters and hope someone will bite. By doing this, you are ignoring the competition, and you will go down without a fight.

DEVELOP THE DATA BASE TO FIT THE RFP: To win, you are obligated to spend your resources according to what the RFP requests. You must avoid overdeveloping those areas where you are strong simply because you are comfortable with them. You win when:
- The proposal team develops the data base to satisfy the RFP requirements. The RFP steers your efforts. You pragmatically match your efforts to the RFP. It is more important to satisfy the customer than yourself.
- The team always follows an RFP—the strawman, the draft, or the real thing. With the strawman, you are guessing. With the draft, the customer is guessing. With the real thing, neither of you is guessing. But always steer your efforts toward the customer.

You lose when:
- The team develops the data base independently of the RFP, then tries to make the RFP fit it, instead of the other way around. Amazingly enough, this happens most of the time. When a team demands this technical freedom, it is in the wrong business. It should be in research, not proposals, where responsiveness to someone else's requirements is what counts.
- The team doesn't address an RFP until it gets the real thing. By then the proposal is out of balance, and it's too late to plug the holes. You have written about those things

166

THE PROPOSAL
CHALLENGE:
POSITIONING
YOUR PROPOSAL
TO WIN

you like or understand and have ignored the other 50 percent of the proposal. What you end up with is a finely tuned mismatch.

MANAGEMENT ASSERTS ITSELF WITH TOP-DOWN DIRECTION: Management support can make up for all sorts of shortcomings. What management wants, you win. There is a lot of evidence to support that. It simply means that management makes sure that everything is done right. You win when:

- Management takes an active role in the proposal through reviews and frequent visits to the proposal area.
- Management, through the leader, provides top-down direction to the proposal team. Everyone knows the proposal strategy and where the winning messages should go in the proposal.
- The leader and division proposes to cost and allocates costs according to the customer's budget. Nothing is left to chance; everything is scheduled, including cost. You control the estimate and negotiate the tasks the functional groups can do for the money the customer has. You end up with competitive costs that won't kill your innovative approaches.
- The leader draws up the scenarios for the proposal before he allows anybody to start writing. Everybody knows what they will write about before they start.
- The leader makes an early draft to find the holes in your approaches. The first draft is always bad, whether it's done upstream of the RFP or just before proposal submittal. Winners get it out of the way, find the holes, and go on to a winning proposal.

You lose when:

- Management gets involved at the last moment, if at all. You can't win unless management is involved. Lack of management involvement implies that the proposal is on the back burner.
- Management and the proposal leader don't try to steer the proposal but accept whatever the system generates. Without management's push, the system always generates a

safe, padded proposal. This is a sorry mistake in today's competitive environment.

- The leader makes no effort to control the estimate and accepts a grass-roots estimate. What incentive does a functional manager have to minimize his bid unless it is to please management? Certainly the low bid is going to mean less people on the effort. Grass-roots estimates are padded and excessive, and that says they are losers.

- The team starts to write the proposal without an overall plan, usually late. Everyone drifts into and out of the effort. Without management's direction, the proposal has big holes. Without a plan, you will rarely succeed at anything.

- The first draft is the last draft, and it's always terrible. This is almost always a sure sign of a loss. For every example where you squeezed out a winner with an exceptional bunch of people, there are ten examples where you lost. Get it down on paper, then sit back and carefully critique, edit, and rewrite what you have to offer.

IF YOU CAN'T TELL, "WHY US?" YOU LOSE: In winning proposals the cover letter of commitment from the chairman of the board starts with the reasons why you should be selected and why the competitors shouldn't.

In losing proposals the cover letter starts with, "We are pleased to submit this proposal in response to your RFP."

IT TAKES A WINNING ATTITUDE TO SUCCEED: On winning proposals everyone from the division manager to the proposal leader to the most minor contributor is win-oriented. The leader writes the summary first, last, and, often. Management insists that you start with a proposal strategy to win. You submit one fully responsive proposal, keep your technical mind open, and respond to the customer's requests.

On losing proposals you write a subject report instead of a proposal, one that is restricted to the features of your approaches and ignores the customer's concerns for benefits. You profess to be technical professionals, not businessmen. The summary isn't written until the last minute, and then not

168

THE PROPOSAL
CHALLENGE:
POSITIONING
YOUR PROPOSAL
TO WIN

by the leader. You haven't been win-oriented. Sometimes you lose by submitting alternate proposals along with the baseline proposal. Finally, and this is the most common, the team members confuse their conceptions with the customer's perceptions.

SUBSTANTIATION IS A MUST: There is no need to waste words here. On winning proposals you substantiate all of your claims. On losing proposals you don't.

WINNING REQUIRES SUPPORT FROM EVERYBODY: On winning efforts functional groups provide key people to the proposal leader upstream of the proposal. The proposal leader has rapid and frequent access to his functional leaders.

On losing proposals the functional groups don't man the proposal until the formal release of the RFP. The leader has a difficult time getting to see his functional leader, and this prevents bold, timely decisions and leads to a garden-variety proposal.

WINNING IS A TEAM EFFORT: You win when:
■ The team gets started early, before the RFP, and stays with the proposal until submittal. You take your people out of their normal work routine and create a special group for them. A proposal is nothing more than a panic program, and it takes all kinds to win. So put them all together. The leader holds brief coordination meetings every morning. The team works to a detailed set of schedules: proposal, estimate, and data base. The leader uses disciplined procedures and insists that all team members do likewise. The leader and team members use techniques such as competitive theses that clearly reveal your approaches and tell why they implement benefits to the customer. And when you can't find any benefits, change to a more responsive approach.

You lose when:
■ The leader never brings the team together. If the team members never meet, they won't be able to resolve their problems completely and interact properly.

- The team rarely or never coordinates its activities. The strongest person usually dominates regardless of what the RFP calls for.
- No detailed schedule exists, only major milestones, which you will never meet. You are continually in trouble because you don't schedule the minor milestones that lead to the major ones. In addition, you don't know that you are getting into trouble; you find out only when it's too late.
- The leader lets everyone do his or her own thing. An appreciable percentage of proposals are conducted this way, but rarely do they win.
- The leader fails to clarify your approaches and revels in high-fog presentations. This prevents a clear analysis of how your approaches will implement benefits to the customer. You never really know what the approach is. And if you don't, the customer won't either.

WINNING PROPOSALS ARE RESPONSIVE PROPOSALS: A winning contractor recognizes that strong people like to do it their way. Management assumes that there will be deficiencies and biases in the proposal unless it takes action. So management appoints a dispassionate third party from within its ranks to simulate the customer's evaluation of the proposal. You win when:

- Management holds Pink and Red Team reviews staffed by dedicated, objective third parties. Our experience is that Red Teams have the most profound effect of all in fine-tuning a proposal. Fine-tuning is essential to evolving a superior approach and getting the absolute most out of what you have to offer.
- The leader provides the Pink Team with a complete draft. You want to find out early if you are going to encounter any trouble along the way.
- The leader provides the Red Team with a clean, first-class draft. You don't want this team to be distracted by cosmetics; they should be free to concentrate on the proposal's contents, not its appearance.
- The schedule provides enough time between the Red Team's work and the RFP deadline to incorporate the Red

170

THE PROPOSAL
CHALLENGE:
POSITIONING
YOUR PROPOSAL
TO WIN

Team's criticisms in the proposal. Otherwise you can't benefit from it. Keep in mind that Red Teams are expensive, maybe not in direct dollars if you use managers, but in time that could have been spent on other programs. There's no sense in paying that price if you don't benefit from the results.

■ The proposal team responds totally to the review teams' comments and fixes all deficiencies. You produce a responsive, finely tuned proposal.

You lose when:

■ The division doesn't use third parties to review the proposal. This shows a certain arrogance. The proposal team provides the Pink Team with incomplete information and the Red Team with an incomplete draft. The Red Team spins its wheels on editorial and cosmetic issues and never focuses on what counts—the subject matter. The schedule at Red Team time is so tight that there is no time to fix deficiencies. So why did you bother at all? The leader treats the review teams as advisory teams and responds as he wishes. The opportunity to improve is lost and along with it the competition.

WINNING DOESN'T STOP WITH PROPOSAL SUBMITTAL: You can still pull out a winner and avoid a loser if:

■ You respond to customer signals during negotiations, always keeping your mind open for ways to improve your offering. There are many examples of contractors moving from second or third place to first place simply by correctly interpreting what the customer says during negotiations. This is an art and a very effective one.

You lose when:

■ The leader and team close their minds to changes during negotiations and respond with substantiation only to support your going-in approach. Just as there are many examples of contractors moving up during negotiations, there are also many who lose it all during this period. There are even examples of customers who have done everything possible to get their favorite to shore up a losing weakness, only to be disappointed when he digs in and fights right down to the frustrating loss.

FOLLOW-UP MAY MAKE THE DIFFERENCE BETWEEN WINNING AND LOSING: You win when:

- The team checks all your deliverables for missing chapters, pages, and mistakes. The leader allows time for proposal delivery with a backup alternative(s). You mock up deliverables on big proposals to make sure you can get everything delivered when and where required. Management provides funds for proposal follow-up, sometimes 10 percent or more of the total.

You lose when:

- The team depends on the system to produce perfect deliverables. The leader goes along with a one-shot delivery plan with no fall-back alternatives. The plane is late, the train quits, or the car runs out of gas, and you lose. There is no follow-up effort and no team to answer questions.

It is as expensive to lose as to win, so why not do it right? Shortcuts add delays on the road from Leverage Country to Panicsville. Losers are just as exhausted and a great deal more frustrated than winners. What we have talked about is nothing more than common sense and good management. Proposals are often a painful effort whether you win or lose, so you should always try to make it a winner. It can get to be a habit.

HOW TO MEET THE PROPOSAL CHALLENGE

So far in this chapter we've talked about how difficult proposals are and why you win or lose. Now we will give directions on how to meet the challenges of positioning your proposals to win. For the most part, these directions are just good common-sense business practices. Sprinkled throughout will be many innovative ideas that you may find useful in imple-

172

THE PROPOSAL
CHALLENGE:
POSITIONING
YOUR PROPOSAL
TO WIN

menting a disciplined approach to proposals. Basically your implementing features are professional proposal-development specialists, a disciplined approach, good planning, and an early, firm commitment. The benefit is a higher win-loss percentage. Another fall-out benefit is better contract performance: Good proposals produce good contracts because there has been a true meeting of the minds.

Use Professionals to Avoid Common Mistakes

The easiest way to improve is to stop making the same mistakes over and over again. Don't start every proposal from scratch. Take advantage of past efforts and eliminate the procedures that didn't work on the last proposal. If some part of the proposal consistently produces bad results, make it a policy to change it on future proposals. Let's look at a few examples.

Although alternate proposals seem to have an overpowering appeal to the innovator, they are an often-repeated mistake.

"Look," he says, "With just a few changes in the specifications I can adapt this gadget I've been working on for the last few years to meet some of the requirements of the RFP. Surely the customer will recognize my gadget as the greatest thing ever. I'm sure he will be more than happy to change his requirements to fit my gadget. Yeah, I know I have to put in a responsive proposal in order for the customer to consider my alternative proposal. But that's a snap. In fact, putting in two proposals just doubles my chances of winning."

So what happens? The proposal leader splits his limited resources between two efforts. He turns in a marginally responsive proposal that draws not a single rave. He also turns in a highly subjective alternate proposal that the evaluator doesn't want, doesn't have the resources to evaluate, and doesn't know what to do with.

Listen to your customers. They will tell you that they are as overworked as you and don't have the time or the staff to chase your pet ideas. They pounded out a compromise RFP after many battles. That's the set of requirements they want you to respond to. Sure, you will hear a lot of complaints about the RFP. If you search long enough, you will even find someone who will openly encourage you to submit an alternate proposal. And of course there is that little invitation in the RFP for alternate proposals, the one that the customer's legal people insist on. But when you get right down to it, the customer is going to award a contract for the requirements in the RFP. If he doesn't, he will have to deal with all kinds of in-house squabbles and protests. If your alternate ideas are so clever, go sell them to the customer ahead of time. He'll write an RFP that will single out your approach.

The alternate proposal is analogous to a boxer in the last round who has lost badly in the previous rounds. Since he obviously can't win the match, he says, "Stop the match, let's change the game to tennis." That doesn't go over very well with all those people who came to see a boxing match. If the boxer wanted to play tennis, he should have waited until a tennis match came up or have suggested one prior to the fight. Similarly, if our innovator wanted a response to his gadget, he should get out and convince the customer to write an RFP around the gadget. He is just being lazy when he stays at home waiting for the first RFP he can tag his amended requirements to. And he is making a common mistake, one you could avoid by using professionals.

Before we leave alternate proposals, we should mention that occasionally they do have their place. You may want to submit an alternate proposal if you think it might cancel a competition. That's when the customer comes to see a baseball game and you know that you're going to be the loser. So you have to get it rained out. That is a complicated business though, and one that you should ponder hard and long. You stand a far better chance of getting hurt than helping yourself. But if after careful consideration you decide to go with an alternate proposal, go all the way. Open your proposal with something like this:

> *Here is a fully responsive proposal. We submit it only because it is required. Read our alternate proposal if you want something exciting. And, incidentally, our alternate approach is far less likely to kill the Astronauts!*

174

THE PROPOSAL
CHALLENGE:
POSITIONING
YOUR PROPOSAL
TO WIN

Now that's commitment, and it can really upset the apple-cart. Its strong, bold claims are intended to kill the current set of requirements and aim everything in a new direction. But it can also kill your chances with that customer for a long time, so consider it carefully first.

Using professionals can keep you from making a number of other general mistakes. Among them:

- Let's ignore the proposal instructions and structure the proposal in a way that will show it to best effect
- The proposal leader says he will write the proposal all by himself
- The proposal leader, on a major system acquisition, says he will head the major technical volume as well as lead the proposal
- The proposal leader will write the summary last
- The proposal leader will write the proposal only one time, just before submittal
- We don't have to join forces on this effort
- Coordination meetings are a waste of time.

These are only a few general mistakes, and they are common to every contractor. So how do you avoid them? Simple. If you are big, create a full-time proposal-development group. If you are small, name some person to monitor and preferably participate in all proposals. If you can afford it, bring in a professional who specializes in proposals. That person will speak up much more forcefully on all the issues because he doesn't have to look to you for his paycheck each week. Also from past experience he knows that your management wants candid treatment, and that can come only from outsiders. Professionals see the same mistakes created over and over, and they can actively work to avoid them. They earn their keep by simply avoiding the pitfalls.

Develop Standard Practices for Consistency

Avoiding mistakes is a passive step. You don't have to be creative, just observant of flaws and disciplined enough to do something about them. That's fairly easy, even though a lot of large, supposedly capable companies can't seem to get even that act together. But if you can get a handle on your mistakes, you are ready for a bigger payoff because you will have attempted to realize the full potential of your capabilities in proposal development.

Go on the offensive. While your professionals monitor all those mistakes and catalog them in the no-no file, have them also record all the actions that work. Each proposal leader and his team adopts certain procedures and practices in putting out proposals. If you have no standard procedures, develop some. Some will work and some won't. Your professionals should, as standard practice, use those that work consistently. Bring in a knowledgeable outsider who has dispassionately watched everybody stumble. He will undoubtedly have a large list of procedures, most of which will work with little or no modifications in your shop. Or get a copy of our earlier book, *Creating Superior Proposals*, which reflect decades of experience with all sizes and types of proposals.

Having standard practices is one thing. Implementing these practices is quite another matter. Begin now to create a professional attitude in your company for the proposal effort. It will take many working sessions to change a company from a bunch of freewheelers to a disciplined team. And don't stop once you think you have achieved your goal. Every time a new chief engineer or marketing manager comes on board, it begins all over again. Your worst performers, oddly enough, turn out to be your recent winners. From that one exciting win, they feel they know all the tricks, all the shortcuts. They have forgotten how to do it right. That, plus the glory of being recent winners, makes them almost impossible to deal with.

You also must constantly update your practices. As you become more experienced in writing proposals, you will find the mistakes that are peculiar to your people, your organization, and your product line. You will also find that some of your practices, although correct in principle, are ineffective or difficult to implement. These you will constantly modify to increase the effectiveness of your approaches.

As you gain this experience, you will have to deal with another worry, one associated with the constant changes in

176

THE PROPOSAL
CHALLENGE:
POSITIONING
YOUR PROPOSAL
TO WIN

the managements of some large corporations. Key players come and go. Every time a new one comes on the scene, the proposal group will find itself with yet another challenge. It's becoming almost a standard practice in some companies for key executives to get rid of everybody on the previous key executive's staff. The new guy brings his own people in, downgrades or fires the old bunch, and then looks around for any signs of the old regime. Those signs include standard practices, not the routine ones, but management practices in general and proposal-development practices in particular. Obviously this new guy feels he has been brought in because he knows more than the previous executive, and surely that must include the proposal process, the very heartbeat of the company's future. He views these practices as constraints to his ability to implement his policies. So out they go, along with the proposal group, and you are back at zero. That's another thing that's difficult about proposals: everybody resists a disciplined approach. Discipline exposes incompetence. The rare, qualified competent has enough insight to have developed a few techniques that work well for him. The maverick manager can undo all of the sound practices painstakingly developed over a long period of time by the previous manager.

Improve Bid Decisions to Increase Competitiveness

Obviously avoiding bad starts helps meet the proposal challenges. Don't go in with the idea that you have to reason your way out of a bid. Instead ask, "Why bid?" Conduct a meaningful bid/no-bid meeting and let everyone have his say. Demand that your proposal team come prepared to discuss all the points presented earlier. Its presentation should begin with a proposal strategy for winning and end with a strong set of reasons why the customer should select you. *If your leader and his team can't convince their naturally biased management why you should win, they aren't going to do too well with the customer, who is hearing equally biased input from other companies.*

Have every department who will be affected by the proposal or the contract at the meeting. When all the facts are in, ask for a commitment from everyone. If there is a show stopper, flush it out in the open then and there. The last thing you want is to have some key person sit quietly through the meeting knowing that he and his people can't support the schedule or the specification. If you bid, make it a total commitment. Everyone has to recognize that you are demanding that commitment, not just entertaining them with another presentation.

In most companies bid/no-bid meetings or sales boards are very ineffective. Proposal teams come poorly prepared, department heads are absent, and some don't even bother to send an alternate. There is an almost overpowering tendency for the session to become political. Everyone plays it close to the vest. Agreements to approve or, in rare cases, to disapprove are made prior to the meeting. Soon people just stop coming, and the sales board dies a quiet death. Once again you bid without any filtering or attempt to establish a favorable position. When this happens, you have lost another key chance to meet the proposal challenge.

Start Before the RFP—Or Don't Start at All
We belabor this point, but getting an early start is absolutely essential in meeting the proposal challenge. If you don't start before the Request for Proposal:

- You can't check out your concepts with the customer
- You have no time or opportunity to incorporate your customer's perceptions into your conceptions
- You can't establish a rapport with the customer's technical people through one-on-ones
- You can't evaluate the customer and his program
- You have no time to evaluate your competition
- You have no opportunity to assess your going-in approach through the use of discriminators, competitive theses, and a pre-RFP draft.
- You are in a catch-up mode, developing your approaches and maybe even your data base when you should be fine-tuning the approaches you and your customer worked out together.

178

THE PROPOSAL
CHALLENGE:
POSITIONING
YOUR PROPOSAL
TO WIN

By the time you get an RFP, you should have ironed out everything with the customer. Your team should be in place and working. You should have identified and articulated all your influencers in an early draft. If you have, you are in a state of readiness to meet the proposal challenge.

Play Customer to Ensure Responsiveness

The best way to make sure that you're giving the customer what he has requested and not what you'd like to sell is to simulate the customer's review with a dispassionate third party. You meet this challenge by appointing a Red Team of experts to review the proposal individually and collectively. Some call this team the Murder Board, Blue Team, or Customer Simulator.

The individuals on the team must not have worked on the proposal. They should be the best experts you can find outside of the proposal team. There's nothing wrong with bringing people in from the outside, perhaps from another division, if you are a big company. You might get someone from another company who has no conflict of interest if you are a small or medium-sized company. You could set up an arrangement with that company to reciprocate on some future effort where there again is no conflict of interest. Use consultants: they've been around and know all of the pitfalls. But whomever you select should be dedicated to the review for its duration, and should agree to follow the established ground rules.

Start with the leader. Remember, the best technical person isn't necessarily the best leader. We point this out again because we see the wrong guy selected in the majority of the cases. The leader should have something to say about who is on his team. In fact, if he is the right kind of leader, he will have everything to say about who goes on his Red Team.

What does the Red Team do? It tries to match the proposal to the RFP. If it can't match them, it writes up the deficiencies, just as the customer would do. But unlike the customer, the Red Team does something more for you. It tells you where you have done a poor job in selecting your approaches or presenting them, and it does it before you have blundered in front of the customer. You get a chance to fix your deficiencies and to improve your offering before you send in the real thing. That's why Red Teams can have a profound effect on the quality of your proposal.

The ground rules for positioning to win relative to the Red Team review include:

- The leader and his members must be dedicated to the review.
- You should assign someone to each part of the proposal and to each part of the RFP.
- Be careful what you tell the Red Team. Tell it only what the customer's evaluators will know about the competition: how you and the competitors have performed in the past, who has been working the customer, the background of the program, who is involved, and the customer's hopes, fears, and biases. Don't tell it what you have tried to put in the proposal, what your hopes, fears, and biases are, or what your strong points should be. Let the Red Team get that from your proposal. What you want to determine is whether your proposal is responsive, superior, and easy to understand.
- The team must be at the heart of the innovative matter, not just administratively oriented.
- The team simulates the customer. It tries to match the proposal to the RFP. It doesn't give personal opinions that are in conflict with the customer's requirements.
- The Red Team's output is specific: "Here's what's wrong item by item in the RFP, and here's what you should do about it."

Obtaining a good Red Team review is only half the battle. How you respond to it is the other half. You should make it mandatory that the proposal team fix all deficiencies relative to the RFP. In other words, the Red Team is not an advisory body. You didn't bring it together and spend the money just to ignore its output. If you want to get the most out of the Red Team, you will have to do something about each of its comments and recommendations. If some part or parts of the proposal bother the Red Team, it will probably bother the

180

THE PROPOSAL
CHALLENGE:
POSITIONING
YOUR PROPOSAL
TO WIN

customer too. The terrible truth is that we are all just about alike. What bothers one person will more than likely bother another, regardless of which side of the fence he is on. The same goes for estimators, designers, contract people, and managers.

Propose to Cost for a Competitive Price

One challenge that very few bidders rise to is controlling costs. That's a tough task, and it becomes even tougher when the innovators and other team members procrastinate. The worst thing your people can do is to look away from controlling costs or put off dealing with them. An estimate will accompany the proposal, and if your leader doesn't work it as hard as the innovation, your cost will be high. And that's a terrible way to lose, particularly if your approach is superior. What's difficult about proposals? Well, the mismatch between the leader's lack of interest in controlling costs and the importance of controlling costs just might head the list.

The way to meet the cost challenge is to determine the winning price. Your marketing people should be able to get a handle on that. Many times the customer will tell you what he has budgeted for the effort. Using this information, set cost targets for all tasks, and realize, of course, that you can't do any of this if you aren't upstream of the RFP. Then get your functional groups to tell you how they will do the tasks for the allocated resources. In the majority of the cases there will be a lot of "can't do's," but if you are going to meet the challenge, you will have to make adjustments so that you are responsive but still within the winning price number. It takes a lot of give and take to rework Statements of Work until a group can meet the task within budget. Sometimes it just won't stretch. Then you shuffle the budget, take some from here and some from there so that you can be responsive all around. This is a time for much shouting and not a little arm twisting. But no one said that winning was going to be easy.

Proposing to cost is another dimension of positioning to win. Many losers say, "We were number one technically, but the estimators lost it for us. The costs were too high." That's the worst kind of cop-out. The reason the estimate was too high was because the loser was too lazy to evolve a superior approach. Part of being superior is being affordable. If you don't understand that, you will spend a lot of time outside the winner's circle looking in. You just missed the challenge!

You Have to Sacrifice to Win

Earlier we mentioned wish-list proposals. These are made by those who will not sacrifice to win. Sacrifice applies to all of your resources, starting with the most valuable—people. If you want to win, put someone in charge of the proposal who will make things click from beginning to end. All too often contractors pick a leader who won't disrupt his normal operations. The rationale here is that he may be marginal, but he will have to do. This is okay unless one of your competitors puts one of his live-wire, go-getting innovators on the proposal. You don't have to guess who wins in this case. It's a mismatch all the way.

The same rule applies for the team members. Look at the task and ask, "Who is the best person I have for that task." Never ask who is available or who can do the job without disrupting his normal job. Think back to the times when you wanted to win so badly that you sacrificed someone of real value to lead the proposal; in those cases, you probably won. When you lost, it was because you had assembled a rag-tag team. You probably spent most of the morning calling around to find out who was available. By late afternoon you and your top people had probably gone through the available bunch for the third time and finally talked yourself into believing that one of them could do the job. When it was all over, you lost and you couldn't understand why. After all, you had spent a whole day selecting the leader. But the truth of the matter is you could have selected the winning team in one additional minute if you had been willing to sacrifice for the proposal.

Equally important to people are money, facilities, and time. Put two teams of equal capability into the fight and the one with the most money will win almost every time. Sure, everyone has experienced a few shoestring wins occasionally,

182

THE PROPOSAL
CHALLENGE:
POSITIONING
YOUR PROPOSAL
TO WIN

but for every happy story there is a string of unhappy losses. And speaking of facilities, you should always look twice at the facility that is empty at proposal-writing time. It may be empty because no one else wanted to work there. It's amazing that proposal teams can consistently perform so well under marginal conditions. Comfortable, well-lighted facilities are a big help to those who must concentrate on proposals. If the facilities are in sad shape, you're going to find your team members going back to their own desks. This inhibits the interchange of data that often makes the fine difference between a win and a loss.

Time is of primary importance. Remember, get started upstream of the RFP, in Leverage Country. Make sure you give yourself the time to create and innovate. Also give yourself enough time for the luxury of a false start or two. This can make all the difference, and it will distinguish you from the losers.

Finally, give the proposal your attention. All too often management picks the leader, assigns the team, allocates the facilities, and then says, "Have at it." It won't do anything more until that last look just before the proposal goes out the door. Then management is unhappy because it wasn't done the way it would have liked. But not once did the division vice-president, manager, or even a director wander into a coordination meeting. When the proposal group called for members of the Red Team, everybody was just too busy. They waited until the last minute, and by then it was too late to influence the proposal. They had time only to damn it.

Proposals are far too complicated for just a look-see approval. The manager should be able to influence the proposal, to improve it. But don't *wait* to approve it. If you don't get your oar in early, you will never see a proposal that will come anywhere near to what you had hoped for.

Expertise Can Make the Difference

Most of the actions we have discussed so far can be done with varying degrees of skills. Surely the level of skill matters in meeting the proposal challenge. If you can acquire or build the expertise in proposal development, you can win consistently, even on the difficult ones. If you have been banging around at a 25-percent win/bid ratio, you can gain as much as 50 percent by having the right proposal smarts. Look at it this way. There is probably not a great deal of difference between your people and those of your first-line competitors. Why should there be? They come from the same schools and attend the same seminars and meetings. In some cities, people can even change companies without changing car pools!

Then why do some people win more often than others? Obviously because some people are better managers than others. You put your money into the right leverage areas and develop the fine edge that gives you an innovative advantage. You avoid the shaky opportunities and ferret out the promising ones. You succeed more often if you have people who can evolve the superior approaches. You succeed more often if you present your approaches, propositions, background, and people in the best light. You succeed more often if you manage your efforts to get the most out of your resources. And you succeed more often if you fine-tune your proposal.

The winners always put the customer's perceptions first. Hobby-shop ideas that offer no benefits to the customer are abandoned early. A going-in approach is just a point of departure for the winners. They look for the approach whose features implement the most benefits to the customer. Then they follow through. They know that the most effective way to get there is with top-down direction, the direction that gets everybody pulling in the *right* direction. And they strive for a competitive proposal, not just a subject report. Benefits get equal billing with them. If they don't see benefits, they can earn their keep for a decade by convincing you not to bid.

12

To Bid or Not to Bid: The Most Important Decision of All

Most bad proposals start with a bad bid/no-bid decision, and many start without a clear-cut decision to bid. A lot of losers just drift into the bid. The losers' bin is full of wish-list proposals. Wish-list proposals are devoid of innovative approaches, and have no discriminators that could produce a win. Usually, management's wish for success was the only reason for entering the competition. For instance, the manager of an aerospace company reads an article on fiber optics, clearly one of the new, vital technologies. Two weeks later he hears of an RFP for using fiber optics to tie parts of a command and control station together. "Bid," he says, even though his company has never done any basic research in this area, has not been working the RFP or interacting with the agency issuing it, has no innovative approach that can elevate it to the winner's circle, and has no qualified leader to mastermind the win. But they go ahead and bid anyway. They ignore the guy who says, "Hey, wait, we don't have any expertise here," and march on to still another loss.

185

TO BID OR NOT
TO BID:
THE MOST
IMPORTANT
DECISION OF ALL

The management of another company decides to bid a spinoff program from its product line, even though the customer has informed the company that he regards the contractor as having a borderline conflict of interest. The customer's legal people advise the contractor to stay out of it, but management decides to go anyhow. Later, when the proposals are evaluated, after an uneventful negotiation period, management is startled when it loses. It asks for a loser's debriefing and spends the next six months trying to figure out what the customer said in the debriefing.

A third management decides to go after a program because one of its market analysts heard that the requestor was unhappy with its present supplier after twenty-five years. Furthermore, according to the analyst, the requestor wants to go with this new company. So without any more questions, management says go, again without checking to see if it has an innovative approach or a qualified leader. It loses. Of course, the competition scared the incumbent. As a result, he cleaned up his act and did a much better job of listening to his customer's hopes, fears, and biases. Months later, another employee of the contractor has coffee with an employee of the requestor. The requestor's employee expresses surprise over the contractor's proposal. "We had no idea you had any expertise in this area," he says. What he fails to add is that they still didn't know where the expertise was. Furthermore, no one could have unseated the incumbent contractor, at least not without a basketful of overpowering discriminators.

These examples are not unusual, but they aren't the most common shortcomings in the bid decision. The most common could be labeled The Drifter. Management just drifts into the bid. It is too uncertain to make an all-out commitment and too insecure to stop. It procrastinates and keeps the effort going on a shoestring. Finally, management traps itself into a bid because it can't walk away from its nickel and dime investment. When that happens, management calls for that last-minute super-effort that is supposed to snatch victory from the jaws of

186

TO BID OR NOT
TO BID:
THE MOST
IMPORTANT
DECISION OF ALL

defeat. Everybody turns to and works around the clock. When everyone is totally exhausted, they submit their marginal, poorly balanced proposal, which in the vast majority of cases loses. Usually the proposal doesn't even make its way through the first gates of the evaluation process.

MAKING THE DECISION TO BID

Now, having talked about how not to make the bid decision, let's discuss how you *should* make the bid decision. We will use a question and answer format.

WHO IS THE CUSTOMER AND THE PEOPLE INVOLVED?

- Agency or company
- Names
- Positions
- Locations
- History and background
- Relationship with other agencies, divisions, and key customer personnel
- Hopes, fears, and biases

Before you think about the business opportunity, you should take a good, hard look at your prospective customer. It is essential to know who you are dealing with in order to make a good bid decision. Many agencies and companies are "tire kickers": they never get around to buying more than a study or two, and doing business with them invariably costs more than it's worth. Some agencies and companies look for quantum steps forward and breakthroughs without worrying about the risks. Others are so risk-conscious that it rules their every action.

You must know where your potential customer sits in the chain of command so that you will know how to respond or whether to respond at all. Who is who in the customer's house and where is everybody located? Has this customer succeeded in the past, or has he had a string of unsuccessful programs and, more important to you, left some bankrupt contractors in his wake? What drives this customer? What are his hopes, fears, and biases? Do you know enough about this customer (and does he know enough about you) to know that you can meet on common ground?

187

WHAT DOES THE
CUSTOMER
WANT AND
WHAT DO YOU
WANT TO SELL?

WHAT DOES THE CUSTOMER WANT AND WHAT DO YOU WANT TO SELL?

- Scope
- Objectives
- Tasks
- Statement of Work
- Work Breakdown Structure
- Deliverables
- Quantities
- Data requirements
- Unique features
- Background

Once you have decided you want to do business with your prospective customer, take a look at what he wants to buy versus what you would like to sell. If the two don't match—and most likely they won't—you have to ask whether or not you can evolve from your going-in approach to the approach that is superior in the eyes of the customer. You must avoid the temptation of trying to sell your hobby-shop approach when it doesn't fit the customer's perceptions.

In addition to this very fundamental question, you have to look at all the usual data. How big is the effort? What are the objectives? Specifically, what are the tasks, the Statement of Work, and the Work Breakdown Structure (the breakdown of tasks into their supporting elements)? What will you deliver? Are there other, not so obvious deliverables such as data requirements (reports, drawings, reviews, prints) and, if so, how extensive are they? What are the unique features of this opportunity that could benefit you—or ruin you? What is the background? Do you really want to pursue the opportunity?

188

TO BID OR NOT
TO BID:
THE MOST
IMPORTANT
DECISION OF ALL

There are no general answers to any of these questions. You have to look at each opportunity in its own light. For that very reason, some companies don't take the time to look at all. But not looking can be an invitation to disaster. You must always look for the position to win. So look hard at the particulars of what the customer wants before you go any further.

HOW FIRM IS THE BUSINESS OPPORTUNITY?

- Requirement (approved?)
- Funding (approved?)
- Support (who and how important?)
- Enemies (who and how important?)
- Competing concepts or programs
- History

An appreciable percentage of the programs contractors pursue turn out to be No Awards. That's right, nobody wins. If you can avoid those dead ends, you will easily increase your win ratio. It is common for No Awards to amount to 10 percent of your bids, and 20 percent is not unusual. Occasionally, in a bad year your No Awards could reach 50 percent. All you have to do is get involved on one major system acquisition, one of those multiyear, government types that gets canceled after a few years. You and your competitors, who banked all or most of your discretionary funds on success, will look at a zero return on investment.

To avoid No Awards, check for a requirement, a tangible product. You don't want to be caught chasing a development agency's hobby shop any more than you want to be caught pushing your unwanted hobby shop. If there is no real requirement, there can't be a development program. And if there is a requirement, is it matched with funding? We have seen programs with top priority that weren't even in next year's funding. The government is notoriously fickle. A change in Administration can wreak havoc on your beautiful five-year business plan overnight.

189

WHEN WILL THE
OPPORTUNITY
MATERIALIZE,
AND HOW LONG
WILL IT TAKE
TO COMPLETE?

Who supports the program and how important are those supporters? And more important, who opposes the program? If the opponents are the people who matter, you may be looking at a program that is going nowhere. Sure, you might get a lot of studies, but when it comes to payoff time and development and production, you won't be able to break through if the people who count aren't positive about the program.

A competition contains more factors than just the people involved. World events, geopolitics, and competing concepts and programs are very real factors too. Remember, developmental agencies, just like contractors, have competing programs. Make sure the program that you are interested in doesn't fall into the also-ran category. There may be some solidly entrenched other program it must unseat before you can realize a return on your investment. That's tough. There have to be some very big discriminators for that to happen.

Finally, look at the history of the business opportunity. There is no end to the programs that cycle through every few years only to fail to make it to development and production. Some get study money every time they make the scene. But they always fail to negotiate some hurdle in the development process. Before you pick up one of these reincarnated programs, make sure you know why it failed on the last go-round. Some programs go through time and time again, catching some supposedly well-managed contractors each time through and failing the same gate each time. Sometimes it's even the same contractor!

WHEN WILL THE OPPORTUNITY MATERIALIZE, AND HOW LONG WILL IT TAKE TO COMPLETE?

- Request for Proposal (RFP)
- Customer funding milestone meetings, if a solicitation is involved
- Program schedule
- Schedule risks and uncertainties

190

TO BID OR NOT
TO BID:
THE MOST
IMPORTANT
DECISION OF ALL

Usually a program can't get started without an RFP. Sole-source programs are rapidly disappearing. Check your customer's development departments. If he is talking big but isn't working hard on an RFP, you had better take a hard look to see if you want to go further. Also, if this customer is serious, he will show all the signs of the worried developer. Somewhere in his house you will find tons of schedule information, including funding milestones, and all sorts of planning information. Your customer is going to be very concerned about schedule risks and uncertainties. And you should be too.

HOW DOES THE CUSTOMER WANT TO CONTRACT FOR THE WORK?

- Type of contract
- Terms and conditions
- Unique factors
- Payment schedule
- Contracting officer or person

Before you leave the customer and his program and look at yourself and your competitors, there's one more checkpoint for you to negotiate. Can you live with the contract features? In many instances contractors have spent a great deal of money developing a highly competitive approach only to no-bid at the last moment. Why? They finally got around to looking at the type of contract the customer required. It was a firm, fixed-price contract for a development program, and that was against corporate policy. Or perhaps the terms and conditions were intolerable. We know of one case where a company spent more than $800,000 on a proposal effort and then withdrew two weeks before the proposal was due to be submitted.

Is there something very unique in the contract arrangements that strongly indicates the opportunity is wired for the guy down the street? Perhaps the payment schedule is strange or the contracting officer is your archenemy, the guy who just can't come up with a structured effort no matter what. Probably all of that information is available on day one or very early at least. Dig it out. It should be a part of your bid decision.

WHY DO YOU WANT TO PURSUE THE OPPORTUNITY?

- Applicability to product line
- Amount of profit in the contract
- Potential follow-on
- Other factors

Now that you have taken a look at your prospective customer and know what he wants to procure, you should take a hard look at yourself. Ask yourself the questions, "Why should I go for it? Is it applicable to my product?" Watch for hobby-shop people in your company who delve into efforts that are not applicable to your product line. Also avoid the efforts with little or no funding, those dead-enders that have no future. If there is no follow-on, and if it will cost a lot to win, maybe you should walk away. We say *maybe* because other factors that are valid could cause you to bid, such as increasing your technology base or making important contacts.

ARE YOU WELL PREPARED TO PURSUE THE OPPORTUNITY?

- Previous applicable contract or independently funded activity
- Knowledgeable people
- Innovative approaches
- Standing with customer
- Contribution to creation of business opportunity and support of opportunity
- Support of customer
- Pre-RFP activities

Wanting to pursue the program is one thing, but being prepared for it is quite another. How will the customer perceive you? Do you come across as a leader in the field? Have you

192

TO BID OR NOT
TO BID:
THE MOST
IMPORTANT
DECISION OF ALL

been working it hard? If the business opportunity is immediate, you have to have an acceptable data base behind you to bid. If not and you would like to get into this business, don't bid now and waste precious dollars. Develop the data base with the intention of bidding on a similar program some months or even years in the future.

You must have the people resources to bid. Rarely can you successfully bring them on board at the last moment. The problem is that the customer has to know them and react to them. He has to know that they are capable, that they fit into your organization, and know how to make things happen. Having the right people is so important that you can sometimes get away with featuring recently hired personnel by showing the customer how they will complement your staff and bring expertise to his problem. You also have to show the customer how you are going to compensate for the new hire being unfamiliar with your systems and personnel. All you have to do is address the discriminators and substantiate your claims.

Before you get too excited about this new business opportunity, look at your going-in approaches. How innovative are they? Do they offer benefits to the customer and give the reasons why he should select you? Innovative approaches are the most important features in your proposal because they give you the winning edge more consistently than anything else. But, as we pointed out before, does the sheer technical brilliance blind you to its utter uselessness? Winners provide features that benefit the customer.

Also, what is your standing with the customer? Is he biased against you? If so, is your arsenal of features, neutralizers, counters, and exploiters sufficient to overcome this handicap? You should go all out on neutralizers. If you can refute whatever weaknesses the customer perceives you as having, the bright light of your features will shine through. Otherwise it will be a wasted effort.

An essential part of being prepared is having contributed to the business opportunity. That's another way of saying you were upstream in Leverage Country. You supported the customer in surveying the activity and fed him data to help him put the RFP together. You were always Johnny-on-the-spot with draft Statements of Work, Work Breakdown Structures, schedules, and specifications. No task was too menial or too extensive. Your idea was to have the customer build the RFP around your approach, and even though he knew this and worked to keep all his options open, you nevertheless get the right flavor in the RFP and go in with a good image to boot.

WHO ARE YOUR COMPETITORS?

- Names of companies
- People
- Approaches
- Ranking
- Relative standings with customer
- Unusual factors

You won't be completely prepared until you form a basis for comparison. That basis is your competition. How do you stack up? Who are the competitors and how long have they been in the business? If they have been working the program for years, have a broad and good relationship with the customer, and have some exciting new ideas, you are in for a battle. But they may be having their troubles, or you may be way ahead with your innovations.

Never underestimate people and approaches. What kind of teams have your competitors sacrificed to the effort? And how do your approaches compare to what you know or think the competitors will go in with? Rank your competitors. What you are interested in is how you stand in relation to them in the eyes of the customer. Make up a cross matrix of all the competitors. It will tell you whether or not you can bid in a truly competitive mode. Ranking your competitors is like looking your opponent in the eye. The more familiar you are with the opponent, the more psyched up you are for the battle. That always helps to produce a winner.

- If a proposal is required, what is the strategy (how can you win)?
- Going-in approach
- Technical efforts required
- Leaders and key people requirements
- Facilities
- Dollars
- Other resources
- Proposal schedule and activities
- Proposal and program organization

Now that you have examined all of the players and the competing approaches, you are ready for the final question. What sacrifices do you have to make to win? Answer this question objectively and dispassionately. You have to develop a strategy for winning, and that means evaluating your going-in approach to determine what you have to do to it to make it fit the customer's perceptions. What kind of an effort will that require? How many people will it require? Do you have the right leader, and are you willing to sacrifice that leader to the effort for the duration of the program?

How about facilities? Are you willing to set aside a comfortable meeting place for putting together the proposal? Do you have an adequate budget for the effort? Remember, you can't drift in on a hope and a prayer. Your bid decision must be made on the premise of winning, and that requires a full commitment.

Any number of other specialized factors also must be considered. Every program has its own assortment. It could be a tough schedule, peculiar organization, or an unusual activity. Based on all of these factors, make a conscious decision to bid or not to bid. Most companies decide to bid far too often. Many feel it's almost a crime not to bid, whatever the circumstances. Nothing could be further from the truth. Bid only if you can win. And if you do bid, make it a total commitment.

13

To Maximize Your Win Probability, Select the Right People and Organize Them Properly

Before you select a team to write the proposal, you should know what a good proposal is. Put in the most simple terms: The good proposal is one that wins. So when you start to select people from your organization, look for those who have a track record of winning. They may not be the best technical people in your organization, and you may not even like them, but you select them because they have a proven track record as innovative leaders who produce winners. Obviously they are doing something right.

It is amazing how many managements will stick with a

losing team, sometimes for years. All too often we find the same losers going from proposal to proposal. These are solid, hard-working people. In fact, the only thing wrong with them is that they don't win. They are available, though. The fellow who isn't available is the one who just won the last big job. Remember Chapter 11, where we talked about why some people win and some people lose? Well, people make the organization; organizations don't make people. Selecting the right people from your organization is absolutely the most leveraged management action you can take.

Why is it so difficult to assemble a winning team? Why do some people succeed and others, seemingly equally talented, fail? Why do some companies win 80 percent of their bids and others win only 25 percent, or less? And what kind of people should you select for your proposal team? Obviously some have to be at the heart of the innovative matter, experts in the subject matter of the RFP. Also, somewhere on that team there has to be a person who has a great deal of experience in working proposals, someone who will keep you from making the same mistakes that some inexperienced clod would fall into. Your team must have as its leader someone who can manage problems, people, and systems. In short, your team has to be a mixture of many types. This is always the case with any complicated program, and a proposal is nothing more than a complicated program with an additional ingredient—panic.

COMMIT YOURSELF TO WINNING

Losing is never fun, and it certainly isn't profitable. You waste assets and diminish morale. Winning means that you are doing something right. If you work proposals, you have to believe that the winner wins because he did the best job of convincing the customer of his superior approach. If you don't commit yourself to winning, writing proposals will be a frustrating experience for you every time. You will spend most of your time trying to rationalize away your losses instead of learning from them. The woods are full of the "we was robbed" gang. The truth of the matter is, when you lose, almost invariably you did not have the superior approach. The customer wasn't a bad guy, and there was no "fix" that locked you out.

People on your proposal team have to have the discipline to evolve a superior approach. That is, an approach that's superior *in the eyes of the customer.* The customer's perception is the only reality. That's very tough for some people to believe. They have firm ideas about how to do the job, and it is hard for them to evolve an approach that some other party perceives as superior. If the team members are not emotionally committed to evolve an approach that the customer deems superior, they will have a hard time following the positioning-to-win discipline. The team will not have much time to adjust either. On a proposal it has to respond fast. It has to be alert to every signal, both from the customer and from management, and it has to react before the customer begins to shift his attention to someone else—your competitor. The point-design guy who believes that his design is right the way it is and who won't change his mind has no place on a proposal team. You must have people who will listen and react to the customer's perceptions of your conceptions. That's evolving a superior approach, and that's what it takes to win.

Knowing how to evolve a superior approach is the major part of the winner's secret. Making it obvious to the customer is the other part needed to position to win. Some people still feel that highlighting good points is somehow improper. How many times have you heard someone say, "My customer doesn't like for me to point out my features and go through all that stuff about telling him how it benefits him. He would rather search it out for himself." This attitude not only doesn't make sense, but it rarely, if ever, leads to a win. What customer wants to do unnecessary work and spin his wheels looking for what should be, or could be, plain to see if the bidder just took the time to show him how his approach implements benefits to him? Your team members have to know how to make the most of their offering in order to position to win.

The winning team always takes the time to learn how to

drive out the argumentative headlines that show "Why you?" If your team members won't do this, don't use them on proposals. Only people with expertise in the subject matter can do this. They know how to fashion these argumentative headlines around your benefits and features. To be a winner, you have to learn to address your weaknesses as well as your strengths. If you look away from your weaknesses, you will lose some points by default. And you don't want to find out how many you can afford to lose. No matter how serious the weakness is, you had better address it with competitive theses rather than ignore it altogether. If you can't come up with a good neutralizer for your major weaknesses, don't bid.

Those who win consistently are totally honest. Most contractors have little trouble with honesty. However, occasionally we do see a feather merchant at work. Feather merchants rarely win; only superior approaches consistently win. The beauty of the discriminator discipline in positioning to win is that you aren't just learning how to propose it better. *You are developing something better to propose.*

Winners use the discriminator discipline to overkill with substantiation. They learn to make a claim and then prove it in every way possible.

The secrets of winning never change:

- Force yourself to evolve a superior approach
- Clearly state how your approach implements benefits to the customer
- Use argumentative headlines to highlight your messages
- Address all strengths and weaknesses, preferably in the first paragraph of each chapter
- Be totally honest
- Answer all questions, both stated and implied
- Substantiate every claim

START WITH THE LEADER

There are two leaders in any proposal, or at least in winning proposals. The first, and the most important, is the proposal leader. He or she is the person with all of the innovative smarts that will shape your approaches. The other leader is the proposal specialist. He or she is the person with all of the proposal smarts. The proposal leader has to have the last say and make the decisions. He or she is the boss. But if you have selected the right person as the proposal leader, he will make sure that the proposal specialist's procedures are carried out. This will ensure the successful packaging of all of those bright ideas that the creative people dream up.

Many people think that the proposal specialist and the proposal leader are one and the same, but there are important differences between them. To assume they are the same is a fatal mistake and a common cause of proposal failure. To be competitive, your proposal leader must be close to the heart of the innovative matter that forms the basis of your proposal. This person is the innovator. Usually he or she is a specialist drawn from one of your functional groups. The leader will take the program through the exploratory phases and the proposal definition phases, then continue to guide the program through all of the remaining phases. If you have made a good choice, you will probably want the leader to manage the program even after the contract is awarded.

In choosing your proposal leader, look for the following qualifications:

- Strong and disciplined but not bull-headed
- Able to communicate and accept criticism and direction
- Flexible and willing to step outside his discipline
- Staying power and the ability to pace himself
- Good attendance record
- Not averse to working long hours and on weekends
- Able to delegate but always retain control of the team
- Able to see the big picture while tracking details

This proposal leader has to be at the heart of the innovative effort. We cannot stress this enough. If the proposal is for a new missile, the leader could be a missile designer or a systems integrator. If the most unique part of the missile is the guidance set, the leader could be an avionics specialist. If the proposal is for a new engine, the proposal leader could be a propulsion expert. But one thing is certain: the proposal leader should not be a pure administrator. You will not be able to evolve a superior approach if your leader has no expertise in the subject matter of the proposal.

The proposal leader must be strong and disciplined but not bull-headed. A good proposal team will be comprised of many strong-willed, difficult-to-manage people, so a strong personality is essential to a successful effort. But the proposal is a complicated new venture with a lot of give and take, so there is no place for a leader who is unreasonable.

The proposal leader has to be able to communicate and take criticism and direction from many people. There is no place for an introvert. The leader certainly doesn't work in an ivory tower: All his moves are visible to all levels of the organization, from the lowest person on the totem pole to the big man himself.

Perhaps one of the most demanding requirements of the proposal leader is flexibility and a willingness to step outside his discipline. The systems integrator who becomes a proposal leader must learn to communicate and direct all the disciplines involved in the proposal. These often include schedulers, estimators, production engineers, factory operations personnel, management systems people, designers, packagers, and sometimes even management.

It's a tough job being the proposal leader. Luckily, however, the maximum push interval in writing the proposal is usually no more than ninety days. But the pre- and post-RFP activity may be extensive and of long duration, perhaps up to a year or more for major system acquisitions. So staying power and the ability to pace himself is important. He has to provide leadership throughout the life of the proposal. He also has to drive out the discriminators and, under the direction of the proposal specialist, provide the expertise to classify the proposal influencers. More than anyone else on the team, the leader must be able to single out influencers and write effective competitive theses. If the proposal leader is absent for any length of time, the proposal will drift. Unscheduled absences are particularly bad, since no alternate member can effectively stand in for the leader. Being a proposal leader involves long hours and a lot of weekend work. It's not a job for the prima donna or the nine-to-fiver.

Finally, the proposal leader is responsible for delegating as much as he can while maintaining control of the team at all times. This isn't an easy task, but the proposal leader is at home in the forest or among the trees. He thinks "overview," but he also must care about details. On a typical day he may have to meet with top management, attend design reviews, establish program policy, and review the covers for the proposal books. The proposal leader has his hand in everything. And in some things such as the executive summary, he has to play a major role.

All of these qualifications are demanding, and they are a big order for many people, particularly those who have never led a proposal before and especially those who have never even worked on a proposal. The sole qualifications of some may be that they are at the heart of the innovative matter, have special expertise, and have a talent for leadership. But the record shows that if these people accept the support of a qualified proposal specialist, they can become excellent proposal leaders. The win record of the first-time proposal leader is just as good as that of the experienced leader (and far better than the leader who just won a contract) when he is teamed with a qualified proposal specialist. The leader who has just won feels he knows all the shortcuts, and he may try to take many of them the next time around. He forgets that what produced that gorgeous insight for winning was the painstaking attention to detail. No two proposals are ever the same, and *only the discriminator discipline will hammer out a winner.* Of course, when you take shortcuts in the discriminator discipline, you aren't exercising competitive convergence and you are decreasing your win probability. It doesn't take much to relegate you to the also-ran category.

Now that we have talked about the proposal leader and the characteristics that are so essential for him to have in positioning you to win, let's look at the other half of this winning combination.

How do the proposal specialist and the proposal leader work together? That is usually the first question a new proposal leader asks when he comes to the specialist for help. The proposal leader knows he needs help, and he expects the proposal specialist to provide that help. But the leader's real question is, what does a proposal specialist do?

The specialist does just what the name implies: he specializes in proposal development. He knows every mistake that can be made on a proposal, and he has probably made most of them himself, sometimes more than once. He knows what works and what doesn't. He learns from each proposal leader so that when he comes on to a new proposal he can pass on to the current leader the accumulated experience of the division or company (or many companies, if he comes from the outside). In addition, the specialist knows the current procurement practices and, more important, how they are changing. The proposal leader who worked on a proposal last year may be surprised to discover that everything has changed since then. Since these practices change constantly, you can't position yourself to win if you don't keep up with them.

The greatest skill that the proposal specialist brings to the effort is his ability to drive out messages and to articulate these in argumentative headlines and competitive theses. He also provides management expertise that allows the proposal leader and the team to sequence their activities and thus make the most of their resources.

Look at the differences in background between the proposal leader and the proposal specialist. The proposal leader is boss because he has the innovative expertise required to drive out the winning approach, but he may have no proposal experience. On the other side, the proposal specialist may have no expertise in the proposal subject matter, but he has an extensive background in packaging whatever you have to offer. He is skilled in competitive convergence. As the proposal leader's alter ego, he can enhance the innovator's expertise with a disciplined process.

Proposal specialists usually come from program management positions. Typically they are technical people by education and program people by trade. But most important, they know how to apply the competitive convergence discipline to proposals. Generally, they have done everything from leading programs to managing proposals. In addition, they have written executive summaries, technical chapters, and management volumes. With all of this experience, they've learned how to get responsive, competitive proposals out the door. They have learned something different from each proposal leader they have worked with, so their experience is wide ranging.

LEVERAGE YOUR TALENTS THROUGH YOUR PROPOSAL TEAM

Your proposal team is a unique group designed for a mini-crash program, which is exactly what proposal development is. The team is assembled upstream of the RFP. By RFP time, it could have as many as several hundred people manning the program. But after the proposal is submitted, only about 10 percent remain on the team. Perhaps only that 10 percent continues with the program after the contract is won. The other 90 percent go back to their functional groups, perhaps to go on to another proposal sometime later.

Organizing proposals is not like organizing technical functional groups. Functional-group disciplines tend to be constant for all efforts; proposals aren't. Every proposal is different. For each new proposal, your mix of people must be different. A normal organization is a relatively stable set of functional groups designed to service its product lines. Every time an opportunity knocks, the first thing you will do is assign the proposal to one of these functional groups. But you do this only for contract-change orders and narrow, highly specialized technical studies. The rest of the time, you have to create a specialized, short-duration group to respond to the RFP—in other words, a proposal team (see Figure 13-1).

FIGURE 13-1. THE PROPOSAL TEAM IS A UNIQUE
ORGANIZATION OF SPECIALISTS

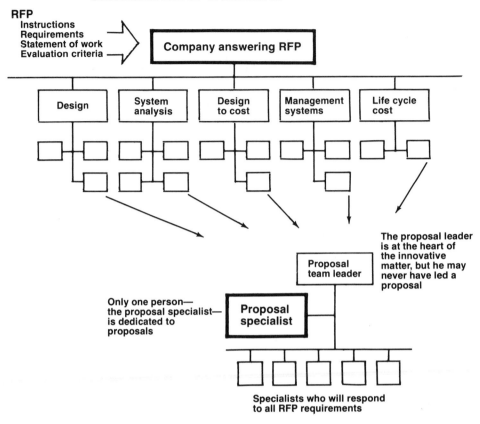

Putting together a proposal team is another of those many factors that make proposals difficult and challenging. It isn't a matter of sacrificing one or two key people for a period of months: you have to pry many key people loose from each of your functional groups. Many times you won't be able to find all of the talent you need within your company. On high-technology thrusts, those that extend the state of the art, you will usually have to go outside the company. Sometimes you may need outside help for as much as half of what the RFP requests. If it was difficult to pry those highly talented people out of your own functional groups, imagine how difficult it will be to get the same response from another company. If you don't have your top management on board working hard, you won't succeed. It takes coordination between top managements to get in-house team members and outside subcontractors committed to the job. Many times the only person on this team who has played the proposal game before is the proposal specialist. For everyone else, even the proposal leader, this may be the first time out.

For this quickie organization to operate smoothly, the functional groups have to keep their hands in because they are responsible for the technical integrity of the effort (see Figure 13-2). The members of the proposal team aren't free from the influence of their functional group; the functional group is still responsible for their actions. In fact, the supervisor of the functional group must supervise the efforts of proposal team members. The proposal leader, on the other hand, directs their efforts toward satisfying the requirements of the RFP. Thus the supervisor is responsible for the "how" and the proposal leader for the "what." This matrix organization provides the top-down direction that keeps everyone pulling together.

But how do you organize this unique group, and how does it work together? Even though every proposal is different, there are general ground rules for organizing the proposal team. One important rule is to organize the team to respond to the deliverables, (see Figure 13-3). Assign someone to each volume, each chapter in each volume, the letter of transmittal, orals, mockups, and whatever else is required to respond to the RFP. You will have some trouble here because there will be an overpowering tendency to organize along functional lines. If you let this get out of hand, you stand a good chance of doing nothing more than duplicating your functional organization while overlooking certain requirements of the RFP. What you want to do is leverage your talents by optimizing your organization relative to the RFP. This will give you a rare chance to innovate on something other than technical matters.

Before we leave the organization of proposal teams, we will answer a frequent question: Where does the proposal specialist fit in the functional group? Everyone else has a definite home. The engineers fit into the Engineering organiza-

FIGURE 13-2. THE PROPOSAL MATRIX PROVIDES
TOP-DOWN DIRECTION.

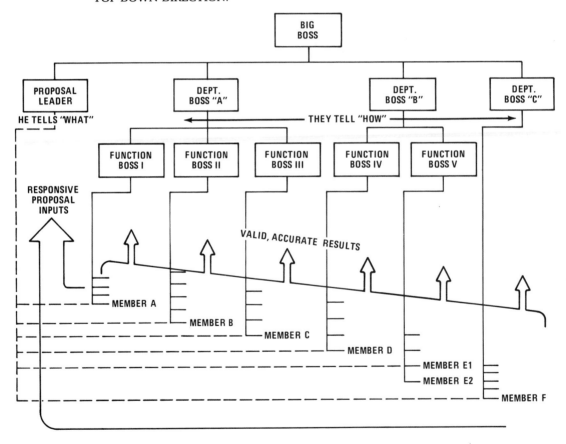

tion, the machine shop guy fits into Operations, and so forth. The answer is anywhere in the functional organization, from the top to the bottom.

ORGANIZE YOUR REPORTING LEVELS

Figure 13-4 presents various levels of assignments. Level 1 has the proposal specialist in the position of alter ego to the division manager, the big boss. This is an ideal arrangement, and it certainly leverages the time your top management spends on proposals. Managers should put in much more time on proposal development, not just from the standpoint of

FIGURE 13-3. ORGANIZE YOUR PROPOSAL TEAM TO FIT THE DELIVERABLES.

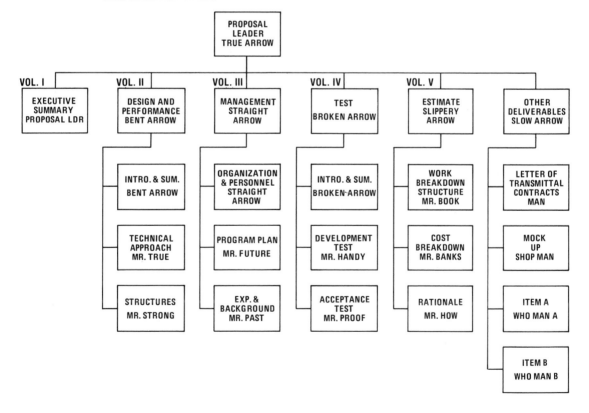

FIGURE 13-4. EMPHASIZE PROPOSAL DEVELOPMENT BY ELEVATING THE REPORTING LEVEL.

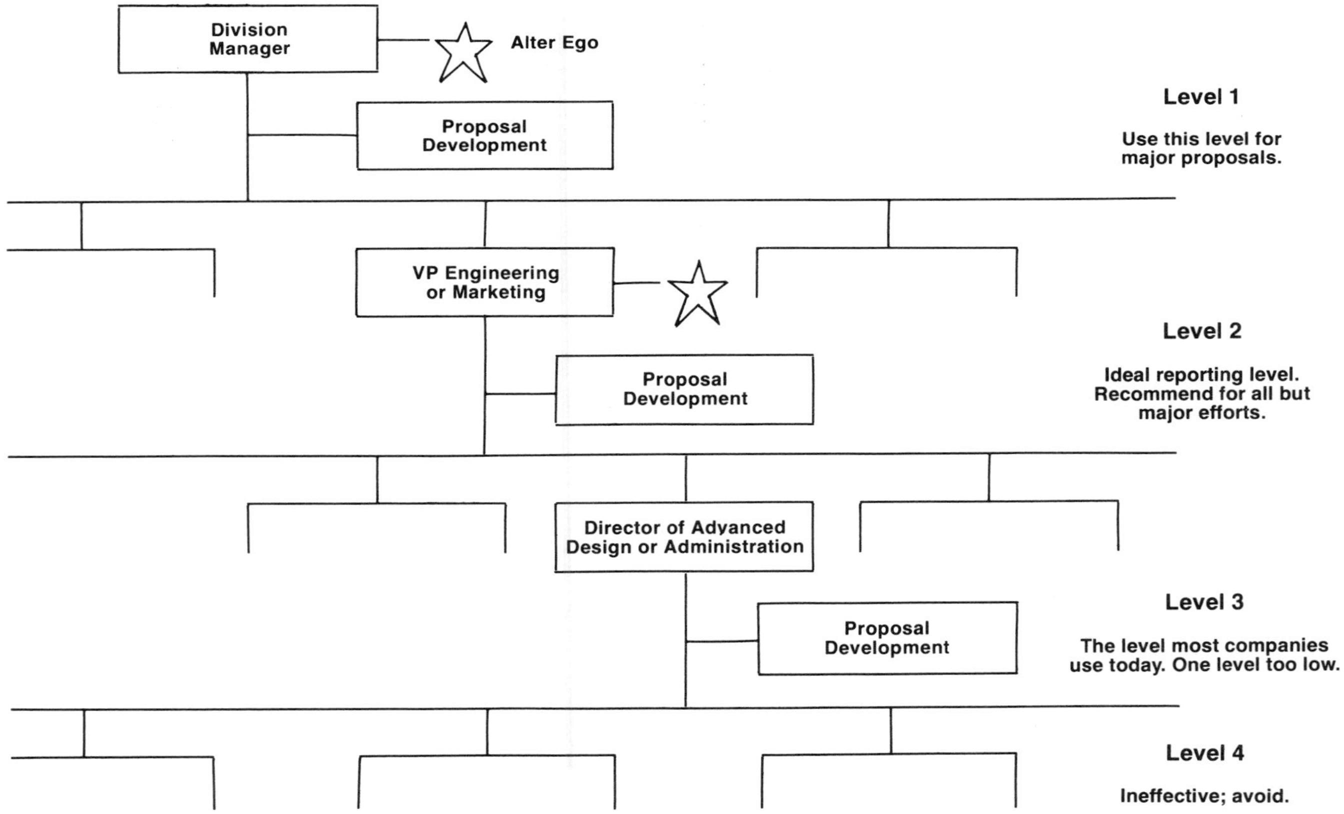

Level 1

Use this level for major proposals.

Level 2

Ideal reporting level. Recommend for all but major efforts.

Level 3

The level most companies use today. One level too low.

Level 4

Ineffective; avoid.

Alter Ego

Division Manager

Proposal Development

VP Engineering or Marketing

Proposal Development

Director of Advanced Design or Administration

Proposal Development

ensuring the viability and fidelity of the content, but to assure the competitiveness of the proposed approaches. This is hard for the general manager because he must oversee so many other functions, such as performing on the contracts already in-house, avoiding a pending strike, or hobnobbing with the corporate people. But he could solve all that by having the proposal specialist or the head of the proposal group represent him on proposals. He would certainly win more often if he did this. It would be top-down direction of the highest kind.

The outside consultant enjoys this kind of relationship regularly with the heads of many of the top aerospace corporations when they are working on a big one. He drives out the messages they want to see in their proposals. Then he takes that to the proposal team and drives it home as the alter ego of the division manager. It always works well, perhaps because he is from the outside. He can be much more candid in his dealings with management and functional supervisors.

If general managers wanted to put more emphasis on proposal development, they could elevate the head of their proposal development group to be a member of their staff. It would be far easier for managers to initiate the proposal development discipline from a position of strength and equal standing than to go through the back door from the bottom up. But except for the really big ones, where the manager uses a consultant, proposal development groups usually answer at Level 2 or 3, and many of them find themselves even at Level 4.

Level 2 probably is more realistic. If indeed the marketing function is a strong force headed by a qualified and dynamic leader, proposal development might well reside in the marketing function. In fact, it probably belongs there for all but the very biggest efforts. It would be a simple matter for the general manager to designate a given proposal effort as so important that during the course of the effort the proposal development fellow would report directly to him. But it is imperative that the general manager be totally committed to the full proposal discipline. He does that by providing his full support and giving liberally of his time, making it clear that no other function in his organization can ever make an end-run around the proposal development discipline.

What all this adds up to is a realization that many in management fail to appreciate the whole proposal development process. Doubtless there are more mistakes than correct steps taken on proposal efforts. It is entirely possible, especially in some of the bigger competitions involving a dozen or more volumes and tens of millions of dollars, that the winner is the competitor who made the fewest mistakes. He doesn't win; he's just the last one standing in the ring after the others have knocked themselves out! Thus a savvy and aggressive management has a lot of leverage available in positioning to win, particularly regarding personnel and organization.

14

Follow Proven Procedures in Positioning to Win

The proposal specialist spends much of his time at the beginning of every proposal just heading off mistakes. While he is doing this, the proposal specialist, with the leader's concurrence, sets up operational practices specially designed for a fast-reaction matrix organization and gets everyone together. The team that collocates is far more effective than the one whose people are scattered all over the place. Collocation gets the team members out of their normal environment and away from their usual tasks. If they are to be key members of the effort, they must dedicate themselves wholeheartedly to the proposal. They must interact with the other specialists working on the proposal, some of whom they have not worked with before and indeed may never have even met before coming on the proposal. But now, in the short time that they will be working on the proposal, usually thirty to ninety days, they have to establish a rapport and learn to work together efficiently.

And work together they must. All of the proposal tasks must be defined and scheduled. Progress against detailed schedules must be monitored daily. Each day starts with a coordination meeting where progress is monitored. Every problem and shortcoming that can't be solved on the spot is identified as an action item. Every action item gets an assignee and a due date. If a subject is too involved or specialized for the coordination meeting it is scheduled for a splinter meeting. At these meetings specialists in the subject matter hammer out details without holding up the other proposal team members. Coordination meetings are brief: at the beginning of the proposal they may be as long as an hour, but for the most part they last less than half an hour.

The proposal specialist knows that you achieve accountability for completing action items by requiring documentation of results. You have probably heard the assignees say, "It's already done." Then, later on, the people who were to use the data say, "We never got anything usable." When you try to put these two factors together, you find out that the assignees were really saying, "We've got it figured out in general," while the users were looking for documented specifics. It always takes the assignees time to add the specifics. Often when the assignees try to implement their plans, they find out they can't get there without inputs from other people. That's the basis for additional action items.

Everything looks okay until the assignees try to get specific. So the proposal-specialist makes the assignees get specific early by designating the format of the outputs (see Figure 14-1). It's amazing what detailed reactions you get to a documented action item. Everybody seems to come out of the woods to point out the shortcomings, deficiencies, and inadequacies of the results. That may make some people uncomfortable, but the proposal specialist knows that it is the beginning of getting the job done right. Now you have everybody involved and you are on the way toward finding the best solution. But you never get anywhere until the problem—the action item—is identified and solved.

The proposal specialist insists that every problem results

FIGURE 14-1. ACHIEVE ACCOUNTABILITY FOR ACTION
ITEMS AND DOCUMENT THE OUTPUT.

ACTION ITEMS

What	Why	Who	When Sched-ule	When Ac-tual	How
1. Produce technical data base schedule	For proposal substantiation	Scheduler	3/1	3/1	Detailed schedule signed by functional and proposal leaders
2. Flight test plan	For estimators and write-ups	Flight tester	3/7	Open	Memo, including schedule signed by flight test supervisor and proposal leader
3. Get system integrator on board	To cover open section	Proposal leader	3/1	3/1	Get concurrence from supervisor in memo
4. Vendor Statement of Work	To get requests to vendors	Material leader	3/10	Open	Specifications approved by contracts and proposal leader
5. Arrange for special badges	For security purposes	Proposal development specialist	3/3	3/1	Get badges and distribute
6. Preliminary competitive thesis	To provide top-down direction	Proposal development specialist	3/5	3/5	Approved by proposal leader
7. Final competitive thesis	For proposal team	Proposal leader	3/8	Open	Memo by proposal leader
8. Define test drawing article	For estimators and write-ups	Designer	3/12	Open	Drawings signed by functional leaders and proposal leaders
9. Clarify contract terms	For materials Statement of Work	Contracts person	3/9	3/9	Memo to all

in an action item designed to solve it. Every action item is assigned to one person and is scheduled for completion on or before its due date, and the sooner the better. The documented results also must satisfy the people who need the results.

The proposal specialist has assimilated all of the good procedures used by past proposal teams, and these he passes on to the next proposal team. Generally, since they are logical, practical, and time proven, the team will accept the vast majority of them. But it will make some changes and introduce a few new wrinkles. The ones that work go into the proposal specialist's goodie bag, to be passed on to the next team. The ones that fail are also passed on—as mistakes to be avoided.

In successful proposal development everything centers around the customer's RFP or, if it hasn't been issued, a strawman RFP. The proposal team is organized to match the deliverables called for in the RFP. Someone is assigned to head up each volume and each chapter within each volume (see Figure 14-2). If appendixes are required, someone is assigned to them. Team members are also assigned to the letter of transmittal, Vugraphs, mockups, and anything else that may be required by the proposal instructions.

The RFP's evaluation criteria, statement of work, and background material drive the proposal team's and your supporting organizations' efforts in identifying the discriminators of the competition. Your field offices and marketing organization provide the information on the competitors' going-in approaches. You use this information to draw up your lists of discriminators and classify them as influencers.

The snags in the proposal development process begin to crop up after the discriminators are drawn up even when everyone thinks the discriminators are so great. They begin to forget the real purpose of the discriminators and treat the proposal just like a subject report. You would be lucky at this point if you could identify an approach, much less find out how it might differ from your competitors' approaches or how it benefited the customer. A good practice for making sure that the discriminators are addressed in the proposal is to write a competitive thesis on each critical discriminator (see Chapter

FIGURE 14-2. FOLLOW PROVEN PROCEDURES TO DEVELOP SUPERIOR PROPOSALS.

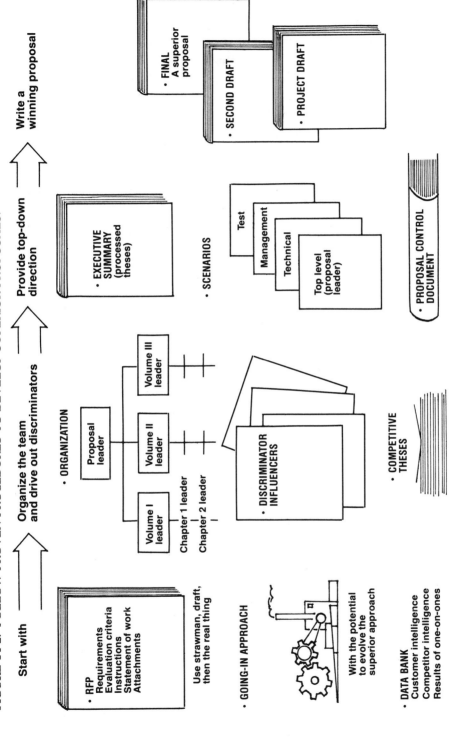

10). These theses are built around your proposal influencers (see Chapters 4 through 8).

Your competitive theses respond to the key discriminators discussed in Chapters 2 and 3. What you really have when you finish is a good picture of the story, claims, and positions that your proposal must substantiate. It presents the challenge to your team. These theses don't have to contain the substantiations, but they do have to identify them. In fact, all of the information can be put in the figures, tables, and illustrations (see Chapter 16). These figures, tables, and illustrations are assigned as tasks for the experts, and these tasks must substantiate the competitive approaches contained in the theses. Use your theses as the basis of an executive summary. Write one even if it isn't formally requested by the customer and distribute it to everyone working on the proposal.

PREPARING PROPOSAL SCENARIOS

The next step in the proposal development procedure is to drive the competitive approach into the proposal outline. Top-down direction is essential here. The proposal leader, his volume leaders, and their chapter leaders prepare a scenario of what they are going to write. The proposal leader's scenario provides direction to his volume leaders, and their scenario provides further top-down direction. The trick is to use scenarios to impart top-down direction to the other proposal writers. Thus the proposal leader must put out his scenario first and coordinate it with his management and all of his key proposal team members. When everyone is satisfied that this top-level scenario contains the main features, neutralizers, counters, and exploiters, you go to the volume-level scenarios. These in turn are carefully reviewed and modified until they track the top-level scenario. Then it's off to the chapter-level scenarios and, if you want, to lower levels, although most teams stop at the chapter level.

To keep everything straight, assemble all of the outlines, discriminators, influencers, argumentative headlines and theses, and scenarios, along with proposal administrative matter, in a Proposal Control Document. Administrative matters consist of such items as the proposal development schedule, the estimating schedule, the technical data-base schedule, names, locations, and telephone numbers of team members, and policy statements that affect proposal strategy. Give the Proposal Control Document to any newly assigned team member to bring him or her up to speed on your proposal strategy for winning. The RFP and the Proposal Control Document are the only things a team member needs to prepare his part of the proposal. The RFP tells what's required to be responsive. The Proposal Control Document tells how you are organizing your response, who is responsible for each part of the response, and the schedule for preparing the response. It also provides top-down direction for implementing the response.

Once you have figured out what you are going to write, you are ready to do the first draft. The procedures for positioning to win have prepared you for the actual writing. You now have all of your messages sorted out, and all you have to do is put them on paper. But this isn't easy. "Write," the leader finally says. Choke! Nothing comes out. Where do you start? It happens all the time. The best thing to remember is that you have done all the planning right, so you are indeed ready to write. Allow yourself the luxury of the false start and begin the draft according to the plan and the top-down direction. Once it's on paper, you can revise it and clean it up. But get it on paper first. Remember, you have planned for some review teams downstream to help you make it right. The object now is to turn out a complete draft, a complete presentation of your approaches, propositions, capabilities, plans, and background.

Figure 14-3 shows the stages of the proposal process from the time you have your influencers until your proposal is in the hands of the customer. It emphasizes review teams and proposal cosmetics. These procedures are designed to save you money and time and eliminate unnecessary steps. Your program and marketing people review the influencers. This is a time for management to get its hands in upstream, in Leverage Country, where it will do the most good. Reviewing the influencers allows them to contribute to the proposal at the start, not when it's cast in concrete.

Scenarios work much the same way. They are intended strictly for the review of your program office and proposal team. Figure 14-4 shows the proposal scenario form. The top part of the form provides housekeeping information and who it applies to: the whole proposal (top level), a volume of the proposal (volume level), a chapter of one volume (chapter level), a section of one chapter (section level), and the number and title of the part addressed. It shows when the scenario was issued, who issued it, where he is located, and his telephone number. This information is followed by the proposal title, the customer, the RFP number, and the submittal date.

Next, the scenario form shows the RFP requirements, which include the instructions, evaluation criteria, and

FIGURE 14-3. THE WINNING PROPOSAL INCLUDES SCENARIOS, REVIEWS, AND DRAFTS.

Draft	Definition	Use of Review Teams	Proportion of Rough Art to Final Art	Finished Art and Text in Place
Proposal influencers ◇	List of discriminators, including strengths and weaknesses	Program, Marketing Review	———	———
Scenarios ◇	RFP Requirements addressed, argumentative headlines, lead-in paragraphs, and organization of proposal	Program Review	———	———
Rough draft ◇	Complete rough draft, typed, with art on trailing pages	Proposal team	25/75	No
Polished draft ◇	A perfect draft, just as you will give to customer	Dedicated review team	0/100	Yes
Proposal	A fine-tuned Red Team draft	Project review of deliverables	0/100	Yes

specifications. In this section the assignee must address the customer's perceptions, as stated in the RFP.

The assignee then writes the theme and a white paper. The theme includes an argumentative headline of a few sentences (actually, the shorter the better), then tells how the features of your approach implement benefits to the customer. The white paper is the competitive thesis that features, neutralizes, counters, and exploits the discriminators. It goes on to list all of your claims that you will substantiate in the following chapters with text and artwork, including tables. If the competitive thesis won't fit on the first page, continue it on a separate sheet or on the back of the form. This should take about an hour or two to complete. It is important to do it in sequence from the proposal leader to the volume leader and on down the line. Each level gets the direction from the level above it. This top-down direction is illustrated in Figures 14-5 and 14-6.

In the outline section, you tell how you will organize the contents of your proposal, by volume, chapter, or section. If you are the proposal leader, spell out the volumes only. If you are the volume leader, go only to the chapter level. Chapter leaders go to the section level, and so on, until you reach the lowest level of the organization.

Figure 14-5 gives the proposal leader's scenario for the Exotic Bridge Construction study. Jane Doe writes her scenario for the overview of the executive summary. She gives the up-front message, the message she wants everyone to see. Her scenario addresses the intent of the RFP. In her theme she states how the major feature of her approach ("The demonstrated forming and joining process") implements the major benefit to the customer ("More trade studies in greater detail"). The RFP evaluation criteria stated that this is the most important, so that's what she strives for.

Her competitive thesis elaborates on this theme. She develops the theme in a series of claims that the next level of people, Bill, John, Willy, Sue, and Bob, who have Volumes 1 to 5, will go on to substantiate. Let's see how one of these people, John, responds to Jane's top-level direction.

FIGURE 14-4. USE PROPOSAL SCENARIOS TO DRIVE DIRECTION FROM TOP TO BOTTOM.

TOP LEVEL ☐   Do these in succession making sure

VOLUME LEVEL ☐   that each successive layer

CHAPTER LEVEL ☐   tracks the higher scenario.

SECTION LEVEL ☐

ISSUE NO. ___Which___   **ISSUE DATE** ___When___

RESPONSIBLE PARTY: LEADER ___Who___   **LOCATION** ___Where___   **EXT.** ___Where___

PROPOSAL TITLE AND NO. _____

CUSTOMER _____   **RFP. NO.** _____   **SUBMITTAL DATE** _____

VOLUME AND CHAPTER TITLE AND NO. _____

RFP REQUIREMENTS: _____ Where is the need for the proposal, volume, chapter, or subsection called out and what are the instructions, criteria, specifications and other requirements it must meet.

THEME: _____ An argumentative headline of a few sentences, the shorter the better. But tell how the features of your approach implement benefits to the customer. Tell also "Why You?"

WHITE PAPER: _____ A competitive thesis that features, neutralizes, counters and exploits all of the Discriminators. A paragraph of claims that you will substantiate in the following chapters with expository text and art (tables, photographs, and figures).

_____

_____

_____

_____

_____

OUTLINE

NO.	TITLE	NAME	PGS	NO.	TITLE	NAME	PGS
	Tell how you are going to organize the contents of your proposal, volume, chapter, or section. If you are the proposal leader, spell out the volumes only. If you are the volume leader go only to the chapter level. Chapter leaders go to the section level, and so on, until you get to the lowest level of organization.						

FIGURE 14-5. THE TOP-LEVEL SCENARIO COMES FIRST AND STATES THE DOMINANT MESSAGE.

TOP LEVEL ☒

VOLUME LEVEL ☐

CHAPTER LEVEL ☐

SECTION LEVEL ☐   ISSUE NO. _First_   ISSUE DATE _2/25/81_

RESPONSIBLE PARTY: LEADER _Jane Doe_   LOCATION _Bld 2_   EXT. _1234_

PROPOSAL TITLE AND NO. _432 - Exotic Bridge Construction Study_

CUSTOMER _Big Bridge Co._   **RFP. NO.** _32_   **SUBMITTAL DATE** _4/15/81_

VOLUME AND CHAPTER TITLE AND NO. _1. Executive Summary, Chapter 1. Overview_

RFP REQUIREMENTS: _Lead-in letters clearly state how your approach will benefit us and tell how it will maximize trade-study output. Trade studies are most important._

THEME: _Because we start with a demonstrated forming and joining process, we maximize study payoff through more trade studies in greater detail_

WHITE PAPER: We believe the key technology element in your bridge is the beam builder. Though important, all other program elements depend on the successful, timely development of this machine. Beam-builder development risk can be reduced if an existing capability is available. We have that capability. We have successfully demonstrated a continuous forming process, using the exotic material you speicify. No one else has. Having this "leg up" enables us to offer you two benefits. First, we can move to the next level of detail in beam-builder trades. Secondly, without compromising the all-important beam-builder development, we can focus greater effort on identification and trades of assembly and operations techniques. This will maximize · · · ·

OUTLINE

NO.	TITLE	NAME	PGS
1.	Executive Summary	Bill	25
2.	Technical	John	200
3.	Test program	Willy	100
4.	Management	Sue	35
5.	Cost	Bob	unl.

NO.	TITLE	NAME	PGS

FIGURE 14-6. THE VOLUME LEVEL CARRIES ON THE MESSAGE FROM THE TOP LEVEL AND GIVES DIRECTION TO THE CHAPTER LEVEL.

TOP LEVEL ☐

VOLUME LEVEL ☒

CHAPTER LEVEL ☐

SECTION LEVEL ☐   ISSUE NO. _FIRST_   ISSUE DATE _2/26/81_

RESPONSIBLE PARTY: LEADER _John Smith_ LOCATION _Bld 2_ EXT. _2345_

PROPOSAL TITLE AND NO. _432 – Exotic Bridge Construction Study_

CUSTOMER _Big Bridge Co._   RFP. NO. _32_   SUBMITTAL DATE _4/15/81_

VOLUME AND CHAPTER TITLE AND NO. _2. Technical, Chapter 1, Summary_

RFP REQUIREMENTS: _Lead-in to RFP Statement of Work requires that we state our technical approach and show that it will do the job. Proposal instructions ask us to describe approaches and advantages in Summary. Evaluation criteria establish trade studies as number-one priority._

THEME: _Starting with our demonstrated beam builder, Exotic 1, enables us to focus the trade studies upon other significant drivers in the exotic bridge to provide more data for your funds._

WHITE PAPER: Trade studies will be the dominant part of our study. These studies will be directed to the selection of the concept best suited for the bridge. The trade-study scope is broad because of the interplay between material, structural options and processing techniques.

We can accommodate this scope within the study efficiently as a result of the substantial progress in materials evaluation and process development already attained in our technology program.

Our Exotic 1 machine, shown in Figure 1, has been widely acclaimed as a breakthrough in its area. Your Mr. Jones, in his talk to the Smarts Society, has stated that it is the machine of the future...

OUTLINE

NO.	TITLE	NAME	PGS
1.	Summary	Dick	4
2.	Technical Approach	Betty	25
3.	Materials	Glenn	50
4.	Processes	Dewey	100
5.	Facilities	Chris	75

NO.	TITLE	NAME	PGS

John has been assigned to Volume 2, the technical proposal, shown in Figure 14-6. His scenario addresses the RFP requirement to illustrate the technical approach and explain how it will do the job. Following Jane's lead, he focuses on the number-one evaluation criteria, the trade studies. Note how his theme carries on the central message put forth by Jane but gets more into specifics. He introduces the Exotic 1 machine and builds his story around it. This is the tack that Jane as proposal leader directed him to take. John stresses the benefits of more trade-study data for the money. His competitive thesis develops the theme in more detail, and he makes suggestions for the art that will go into the summary of the technical volume.

Like Jane, John completes his scenario by outlining his volume. Then he assigns the various chapters to team members Dick, Betty, Glenn, Dewey, and Chris. They must follow the direction of his scenario in making up their own. But before John issues the scenario, he must get it approved by the proposal leader. Jane hammers out a common understanding with all her volume leaders before she allows the directive process to continue. In the process, many of the scenarios may have to be changed, perhaps even all of them. And Jane herself may have to modify her scenario to something that all of her volume leaders feel they can work with to influence the evaluators in their favor.

Now it's down to the next level of detail, the chapter leaders. Again the same reviews will take place with subsequent changes. Ultimately, the process works down to the lowest level of detail, where the roots for the substantiation of all the claims will have to be nourished. When this process is completed, the team members are all of the same mind. They are now ready to write a proposal that, while it addresses all of the particulars, will have a single message running through it.

As you write your first draft, you generate art, and the more art the better. As a general rule, a good proposal has one or two pieces of art per two-column-art-and-text-in-place-page (see Figure 14-7). Single-column proposals with art on trailing pages are antediluvian, gone with the dinosaurs. With two-column art and text in place, you can get three to five

FIGURE 14-7. AN EXAMPLE OF HOW EFFECTIVE THE TWO-COLUMN FORMAT CAN BE.

competitor doesn't have a recovery system or has had trouble with his, then he is in trouble. He has to explain why to the evaluator who keeps thinking of that recovery system with all those experienced Tomahawks.

Consider the case where you want to claim success as a subcontractor (see Examples 4, Figure D-3, and 5, Figure D-4).

RECEIVED
SEP 3 1975

AAA INTERNATIONAL
435 Lakewood Lane
Downtown, CA

M5-153-MZT-290-L

August 28, 1975

XYZ Corporation
ABC Aerospace Division
Lindbergh Plant
P.O. Box 10800
Uptown, California 92138

Attention: Mr. A. B. Doer
Program Director
Subject: Palmville Support

Gentlemen:
Excellent cooperation has been provided by your program personnel in support of our manufacturing effort at Palmville since the delivery of the Flying 100 Fuselage. The purpose of this memorandum is to commend all personnel involved at ABC with the coordination support to Palmville for a job well done.

Very truly yours,

AAA INTERNATIONAL CORPORATION
Space Division
Carl N. Receiver
C. D. Receiver, Director
Major Subcontract Management

OUR SUBCONTRACT PROGRAM TEAM CONTINUES TO SUPPORT AFTER DELIVERY.

Figure D-3. The visul impact of the actual letter is far more effective than text talking about it.

These examples show the value of making claims in action titles and providing instant proof in the art. You want to get the point across that the people you have subcontracted to are pleased with your work and the best way is to use art with action titles.

RUTFORD AIRCRAFT COMPANY
3351 Lakes Boulevard, Birdsville, CA 90801

30 July 1971

ABC Aerospace
XYE Corporation
P.O. Box 40000
Uptown, California 92112

Attention: Mr. A. B. Doer
ABC-10 Program Manager

Dear Abe,
Another great milestone was passed July 29 when the first two AC-109 Airplanes were delivered to AAL and DAL. This was two months ahead of the planned delivery schedule. Prior to flight, the airplanes received both Type certification and Production certification. The delivery ceremony received good press and television coverage and was well attended. RUT's Management sincerely thanked all those contributing in making the AC-109 a successful airplane.

Abe, you as Program Manager, and your AC-109 group share in that success, and ABC's contribution played a major part in achieving and beating our first delivery schedule. Your contribution of long hours and hard work over the past three years showed a dedicated approach to achieving the desired goal of delivering a major portion of the AC-109 airplane to us here at Birdsville.

We sincerely thank you and your people for the support and assistance in making the start of a long-range program so successful. Congratulations on a job well done.

Sincerely,
John Gots
J. H. Gots, Branch Manager
Major Subcontracts

OUR AC-109 WORK HAS BROUGHT MANY COMMENDATIONS.

Figure D-4. How could you top this in proposal text?

Action titles can be used even with ordinary art, as shown in Examples 6 (Figure D-5) and 7 (Figure D-6). Here again you make claims and provide instant substantiation. Can you imagine the lack of impact if you hadn't used action titles?

With action titles this ordinary art takes on real meaning to the contracting officer who wonders where you will accomplish his program. Anything "used-car-ish" here? Not on your life. When you submit this art

From Creating Superior Proposals by J. M. Beveridge and E. J. Velton, © 1978.

times as much material into a fixed number of pages, depending on how much you can reduce the size of the art without sacrificing readability. Postage-size art can be very readable, and when detail is not important, it can be far more effective than full-page art (see Figure 14-7).

For your rough draft, full-page art is acceptable. You should have the first draft of your art begun by the time you have written the text for the first rough draft. One-quarter of the artwork in the first rough draft should be final. The rest of the graphics in the draft can be rough.

Submit your rough draft to your review team that has been set up to simulate the customer's evaluation. After the team has gone over the draft, you will have to go back to the drawing board with much of your material. But you haven't lost any time or money. In fact, you are way ahead of the game. By doing an early draft, you found where all the holes are. The review team helps you to direct your efforts without having expended too much of your funding and time.

The next step in the positioning-to-win procedure is the polished draft. This will be your first art-and-text-in-place rendition of your proposal. Having just gone through a simulated customer review (and revised accordingly), you should feel confident at this point to invest the money in a polished draft. Also you will want to get your proposal on tape or disc to shorten the time required to publish the proposal. Because you are going to bring in a heavy team of directors and vice-presidents for this next review, you won't want them to be distracted by a sloppy proposal. So you show them what you are going to present to the customer. This new bunch of reviewers, the Red Team, is going to judge what you feel is the finished product for the customer. This review team will still find things wrong with your proposal.

Now it's down the homestretch with a fine-tuned art-and-text-in-place proposal. After it is reproduced, go over it again and inspect every page. Look for any missing, upside-down, or partially printed pages. Don't cut short your effort at this point, but make the most of it. It's all a part of positioning to win.

15

For Best Results, Use the Classic Approach to Proposal Development

In this chapter we will treat the most successful approach in positioning to win. We call it the classic approach because it employs the full positioning-to-win discipline. We will develop the approach while elucidating a real-world case study in parallel.

In Chapter 16 we will treat two specialized approaches for positioning to win. One of the approaches we call *challenging the discriminators*. It's a professional way for an experienced leader to handle an inexperienced team on a highly complex subject that spans many disciplines. This approach affords the opportunity to examine the viability of the proposal team's approach while writing the executive summary at the same time—and on a subject you know nothing about! The second approach we call the *hybrid approach*. It sometimes is an

230

FOR BEST
RESULTS, USE
THE CLASSIC
APPROACH TO
PROPOSAL
DEVELOPMENT

acceptable shortcut, but it also should be used only by those with proposal-development expertise. It's an approach that a small company might use when it can sacrifice only one experienced person to the proposal effort, but where the input has to come from many functional personnel, all of whom have other jobs they can't leave completely. Instructions to them must be piecemeal. They have to do the job step by step. To lay the whole exercise out for them at one time and expect them to phase it in with their other activities would produce inconsistent results with big gaps. You do it step by step using a combination of development techniques. But keep in mind when we discuss either the challenging-the-discriminators or hybrid approaches that they are far less than ideal. Do it right with the classic approach. If you must resort to the chancier, second-best approaches, use an experienced proposal-development specialist. Otherwise you don't stand a chance.

THE CLASSIC APPROACH
TO A HYPOTHETICAL PROPOSAL

Proper proposal development consists of a number of sequential steps that allow for progressive team buildup, development of the approach, and active management direction. The steps permit freedom to develop superior approaches with the customer while providing checks and balances against over-enthusiastic ventures that have little chance of success.

We will describe this approach through a hypothetical proposal for a study contract of approximately $200,000. The phases of development are:
- Exploratory
- Project formulation
- Bid requirements
- Commitment
- Direction
- Writing and estimating
- Polished draft and estimating
- Final proposal
- Follow-up
- Contract

To visualize the time frame in which you should operate, look at Figure 15-1. Remember, you are working with a study proposal, not with a big system development or procurement proposal. For a study proposal, time is short and resources are limited.

To begin, someone in your company sees a budding business opportunity far upstream of the RFP release date. Ideally that person should be at the heart of the innovative matter if you are to ride to a win. That person will be the proposal leader in bidding and probably also be the program manager once you win the contract. For now we'll call him the proposal leader.

The proposal leader contacts the potential customer's people as early as possible, when they are first conceiving the study. From your in-house studies using discretionary funds, the proposal leader has data and ideas to exchange with the customer's people. Thus rapport is established. The leader develops a going-in study approach that appears to have the potential for evolving to a superior approach in the eyes of the customer. And that touches off the first step of the proposal, the Exploratory Phase, about ninety days prior to the RFP release date.

FIGURE 15-1. PHASES FOR POSITIONING SMALL PROPOSALS TO WIN

Phase	Days Before/ After RFP		Output	Number of Equivalent Heads Assigned
	From	To		
Exploratory	−90	−40	Business assessment	<1
Project formulation	−65	−25	Winning assessment	<1
Bid requirements	−45	−30	Resources requirements	1
Commitment	−30	−30	Commitment	4
Direction	−30	−25	Top-down direction	4
Writing and estimating	−25	0	Rough draft and ROM	5
Polished draft and estimating	0	+20	Draft and cost	4
Final proposal	+20	+30	Final draft and price	3
Follow-up	+30	+90	Contract	<1
Contract	+90	?	Program	?

FOR BEST
RESULTS, USE
THE CLASSIC
APPROACH TO
PROPOSAL
DEVELOPMENT

In the Exploratory Phase the proposal leader is working only part time on the program. But he will bring in other part-time people during the Project Formulation Phase and still others during the Bid Requirements Phase. Things will begin to roll at the Commitment Phase, thirty days before the RFP release date. More people come on part time, and the proposal leader now works full time. Management commits and sacrifices the full-time capabilities of the leader to the proposal for the duration of the effort.

The first five days after commitment are devoted to top-down direction. No one writes or starts to estimate costs until he figures out what it is he is going to write about and until he settles on cost targets. The proposal leader makes sure that the approaches, which he carefully worked out with the customer and coordinated with management, make their way all the way down to the people producing each subsection of the proposal.

Once everyone is pointed in the right direction, the Writing and Estimating Phase starts, about twenty-five days before receipt of the RFP. This phase produces a proposal draft and the first cost estimate on or before receipt of the RFP. A review team compares the rough draft and cost estimate with the RFP and upgrades it during the Polished Draft and Estimating Phase, which starts at the receipt of the RFP.

The Final Proposal Phase starts with a simulated customer evaluation (also called a Red Team review) of the RFP, the polished draft and the estimate about ten days before submittal. The evaluation results in a finely tuned, fully responsive, competitively priced proposal ready by the submittal date. The next sixty days is the Follow-up Phase, ending when the contract is finally awarded.

Figure 15-2 presents these phases in a bar-chart schedule form, illustrating the overlap in the phases. It shows that you have to start early and stay late to win consistently, even if everything else is perfect. And from beginning to end, you have to be disciplined. Before we look at each of the proposal development phases, we will describe the parallel case study to illustrate this process.

Let's assume that the customer is asking for a study of a small surveillance aircraft that has Vertical Takeoff and Landing (VTOL) capability. You have developed with discretionary funds a small, independent ducted-fan approach (see Figure 15-3). Your competitors are proposing (1) a small unmanned helicopter and (2) a small manned helicopter (Figure 15-4). We will describe the activities of the various phases in detail and discuss their general aspects. Along the way we will integrate the surveillance aircraft case study.

The Exploratory Phase

The first step in the classic approach in positioning proposals to win is to determine if you have any place in the competition. You have already discovered the opportunity, and you

FIGURE 15-2. THE PROPOSAL PHASES OVERLAP

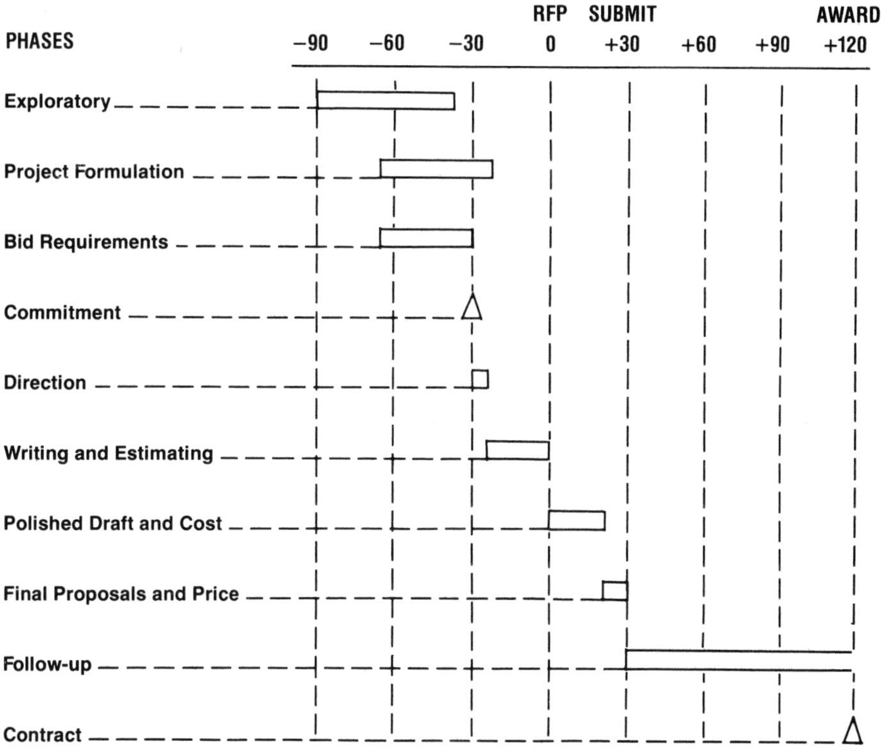

FOR BEST
RESULTS, USE
THE CLASSIC
APPROACH TO
PROPOSAL
DEVELOPMENT

FIGURE 15-3. THE CUSTOMER WANTS A SMALL SURVEILLANCE AIRCRAFT STUDY; YOU HAVE DEVELOPED AN UNMANNED DUCTED FAN APPROACH.

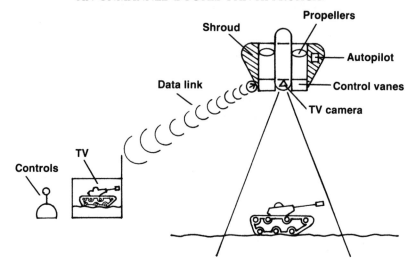

FIGURE 15-4. YOUR COMPETITORS USE HELICOPTERS.

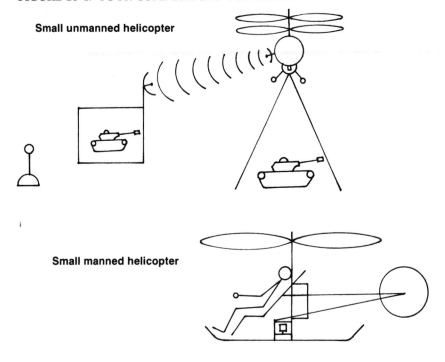

have identified the customer well upstream of the RFP release date. But does your going-in approach have potential? Your proposal leader has to be aware of the perceptions of the customer's personnel because they may vary considerably. It is extremely important that he determine what is valid and what must change relative to the going-in approach. Remember, it's the customer's perceptions that count, not yours. Getting a handle on those perceptions can be a difficult task. But at some point you have to go through a first-bid review. This can be the most important review in the whole process because from the beginning bid momentum builds. It's every bit as hard to stop a bid as it is to start one! With your limited funds, you can't afford a false start. So look at the competition hard and compare it with your other opportunities. Make sure that your proposal leader is off and running (and above all, listening) with an open technical mind, together with the customer's people.

If you get past that first-bid review and decide to continue, you should intensify the customer technical contacts. Establish one-on-ones with the customer's key people. At the very beginning, list all of the discriminators that you can think of. Check the list daily. Every time you add a new person to the effort, orient him or her to the use of discriminators. Your discriminators form the record of strengths and weaknesses of all the competitors, and it's a record that will decide who wins.

How do you know what your unique strengths and weaknesses are? Sometimes all the competitors' approaches are known. You pick them up from the customer's people or from vendors and trade publications. But even if you have no hard data, you know there are alternate approaches. Treat any possible/probable approaches as though they are real. Make your trade studies relative to your competitors' approaches (or possible approaches). If you are wrong and some of your competing approaches never make the scene, you haven't lost anything. But if they do and you don't address them while your competitors lower the boom on you, then you've done a poor job in competing and haven't served yourself or the customer. By picking alternate competitive approaches, you can begin to

FOR BEST
RESULTS, USE
THE CLASSIC
APPROACH TO
PROPOSAL
DEVELOPMENT

classify your discriminators into influencers, an essential step in the classic approach.

Before we go to the next phase, let's take a look at what the exploratory phase yielded for the Ducted Fan contractor. After talking to all of the customer's key people, the contractor found out the following information (Figure 15-5). Most people in the development command liked radar instead of TV, probably because the development command was a radar development center. They didn't develop aircraft, so they preferred drones. One thing they felt strongly about was signature, meaning how easy you are to detect. So a smaller signature with less radar cross-section and heat emission was definitely a plus.

FIGURE 15-5. DUCTED FAN EXPLORATORY PHASE FEEDS BACK IMPORTANT DATA

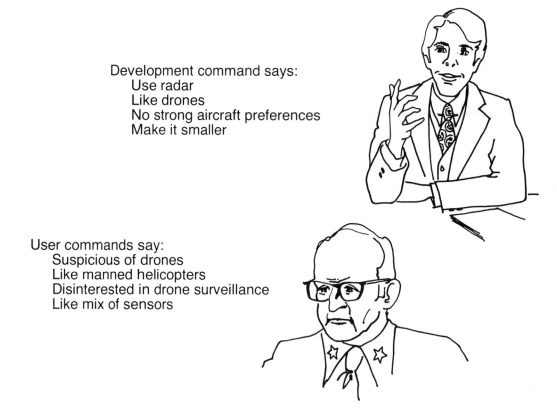

Development command says:
  Use radar
  Like drones
  No strong aircraft preferences
  Make it smaller

User commands say:
  Suspicious of drones
  Like manned helicopters
  Disinterested in drone surveillance
  Like mix of sensors

The information picked up from the user commands was different. Although they didn't openly oppose drones, they were suspicious of them. They liked manned helicopters, perhaps because some of them are pilots and they don't want to be put out of work. They were disinterested in surveillance by drones. They liked a mix of sensors, not just radar, because they felt the mix of data was necessary for battlefield conditions.

Based on the data obtained for the Ducted Fan, the contractor started the winning process with an influencer claims list (see Figure 15-6). The results didn't look bad at all. The unmanned ducted fan had the lowest signature of all the approaches, and it was more compact for less visual signature. The shroud shielded the exhaust pipe from the enemy's infrared sensors, and there were no flapping blades to create the whop-whop noise the helicopter makes. Also the blades were wooden for less radar signature. The Ducted Fan drone wins points in the signature department. Ducted fans were safer too. The shroud protected ground personnel from the blades and the blades from limbs and obstacles. The small helicopter wasn't as safe because it was a menace to ground personnel with its large-span flapping blades. Score more points for Ducted Fans.

There were some problems though. The users were biased against ducted fans because there were no operational ducted-fan air frames. The users felt that if it was a viable air frame, there should be some in service. But they had no questions about the feasibility tests, which substantiated the design and performance claims. Still, they preferred manned aircraft.

Looking further, the Ducted Fan contractor found that in a surveillance role manned helicopters would have poor survivability. Not only did the ducted fan present less vulnerable area, but without a man aboard the machine had infinite courage and could be readily committed to fatal missions so long as the data justified the cost. Compared to the unmanned helicopter, its autopilot was simpler. However, it did have a high downwash because of its high disc loading. The developer definitely preferred radar over TV but that wasn't a draw-

FOR BEST
RESULTS, USE
THE CLASSIC
APPROACH TO
PROPOSAL
DEVELOPMENT

back. The ducted fan could carry radar just as well as the helicopter, manned or unmanned.

There were a lot of things to think about in the influencer claims list. Despite the strengths, the negative user command feelings were a definite concern. But the development command would fund the study program, and they were positive all the way. Management therefore decided to go ahead in the first bid review.

FIGURE 15-6. START THE WINNING PROCESS WITH AN INFLUENCER CLAIMS LIST.

	Features			Neutralizers			Counters of Competitors' Strengths		Exploiters of Customers		
CLASSIFY DISCRIMINATORS	(Aha!)	Ghosts About		(Oh-Oh!)	Ghosts By						
LIST DISCRIMINATORS	Your Strengths	Drone Copter	Manned Copter	Your Real Weakness	Drone Copter	Manned Copter	Drone Copter	Manned Copter	Hopes	Fears	Biases
Shroud reduces signature	X	X	X					X			
Shrouded propellers are safer	X	X	X					X			
Ducted fan better operationally—smaller, more compact, rugged	X	X					X				
No operational ducted fans				X	X	X					X
User likes manned helicopters				X		X	X				X
Manned copter has poor survivability	X		X					X			
Unmanned copter has a complicated autopilot		X						X			
Ducted fan downwash is higher				X	X	X		X			X
Developer prefers radar							X				X

The Project Formulation Phase

239

THE CLASSIC
APPROACH TO A
HYPOTHETICAL
PROPOSAL

Once you pass the exploratory phase, you step up your customer contacts. You are trying to determine if you can produce a winner. Along that line, your proposal leader is working hard to make your approach the customer's approach. That means giving up a lot, changing a lot of your pet ideas, and incorporating the customers suggestions into the approach. The whole idea is to capture the customer's perceptions into your design and thereby evolve the approach that the customer perceives as superior.

By now your team is hard at work writing the competitive theses for each of the major discriminators and formulating argumentative headlines for your major claims. The whole idea is to test the effectiveness of your influencers. Can you come across strong for the strength features? Are your neutralizers plausible? Are your counters sound? Will they backfire on you? Have you addressed the customer's hopes, fears, and biases?

This is worth a second bid review. If you can't articulate your influencers in a good set of competitive theses, you had better think twice before going further. You will have to make some major changes in your approach to become more competitive. But if the competitive theses sound like winners, and if you can substantiate all the claims you make, then it's time to start building the team, to add the expertise needed to build your data base and interact with the customer. Remember, the door is still wide open. It won't close for another couple of months.

What actually happened to our Ducted Fan contractor in this real-world case study during the concept formulation phase? The contractor made some big changes and shaped his proposal strategy (Figure 15-7). The biggest change was to substitute radar for a TV sensor. That's what the developer wanted. For awhile the contractor thought about multiple sensors, to satisfy the user commands. However, since the developers were in the driver's seat, responding to their perceptions seemed to be the soundest move.

The marketing strategy was to present the ducted fan as a

FOR BEST
RESULTS, USE
THE CLASSIC
APPROACH TO
PROPOSAL
DEVELOPMENT

unique drone concept. That was an attempt to make a case for a new type of air frame for this new type of mission. As a companion move, the strategy was to attack the conventional helicopter air frame as effective only for manned application, and then only for multiperson sizes. Ghost stories were developed that featured busted heads and tangled blades for the small helicopters, this in contrast to the safe ducted-fan drone with its shrouded propellers and infinite courage.

There was the continuing concern about the user commands' negative feelings toward drones in general and ducted fans in particular. To overcome this, an active campaign was started to convince users that the ducted fan fit the drone role. It would succeed where other, manned derivatives had failed.

FIGURE 15-7. CONCEPT FORMULATION PHASE INCLUDED CHANGES IN APPROACHES

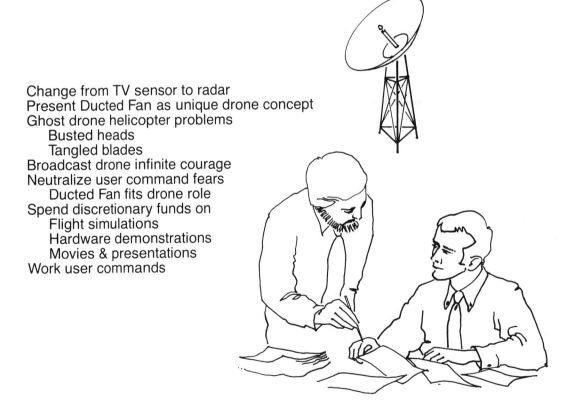

Change from TV sensor to radar
Present Ducted Fan as unique drone concept
Ghost drone helicopter problems
    Busted heads
    Tangled blades
Broadcast drone infinite courage
Neutralize user command fears
    Ducted Fan fits drone role
Spend discretionary funds on
    Flight simulations
    Hardware demonstrations
    Movies & presentations
Work user commands

A lot of money was spent on flight simulations, hardware demonstrations, and presentations, far more money than the study contract justified but in line with the long-range business potential, assuming the customer adopted drones into the inventory.

The Bid Requirements Phase

Now comes the time for determining what it will cost to bid. So far a lot of people have been charging a few hours a week to the program. They have been actively interacting with the customer and formulating the approach. It looks good. Soon you are going to have to commit yourself to the effort and dedicate appreciable resources to the proposal. But how much, what types, and for how long?

You start to work the RFP with the customer. If the customer is unreceptive, watch out. Something isn't right. There can't be a competition without an RFP. So your proposal leader and his part-time people question the customer about the RFP and help put it together. They encourage the customer to issue draft RFPs so that you will be able to get the most mileage out of your resources.

What you are really interested in are the requirements of the RFP. Are they for real? Is the schedule realistic? What kind of contract will be requested? How much money does the customer have? What are the proposal instructions, the evaluation criteria, the Statement of Work, the Work-Breakdown Structure? You need this information before you commit yourself. You also need it to direct your effort until you get an RFP from the customer. If yours is to be an efficient effort, you have to make sure that everyone is addressing the same program. So you put out an internal strawman RFP. Now you're ready for the decision to commit. But let's check the results of the real-world case of the Ducted Fan contractor.

The Ducted Fan operator worked the RFP hard during this session. The object was to make sure that there were no requirements in the RFP that the ducted fan couldn't meet. Primarily these consisted of low disc loading and downwash

242

FOR BEST
RESULTS, USE
THE CLASSIC
APPROACH TO
PROPOSAL
DEVELOPMENT

characteristics, characteristics typical of the helicopter. In this regard, the Ducted Fan contractor was successful.

The contractor also tried to get low signature and safety requirements that only the ducted fan could meet into the RFP. In this the contractor was only partially successful. Signature requirements were lowered, but not beyond the realm of possibility for helicopters. The safety requirements came out loosely worded, almost generalizations. Helicopters would have no problems there. Along the way the Ducted Fan contractor picked up all the information about the customer's plans. He put together a strawman RFP. So, like you, he was ready for the commitment phase.

The Commitment Phase

You have to commit well in advance of the RFP release date. On large proposals this could be a year or two in advance. On our relatively modest proposal, a month is adequate. This gives you time to turn out a draft by the time the RFP is released.

The question is will you commit the resources to win? It's time to take one last look at bidding. If you go beyond this point, you are committed. You should look at this milestone like jumping out of an airplane or diving into a cold lake. Once you leave the airplane or the shore, you're committed. There's no turning back there or with this proposal. You are going into high gear, and you will add the people necessary to produce a full-blown proposal. The customer's door will close in thirty days, when he issues his RFP, so you want to intensify the one-on-ones with his technical people to make sure you have incorporated his perceptions into your conceptions. You have to find that superior approach. So you review your influencers and search for the major disaster glitches that could throw you off track. As a part of the third bid review that accompanies commitment, you update all of your competitive theses. Your theses, along with data prepared in the Bid Requirements Phase, form the data you use to make your judgment. Are you competitive? Should you go all out? The decision should be clear cut. A classic mistake in most losing proposals is that the contractor drifts into the bid without a clear-cut commitment. He never really sacrifices anything to win. And the reason he made no sacrifices (and therefore no commitment) was because he never felt he had a good chance to win. He cheated the effort, and as a result he didn't win.

Assume that you decide to commit. How about our Ducted Fan contractor? He, too, decides to commit. His strategy to feature the ducted fan as a unique VTOL drone air frame was developed sometime ago. He has his technical people checking every design development with the customer's development people. It's an overkill operation for him because he sees the possibility of a new product line. He makes an all-out commitment.

The Direction Phase

The inclination after commitment is to start writing, and that's the wrong thing to do. First, you have to figure out what you are going to write about. And you have to make sure that everyone follows the same direction. You have to give direction from top to bottom. On this small proposal your equivalent head count might jump from one to four or five. That could mean up to a dozen contributors to the proposal, assuming that most are working on it part time. Even that number is difficult to coordinate and direct. If they are strong people, the kind of people you need, they will go in their own directions unless you exert strong leadership.

The first thing you do is call a kick-off meeting to bring everybody up to speed. You distribute the influencers and competitive theses you have been writing since Day One, and you lay out a strong request for more of the same from the new people coming on the program. You give everyone the outline and make assignments. You pass out proposal development, estimating, and data-base schedules and establish a place where everyone can collocate while doing their part on the proposal. You announce that short coordination meetings are going to be held every morning to ensure that everyone is pulling together and that all the problems are being properly addressed.

FOR BEST
RESULTS, USE
THE CLASSIC
APPROACH TO
PROPOSAL
DEVELOPMENT

The best way to provide top down direction is to have the proposal leader, his volume leaders, and their chapter leaders prepare a scenario of what they are going to write. As detailed in Chapter 14, the proposal leader's scenario provides direction to his volume leaders, and their scenarios provide direction to the chapter leaders. It is a sequential operation that provides top-down direction (see Figure 15-8). The trick is to use scenarios to impart top-down direction to each level of proposal writers. Thus the proposal leader puts out his scenario first and coordinates it with his management and his key proposal team members. After everyone is satisfied that this top-level scenario contains the main features, neutralizers, counters, and exploiters, you go to the volume-level scenarios. These in turn are carefully reviewed and modified until they

FIGURE 15-8. GIVE TOP-DOWN DIRECTION TO DEVELOP YOUR MESSAGES.

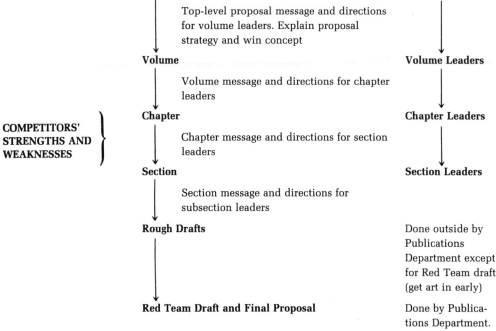

track the top-level scenario. And then it's off to the chapter-level scenarios and, if you want, to lower levels, although most people stop at the chapter level.

This is the same kind of activity that our Ducted Fan contractor also is doing. That and more customer one-on-ones. This isn't the time to slack off on customer contacts. As long as the door is open you want to strive to get the customer to make your approaches his approaches. The best way to do that is obviously to develop the approaches jointly with him.

Don't hurry the Direction Phase. No proposal ever suffered from too much up-front planning. To do anything less than a thorough job is to compromise your winning position severely.

The Writing and Estimating Phase

Now, at long last, you are free to write. Give yourself the luxury of a false start or two and have at it. But follow top-down direction and the scenarios. Don't deviate from the outline without working out the why and how with the proposal leader.

In making your estimate, use a propose-to-cost approach. Rarely will you enter a proposal without some sort of a handle on what the customer is willing to spend. If you have absolutely no idea, you're probably in the wrong business. But assuming you aren't, you will have to constrain your functional people to a budget that is consistent with the customer's budget. Don't be capricious. Distribute the budget limits to your functional groups. Have them propose to cost and tell you what they can do within the budget. That's the opposite of a grassroots effort, where you are forced to accept what the system generates. Without exception, that's always high. It is a difficult job to pare a bid down to size. And if you win, controlling cost overruns is almost impossible.

In this phase of activity, a great deal of activity is going on and there are all sorts of problems. So collocate your people. Hold coordination meetings and keep action items. Schedule splinter meetings to address each problem. Above all, maintain the schedule and adhere to your strawman or (if you are

246

FOR BEST
RESULTS, USE
THE CLASSIC
APPROACH TO
PROPOSAL
DEVELOPMENT

lucky) the customer's draft RFP. Drive out a proposal draft and cost estimate at RFP receipt and use a dedicated review team of managers to critique it. And so long as that door to the customer is open, check it all out with the customer. If you ever managed to keep an open mind, continue to do so now. If you do a perfect job, by responding to the customer's people you can get them essentially to write some of the sections of your proposal. What better way to set an evaluator up and assure yourself of the perfect score? This is exactly what the Ducted Fan contractor is doing. In fact, from here on out the activity is the same for your proposal and the ducted fan. The door to the customer is just about to close.

The Polished Draft and Estimating Phase

The RFP is out now and the door is closed. You no longer have access to the customer. You have a proposal draft, addressed to your strawman RFP. You also have the real RFP. The first thing you do is determine the differences between your strawman RFP and the real one. Then you evaluate your rough-draft proposal against the real RFP, paying particular attention to those areas where there were differences in the RFPs.

During this phase you are going to turn out a cosmetically perfect version of the proposal, just like you will give to the customer. In fact, it should be a draft your proposal leader is willing to give to the customer. The proposal leader and the team have incorporated the comments that resulted from the review of the rough draft at the end of the Writing and Estimating Phase and the beginning of this phase. To the best of their knowledge, the proposal leader and his team have substantiated all of the claims. Now they feel they are ready to turn this polished draft in to the customer. But you provide the ultimate fine-tuning step—a customer-simulated (Red Team) review by top management of a cosmetically perfect draft. You and your managers play a dispassionate third-party role.

The results of this Red Team review are always the same: You find that your proposal team, no matter how capable, has drifted away from the RFP. People wrote about what they liked and were good at, not what the customer asked for. In some places the proposal is thick with information where little is called for. In other places it's thin, almost nothing, where the evaluation criteria gives a lot of weighting. It's highly likely that you even find a few places where you have not been responsive to the RFP. The important thing to keep in mind is that you found those omissions and deficiencies in-house; there are still ten days to go before you deliver it to the customer. You have time to recover. The Ducted Fan contractor conducted a similar effort and he, too, is ready for the final proposal phase.

The Final Proposal Phase
By now you have started to off-load some of your people. You hold on to the best, though, to wrap it up right. The first thing you do is incorporate the comments of the Red Team and fix the deficiencies it exposed. You beef up the sections that need it and pare down those that are overdone. And you fine-tune the proposal, making the absolute most out of what you have to offer. If you did everything right up to the time the customer issued the RFP and closed the door, you have the superior approach, an approach the customer is familiar with, wants, and expects. All you have to do is ensure that it is responsive and presented in its best light.

You follow it right to the end, too, leaving nothing to chance. You take one last look before you approve it for printing, and you inspect every document and piece of paper you send to the customer. And you make sure it gets there on time, sending it out early enough so you can follow up with a back-up delivery in case the primary package gets lost. You don't really rest until the customer has it in his hands. Then it's time for a breather before starting the follow-up activities. The Ducted Fan contractor did all of this too, so he is off for a little R&R before starting his follow-up.

The Follow-Up Phase
Many a competition has been lost between the time the proposal was submitted and the contract awarded. There are technical negotiations, orals, site visits, cost negotiations, and

248

FOR BEST
RESULTS, USE
THE CLASSIC
APPROACH TO
PROPOSAL
DEVELOPMENT

proposal updates. And you might even turn in a completely new proposal if you want to! While it's highly unlikely that that would do you any good, it is very likely that competitors can improve their standing between proposal submittal and contract award. That's what you have to be tuned to during this period.

You start in a fairly mundane fashion, making sure the proposal gets to the customer. Don't laugh. More than one submittal has been judged nonresponsive because they came in late. We've seen it happen, first hand. But once the proposals are in, the heady part of postsubmittal competition starts.

If technical negotiations are held, particularly if it's a formalized government four-step procurement, you have to be all ears. Don't reject anything, and do more than just react to the questions. Look behind them and reveal the concerns that generated the questions. Those are far more important. They may reveal the major faults in your approaches in the eyes of the customer.

For instance, if the customer asks why you didn't list the number of months your new-hire program director was with your company, he isn't looking for a response that says you overlooked this and hoped he wouldn't notice. The customer is concerned about how a new hire will manage a program in your company without a few years of experience to learn how the system works and who the people are who make it work. That's his real question. How are you going to answer?

If the customer bores in on details about some aspect of your proposal, it may be because he is very uncomfortable with that aspect. You have to be alert to his concerns and able to analyze all his questions and comments so that you can know where to dig in and where to switch. As always, you are trying to evolve the superior approach. Before the RFP you communicated openly with the customer. If you heard him right then and reacted properly, you at least should be close. But things could have changed somewhat since the door closed. New people may have come on the scene. So you still have to listen, but this time you have to listen to far more subtle language and oblique messages. Most of all, you have to keep your technical mind open, right down to the time the program is phased out.

You and your proposal leader have to control the answers to the questions, presentations, and site visits. Also you must keep a tight handle on these final phases because they may decide who wins. And that goes for the Ducted Fan contractor too.

The Contract Phase

If you have done everything right up to this point, if you have competed to the hilt at every turn, and if you never closed your technical mind, you are going to turn in the superior approach in your best and final offer. That's what wins, and that's the only thing that wins. If you had the superior approach and didn't win, it is more than likely because you did a miserable job of listening. You failed everybody—yourself, the customer, and the competitor who won.

SO WHAT REALLY HAPPENED TO THE DUCTED-FAN CONTRACTOR? In a nutshell, he won the battle but lost the war. Because he listened to the developer's perceptions, he won the study contract. He did a good job too. And because of that, he won follow-up studies. There was even a funded demonstration effort. A couple of million dollars ultimately were awarded to study and demonstrate the acceptability of the ducted fan as a surveillance drone.

There was just one problem: No one ever convinced the user commands that they needed drones! That didn't matter so long as the program was in the study and demonstration phase. But before it could go into full-scale development and production, the user had to state a requirement (a need) for it. And to do that he was going to have to give up something else or cut back on something he already had in his planning cycle.

The simple truth was that he didn't want to cut back on anything. What he wanted was about twice as many helicopters as he could afford. If he came across a few more dollars, he would have bought another helicopter or a few parts for the ones he had. If he had the funds to develop anything, it would

FOR BEST
RESULTS, USE
THE CLASSIC
APPROACH TO
PROPOSAL
DEVELOPMENT

be a new helicopter, not those damned ducted fans that those nuts in the development command were pursuing.

The user wasn't interested in anything but helicopters. That's what he thought would benefit him. Mobility was his game. Furthermore, his pilots hated drones. They didn't want to share a cubic inch of their sky with those dumb flying machines. They viewed drones as a menace, something that threatened to take the scarves right off their necks.

There never was a chance of getting the ducted fan into production. That's the lesson of this example. Even if you do everything right, you still may fail in the end.

16

Specialized Proposal Development Techniques That Work–Sometimes

The classic approach to proposal development presented in Chapter 15 is the one approach most of us should strive for. It is the safe approach, and the one that is most likely to succeed. But even in proposal development, there are specialized techniques that can save money and time. And they can work, if you have people with the right experience and expertise. Like any variations from the tried-and-true, these techniques can also get you into trouble. For those special few, these techniques present interesting alternatives for certain proposal undertakings.

THE CHALLENGING-THE-DISCRIMINATORS APPROACH

In the challenging-the-discriminators approach, you do exactly what it says. As always you start with the discriminators that are compiled by the proposal team. You review these to make sure that you are competitive. If you are dissatisfied with the discriminators, take a hard look to make sure your proposal team is well versed in the subject matter. If it turns out the discriminators are weak and that the proposal team was unresponsive, sit down and try to find additional discriminators. Don't go any further until you are sure that you have a good foundation for the competitive evaluation.

Once you have a complete set of discriminators, challenge them. To do this you must have an expert proposal specialist. He or she should have experience in many types of proposals and be able to work with highly technical data. Assign the specialist to the writing of what, in effect, is an executive summary, by stringing the discriminators together in sentences and paragraphs. It is surprising how good a job an experienced proposal specialist can do if he has a complete set of meaningful discriminators to work with.

Next the proposal specialist identifies and flags the claims in the executive summary. Later he will go back to the claims and request substantiating art from the originator. When the proposal specialist gets all the art back from the requestors, he analyzes it to make sure that all points have been covered. He will always find omissions and substantiation that doesn't come close to doing the job. That is one of the values of this approach. By challenging the discriminators you find out if you have a competitive approach. Thus if you don't, you find out at the very beginning.

Perhaps you want to take another look before you decide to bow out. If so, your proposal specialist tries for more substantiation. He will reduce your claims to eliminate those that are unsubstantiated. Then he rewrites the executive summary based on the remaining discriminators, those that your team can fully substantiate. Ask yourself if you are competitive with the reduced list of discriminators. If you are, distribute the executive summary to the proposal team as part of their top-down direction. If you decide that you still aren't competitive, stop. The process of challenging the discriminators is illustrated in Figure 16-1.

To get a better handle on this process, let's look at a

FIGURE 16-1. CHALLENGE THE DISCRIMINATORS BY LOOKING FOR SUBSTANTIATION.

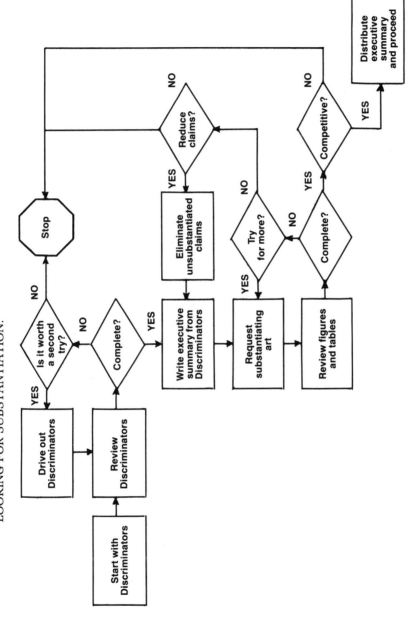

fictitious example to see how it works. Just to make sure that no one is an expert in the subject matter, we will pick an Antigravity Flying Belt program. Assume that your proposal specialist comes on the program cold. After he gets over the shock of finding out what he is going to work on, he goes about it just as he would go about any reasonable and believable project: he starts with discriminators. He finds the usual resistance, but he keeps at it until he is convinced that he has identified all of the discriminators. Then he sits down and looks at what he has (see Figure 16-2). It turns out to be an interesting package.

The first thing the proposal specialist learns is that your company is the leader in antigravity technology. That is impressive in itself, but it is nothing in comparison to the revelation that you have actually developed more antigravity machines than anybody else! The proposal specialist now begins to warm up to the project. He finds out that you have the best team and can ensure successful development. And he goes on to read about your accomplishments and leadership.

The remainder of the claims convince him that you are in a state of readiness with an outstanding manager, directors, supervisors, and team. Futhermore, you have a computer simulation in operation and all of the facilities needed. And you know the customer. You are motivated and ready to move out. How can you lose? The proposal specialist can hardly wait to challenge these discriminators to see if he is living in a funnybook land or if all this is really true.

In order to challenge the discriminators, the proposal specialist first has to write a top-level competitive thesis complete with argumentative headlines, the kind that would go into an executive summary. By stringing the discriminators together he comes up with the following theme and theses. Wherever he comes to a claim that needs to be substantiated, he simply calls out a figure. These will be his key to challenging the discriminators. But first let's look at the thesis.

BECAUSE WE ARE THE LEADER AND HAVE A LARGE INVESTMENT IN ANTIGRAVITY DEVELOPMENT, WE HAVE THE UNIQUE EXPERTISE FOR SUCCESS.

As principal investigator on the Antigravity Feasibility Study, only we understand the total system requirements of the antigravity belt (Figure 1). You won't have to bring us up to speed relative to this system. Figure 2 presents a flow diagram of our comprehensive program. Figure 3 represents the innovative schedule for this program that allows us to meet all your milestones. Figure 4 presents our technical approach, showing how the features of this approach implement unique benefits to you.

Since we are the principal investigator on the Antigravity Feasibility Study, we are motivated to ensure development on time, to specification, and within budget. As you know, we have spent heavily on the feasibility program, and we are anxious to see this technology pay off. Therefore, in us you are assured of a committed contractor.

Antigravity devices are our major corporate thrust. This is shown by the team we have assembled for this product line (Figure 5). The manager is from our Flight Division. He has received awards for unusual flight systems. The chief engineer and the flight director are from our Smart Division, where they worked on the related Flying Truck device (Figure 6). The heads of the projectized engineering, QA, factory, and other departments are drawn from operations within and outside of our company, including government research and testing facilities (see résumés in Figure 7).

Our program plan, schedule, and organization reflect our experience with small flying systems (Figure 8) and antigravity systems (Figure 9). We are working the state-of-the-art designs on our multismarts computer (Figure 10). We've been doing our homework on independent research and development (IRAD), too (Figure 11). And we have all the testing capabilities and facilities needed for this program (Figure 12).

One additional advantage is that we are working with you on the development of other antigravity machines (Figure 13). We know how you operate and vice

FIGURE 16-2. YOUR AWESOME DISCRIMINATOR LIST LEADS TO A TOP-LEVEL COMPETITIVE THESIS

CLASSIFY DISCRIMINATORS

LIST DISCRIMINATORS	Your strengths	Features — Ghosts About (AHA!) Competitor A	Competitor B	Competitor C	Competitor D	Your real weakness (OH-OH!)	Neutralizers — Ghosts By Competitor A	Competitor B	Competitor C	Competitor D	Counters of Competitors' Strengths Competitor A	Competitor B	Competitor C	Competitor D	Exploiters of Customers' Hopes	Fears	Biases
We are the leader in antigravity technology.	X	X	X	X										X			
We have developed more antigravity machines.	X	X	X	X										X			
We have the best team.	X	X	X	X										X			
We can ensure successful development.	X	X	X	X										X			
Only we understand the total system requirements.	X	X	X	X											X		
We are the principal investigator of the antigravity study.	X	X	X	X										X			
We are up to speed; the rest of the industry will have to catch us.	X	X	X	X										X	X		
Our program is comprehensive.	X	X	X	X										X			
We have an innovative schedule that allows us to meet the customer's milestones.	X	X	X	X										X	X		

Statement														
Our technical approach implements unique benefits to the customer.	X	X	X										X	
We have special motivation to succeed.	X	X	X											X
We have spent the most money on this technology.	X	X	X											X
Our manager has outstanding credentials.	X	X	X											X
The directors and functional supervisors are the best.	X	X	X											X
Our organization, team, and management systems are tailored to small flying systems.	X	X	X											X
We have a computer simulation in operation.	X	X	X										X	
We have all the testing facilities needed.	X	X	X											X
We have many other programs with the customer, and we know how they operate.	X	X	X	X									X	X
We have worked out many problems with the customer.	X	X	X	X									X	X
We recognize the schedule difficulties and risks of the program.	X	X	X										X	
Our people are innovative.	X	X	X										X	

versa. Jointly, we have worked out many knotty prob-
lems (Figure 14).

We recognize that the schedule for developing the
flying belt is very hard to meet. The major program
problems and risks are presented in Figure 15, along
with their program implications and proposed primary
and alternative solutions. Our people are innovative
and competitive in all the related technology fields.
They have produced the innovative products and sys-
tems shown in Figure 16.

Pretty impressive? If those claims are true, you have an
airtight case for "Why you?" But how do you find out if you
are dealing with fact or fiction? The first thing you do is
challenge the discriminators with art requests. That's practi-
cally all there is to it. The proposal specialist lists each figure
and tells the message he would expect to get out of a piece of
substantiating art. He then provides a description of what he
would expect the piece of art to be. Finally, he assigns that
piece of art to the originator of the discriminator. Then he calls
everyone to a meeting and places the challenge (see Figure
16-3).

A great deal of negotiating takes place before everyone is
satisfied with the description of the artwork. Figures may be
changed to tables and the titles of the artwork may be
modified, but ultimately the assignees have to substantiate
each claim or drop them. Then it's "sit back and wait time"
until the substantiating art appears. Of course, the proposal
specialist might not be able to judge the technical validity of
the art, so he will submit the art to the functional experts.
However, if there are dispassionate third-party experts on this
subject, the proposal specialist can effectively challenge the
discriminators before moving further into the proposal where
the big bucks are spent.

While Antigravity Flying Machines may seem to be far
out, we have actually tried this approach on such subjects as
Neutral Beam Injector Systems, Fiber Optics, and Reliability
and Maintainability Simulations. In two cases, the discriminators couldn't withstand the challenge and management ulti-

FIGURE 16-3. CHALLENGE THE DISCRIMINATORS WITH ART REQUESTS.

Figure Number and Title	Description	Assignee
1. Only we understand the total system requirements of the Antigravity Belt.	A table that relates system requirements to the data base generated by our experiences. It must convince customer that without that experience a contractor wouldn't understand the requirements.	John Doe
2. We have a comprehensive program plan.	A flow chart with the kind of detail the competitors aren't familiar with and can't provide.	Mary
3. Our innovative schedule meets all your milestones.	A schedule that demonstrates unique knowledge and discredits the competitors in the process.	Jane
4. Our unique technical approach implements the most benefits to you.	A drawing that describes the system with bullets that show how features implement benefits to customer. Obviously this key figure has to substantiate a superior approach.	Willy
5. Our team is the best in the industry.	An organization chart that shows a favored position for the program and uses bullets to show background of members as related to their responsibilities.	Betsey
6. We start with the directly related experience of the Flying Truck.	A photograph of the Flying Truck device with inserts that relate this device to the Flying Belt.	Glen
7. Our personnel are uniquely qualified for the program.	Résumés tailored to show unique capabilities and background for this program.	Tom
8. Management is tailored to small flying systems.	Art that relates plans, schedules, and organization to this program and shows how they were substantiated in similar programs. Show we are uniquely qualified.	Frank
9. Management is tailored to the antigravity program.	See description for Figure 8.	Ethel
10. The multismarts computer program gives us a lead-in problem solution.	Art that reveals a sophisticated program. Designed to give technical types a warm feeling on readiness.	Mr. Smarts
11. Our IRAD provides the most advanced data base.	List the IRAD programs and the major findings. Leave the evaluator with the feeling that we are ahead of everyone.	Shirley

(Continued on page 260)

FIGURE 16-3. (*continued*)

Figure Number and Title	Description	Assignee
12. No new facilities are required.	Show photos of facilities and tell which tasks will be done at each facility. Show how machine loadings will accommodate new tasks.	Roger
13. We are experienced in how you operate; you won't have to train us.	List programs and performance. Show actuals vs. estimated.	Don
14. We have jointly worked out many problems.	List all the problems and clear the air.	Bill
15. We have identified major program problems and risks, along with implications and alternate solutions	A table of problems, risks, implications, and alternatives; far more detailed than what the competition can identify. This table has to plant the ghost about going with any of the other competitors.	Betty
16. Our related-technology products demonstrate our ability to innovate.	Photographs of all the related products with inserts that explain applicability to the current program.	Bob

mately dropped the bids. In the other case, the discriminators withstood the challenge and the proposal won, with the summary worded virtually the same as the challenging thesis.

But let's not stop here. How about the rest of the proposal? Can we use some variation of this to expand the lead-in theme and thesis to cover the whole proposal? Well, it's more involved and takes more leg work, but the answer is yes. This is called the hybrid approach.

THE HYBRID APPROACH

The hybrid approach is an extension of challenging the discriminators, but it is far more involved. It addresses the whole proposal, including the proposal outline and all of the substantiation for secondary as well as main themes. (In challenging-the-discriminators, you restrict yourselves to the executive-summary level; here you are primarily interested in determining the quality of your approach, rather than writing the whole proposal.) We use the term hybrid because the approach consists of a mixture of techniques (see Figure 16-4). It is a good approach to use for small or medium-size proposals. Use it if you have personnel with the expertise and aren't too pushed for time. However, it takes a great deal of skill because one full-time person orchestrates the whole proposal. That person should be a proposal specialist. Otherwise, you may have a nightmare on your hands. The team members for the most part do their regular work until the proposal specialist calls on them. After each step the proposal specialist checks the status, judges what has been accomplished so far, and lays out the next step. Because he is experienced in proposal development, he can direct the effort to the areas that need it the most and avoid spending time on work that should be done later in the development sequence.

The proposal specialist of course starts with discriminators. He puts together a strawman RFP and conducts interviews with all the key people involved in the proposal. In these interviews he draws out and records the discriminators. From the technical person's standpoint, it is more productive to be interviewed in person than to fill out a form. As the proposal specialist records the discriminators, he eliminates those that are redundant. He rapidly gets to the point of recognizing when he is on to something new or just hanging around in Ho-Hum territory. Moreover, he evaluates the contributors in this first go-round and identifies the handful of innovators who will make the proposal go. And because he is persistent, the proposal specialist gets the introverts and the higher-ups to contribute too.

After the discriminators have been listed, the proposal specialist can sort, classify, and analyze them while the other members of the team go back to their regular jobs. In the process, he touches base from time to time with the live-wire innovators and with management to rank the most important influencers. Also he learns who has the expertise regarding each of the key influencers.

FIGURE 16-4. HYBRID PROPOSAL DEVELOPMENT IS A COMBINATION OF APPROACHES

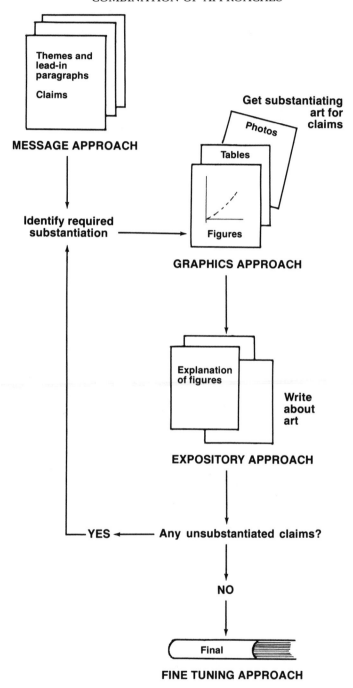

It's interview time again, but this time the proposal specialist has a rapport with the experts, and he can elicit themes and competitive theses from them in record time. Using the list of influencers and the outline for the proposal, the proposal specialist assigns the various chapters in the outline to the experts. Working with the key experts, he derives a proposal theme and the overall thesis, which he checks out with the rest of the team. Then he works with each chapter leader to decide on a theme for his or her chapter, one that tracks the main theme. The chapter leaders each write their competitive thesis and the proposal leader fine-tunes them.

Each chapter has a theme and a competitive thesis for a lead-in. The competitive theses are spread throughout the chapters to feature your strengths and your competitor's weaknesses, neutralize your weaknesses, counter the competitor's strengths, and exploit the customer's hopes, fears, and biases.

Once the proposal specialist has all of the theses, it's time for him to shift gears. Here is where his skill comes in. He reviews and analyzes each theme and competitive thesis for claims, just as though he were challenging the discriminators. He also eliminates redundant claims and does some reorganizing to eliminate repetition. So far the proposal specialist has accomplished a lot without involving too many people. From here the operation will become even more efficient because he has identified the handful of people who really count. He can forget the other members of the team for now. They can add the details later on. Now he will follow a series of stages through to the final proposal:

- Message stage
- Graphic stage
- Expository stage
- Fine-tuning stage
- Red Team review

Up to now, the proposal specialist has been in the message stage. This stage generates the argumentative headlines, themes, and competitive theses. Now he turns to the hybrid approach. He looks for substantive art for the claims contained in the themes and competitive theses. He starts with his live-wire innovators and works out message titles for the rest, using titles suggested by the innovators. What he has done here is to shift gears to the graphics stage. He started out with a lot of text but no substantiating art and ended up with an art-heavy presentation.

Now he shifts gears again, this time to the expository stage, when he asks the members of the team who supply the tables, figures, and photographs to write a paragraph or two describing the art they gave him. Contained in these descriptions will be more claims. The proposal specialist will identify them and then repeat the whole operation—more art and more text until the story is complete and the final proposal is ready to be fine-tuned.

In the fine-tuning stage, the proposal specialist calls in the innovators and key personnel. When everyone is happy with the proposal, it's time for the Red Team review. Then it's back to the drawingboards for a fully responsive, highly competitive, balanced proposal.

When conditions are right, use the hybrid approach. Use it on unsolicited proposals if you have the people to handle it, and try it on small and medium-size efforts too. But don't try it on the biggies. For those, go back to the classic approach.

17

How to Correct Late Starts, False Starts, and People Problems

Now it's time to look at less-than-ideal proposals and see how positioning to win works in real-world situations. It's not a world of black and white but of all shades and all colors. Obviously you can't use the same techniques for every new effort. Occasions will arise where it may be advantageous for management to pursue an opportunity under the worst of conditions. What do you do when management has decided to bid and you know that nothing has been done right upstream? How do you handle highly technical proposals far beyond your expertise when you have a totally green proposal team and the bid period is too brief to bring them up to speed on the fundamentals of positioning to win? Certainly you will handle these situations differently than the proposal that has been positioned to win from the start.

The previous chapters treated three proposal-development approaches for positioning to win: the classic approach

266

HOW TO
CORRECT
LATE STARTS,
FALSE STARTS,
AND PEOPLE
PROBLEMS

and the two specialty approaches, the challenging-the-discriminators approach and the hybrid approach. It would be great if all, or even most, of your proposals were developed the right way, and certainly it would be better for your customers because they would receive better, more competitive proposals. There would be less danger of their passing over the superior but poorly presented proposal. Also the contractors would spend less money and compete more efficiently. But most of all, the right contractor would always win. That should make everybody happy. Even the loser would be better off in the long run. He wouldn't get out of step with his customer, and he would preserve his viability for another competition, when things were slanted more his way.

Unfortunately, this is a dream world. The sad truth is that the majority of proposals are developed haphazardly and without any discipline. The number of unbelievably dumb mistakes that can be made are limitless. But of all these poor approaches, there are two very bad ones that we see often enough to give them special attention here.

THE BACKING-IN APPROACH:
MAKING THE MOST OF A BAD SITUATION

The conditions that may force you into the backing-in approach are worth reviewing because they expose a common trap of trying to do a proposal by concentrating your efforts on fine-tuning. You overdevelop your strengths at the expense of more pressing but less appealing customer requirements—those that expose your weaknesses. Many times the backing-in approach results from a late start or from some drastic, unanticipated change in the customer's requirements. But just as often it results from poor management by good technical people who are not business oriented.

Basically, you build your technical data base for a proposal in two ways. The right way is to build it in response to the RFP requirements. You outline the proposal according to the RFP at the very start. If you don't have the actual RFP, build a strawman RFP. Then you build a cross matrix of the outline with the RFP Statement of Work (SOW), Work Breakdown Structure (WBS), Contract Data Requirements List (CDRL), deliverables, proposal instructions, contract requirements, cost proposal, letter of transmittal, and any stray requirements that appear throughout the RFP. You might even add a few that you have picked up in talking to the "user" side of the customer, requirements that didn't go into the RFP but aren't in conflict with it. You have to be careful here. You must have a high opinion of the person who suggests that these unwritten requirements are real. If you treat them as though they were formally stated requirements, they had better be valid.

Once you have listed all the requirements, analyze them in accordance with your existing data base. If there are adequate data to substantiate your claims in a particular area, you will avoid spending additional money. Of course, these will be the areas you specialize in, the areas that most of your people are familiar with and good at. It is very hard to shut down studies, tests, and analyses in those popular areas. But you look for areas where you haven't substantiated your claims. Most likely these will be in the fringe areas of your strengths or maybe even completely outside of them. These areas will reflect the marginal capabilities of your company, the areas where historically you perform badly. If your company doesn't have adequate strength or expertise, you might have to go outside and buy it or even team up with another contractor.

In building your data base to respond to the RFP, you should put your resources where the holes are. That produces a complete and responsive data base, but it also makes for a lot of unhappy technical people who are forced to work on subjects with less appeal. It takes a great deal of strength to keep this kind of effort in line. You have to monitor it continuously to make sure it doesn't drift back into the mainstream of the technical interests, areas where your data base is more than adequate already. If you continuously orient yourself to the RFP, budget your resources to respond to all of the customer's

267

THE BACKING-IN
APPROACH:
MAKING
THE MOST
OF A BAD
SITUATION

268

HOW TO
CORRECT
LATE STARTS,
FALSE STARTS,
AND PEOPLE
PROBLEMS

requirements, monitor the effort closely, and manage by action items, you will end up with a better proposal and pay less for it.

The alternate approach to obtaining the data base is done strictly on a functional basis during the early part of the proposal effort. With this approach people can invent and create within their discipline without the constraints of the RFP requirements. This approach produces superb technical results in concentrated areas, sometimes at the expense of other supposedly less important areas. Little or no effort is spent searching for administrative and supportive areas that might be required in the proposal. It's the kind of approach that yields technical breakthroughs in specific disciplines. You generate this data base just like you do your independent research.

Of course, at some time in the proposal effort, usually near the end, the proposal team has to stop inventing and start writing. Without orienting the effort to the RFP from the beginning, you almost assuredly will find that the data base you have been generating doesn't fit the RFP! Certain areas, like the technical breakthrough area, will be grossly overdone compared to other areas. The customer evaluation criteria may assign that particular technical area two or three points out of ten, but you have spent 90 percent of your effort and dollars in that area! You have virtually ignored certain areas that are given equal or more weight by the customer. How do you handle the proposal effort from here on, until it's out the door on the way to the customer? How will you find the gaps quickly and assess how big they are so that you can spread your remaining resources to do the most good? You will use the backing-in approach. This approach won't make up for a lack of good upstream work, and it can't recover that most precious resource, time. But it might enable you to organize the remainder of the effort and make the most of what you have. Here's how it works.

You are trying to fit your data base to an RFP. Instead of having the RFP drive the data base, you let something else drive it, probably somebody's hobby-shop idea or a strong engineer's technical interests. At any rate, you have a lot of data that roughly pertain to an RFP, but you don't know where and how well. You have to see how well it fits and where the holes are. Probably you should do this before you decide whether or not you want to bid the RFP.

One way to do this is to back in with a wall-mounted storyboard (Figure 17-1). Pick a room with a lot of wall space. Put up headers for the outline that you obtained from the RFP and space them around the room. Under the headers, put the subject requirements from the RFP that relate to the various chapters. Then put up the themes and messages you think you can support for the chapters. Mind you, this is not competitive convergence in any sense of the word. Rather, it is trying to make the most of a bad situation. Your themes and lead-in paragraphs are more of a wish list than anything else. Since the RFP is already in the house, you are limited in what you could do to try to change to a better approach. You are not in Leverage (pre-RFP) Country. But if you are determined to bid, you are better off in going part way with a logical approach rather than not at all.

Once you have your RFP requirements and messages posted under your chapter headings, you begin to post your data base to the outline. It takes a lot of time and shuffling of data, but as time wears on your team will get pretty sharp about what goes where.

When you are finished, you will find that most of your data base falls under one or two headings. Those are the areas your people are interested in. They are the areas where you spent all your money and made your technical breakthrough. Most of the rest will have a little bit of data, and then there will be one or two areas that are completely missing. You don't know beans about those subjects, and since you didn't use a strawman RFP to drive your data base, nothing was done in those areas.

So now what do you do? First, you had better take a good look at whether or not you want to play this game. Obviously you are starting from a loser's position, and you don't have time to evolve an approach that differs from your going-in

269

THE BACKING-IN
APPROACH:
MAKING
THE MOST
OF A BAD
SITUATION

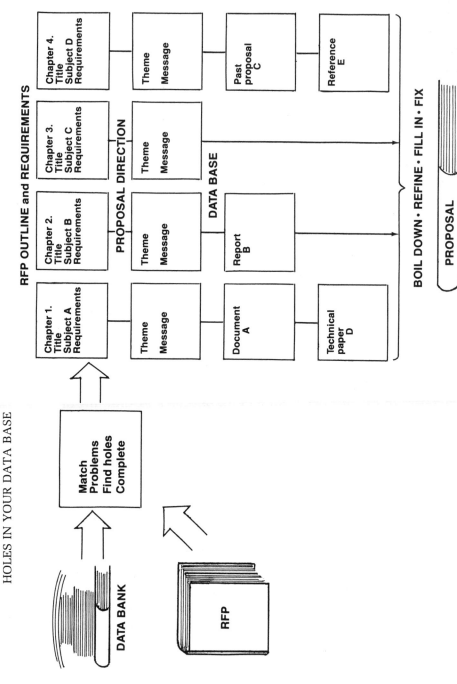

FIGURE 17-1. THE BACKING-IN APPROACH EXPOSES THE HOLES IN YOUR DATA BASE

approach. And unless you have been very lucky, that's probably a long way from what the customer had in mind. Otherwise he wouldn't have written the RFP as he did, so different from the fit with the homework you have been doing. But after this look, if you *have* been lucky or other circumstances justify going ahead, you at least know where the holes are. You can figure out those areas where you can still change to come up with a stronger approach, and you can create the data needed to fill the voids. As a responsible contractor, you had better go back to the wish list of themes and messages you started with and tone them down to what you can substantiate. You don't have nearly the chance of winning that you would have had if you had started right. But you are at least a lot better off than going in blind with a nonresponsive proposal. The backing-in approach has some merit, but it is far from a good way to turn out a superior proposal.

THE CLOSET APPROACH

While the backing-in approach is an example of bad business management in proposal development, the closet approach presents an entirely different kind of problem. This approach is characterized by complete secrecy from start to finish. Those who use it exclude the rest of the company from the effort. They would literally operate in a closet if they could get away with it!

The closet proposal is drawn up by your most talented people. They are the people you go to when you want to get new programs moving. They are independent self-starters, innovative, bursting with smarts, and always ready with a unique approach. And they are hustlers all the way. You can't exist without these brilliant mavericks. But as their program matures, you had better make sure they come out of the closet.

Their track record is mixed: they win the small start-up contracts, and they are excellent at one-on-ones, but they have some major limitations. In short, they think the system stinks—your system, their system, any system. They really fail

272

HOW TO
CORRECT
LATE STARTS,
FALSE STARTS,
AND PEOPLE
PROBLEMS

when large groups and many departments are involved or when business systems and orderly conventional techniques are required. Their forte is innovation, doing things differently. The ordinary is not for them, and they rarely pull down the big ones.

Those who adopt the closet approach run unique hobby shops. They make the contacts themselves and put the approaches together in boiler-room operations with a few trusted subordinates. Rarely do they call on the functional troops for help, and never do they call on the support organizations. They play everything close to the vest. You never know what they are up to, and you never know any of the details of their operations. They go over and around the functional barons, smoothly, without a ripple. They are famous for inventing their own systems. No one can move into their operation without first paying his dues and becoming accepted.

Their win percentage is high, so long as you are talking about innovative study contracts and operations that don't involve many departments and functional or service groups. The more complicated and unusual, the more they succeed. Your management idolizes them because they can seemingly do the impossible. But watch out. They will fall flat on the big one. They just don't seem to know when to stop innovating, and they can't restrict their innovations to technical matters and settle down to systems that have good track records. A new and startling system for every need must be found every time. That applies to proposals too. Out the window go all the standard practices and discipline that have worked on so many proposals to date. In their place go the customized, hip-pocket practices of these innovators. They work in conceptual matters but become inadequate when the activity turns to validation. And they completely break down for development and production.

In the beginning you can tolerate these people, but phase in your proven practices as the program grows. Demand disciplines that go beyond the one person/one group operation. And above all, work like hell to convert these closet types into managers.

18

Axioms for Winning

POSITIONING-TO-WIN AXIOMS

- Start evolving your superior, winning approach by understanding the pivotal differences between you and your competitors as those differences are perceived by your customer.
- Benefits exist only as the customer's perceptions, not yours. Respond to the customer's hopes, fears, and biases.
- Before you can evolve a superior approach in the eyes of the customer, you have to take stock of where you stand relative to your competitors.
- If the customer thinks something about you, or about one of your competitors, then that's your competitive challenge, regardless of whether or not it is true.
- The claims that decide who wins are those that deal with pivotal differences (discriminators) between the competitors.

- Discriminators are strengths, weaknesses, hopes, fears, and biases. They form the influencers of the competition.
- To get the maximum leverage from your conceptual efforts, itemize the discriminators at the start, well in advance of the competition.
- Your discriminator list is a measure of your potential for making your customer work for you.
- Feature your strengths and your competitor's weaknesses. *Features* are your main selling points.
- Without unique strengths you will have a hard time getting into the winner's circle.
- The most effective strengths are technical innovations, and innovations often are the key to a win.
- If all the competitors do their job right—by emphasizing their strengths and exposing their competitors' weaknesses—the evaluators will have an easy job picking the winner.
- If you don't substantiate your claims, your competitors can easily counter your strengths. If you can't prove a claim, it works against you.
- The time to feature a competitor's opinion is when it differs from the customer's opinion.
- You do the evaluator a great service by exposing and exploiting your competitor's weaknesses, just as your competitor does when he exposes yours.
- *Neutralizers* are theses that eliminate or correct real or imaginary weaknesses attributed to you by the customer.
- In positioning to win, you can't refute a real weakness without first taking corrective action.
- Only the customer's perception of your weaknesses count. You neutralize their adverse effects.
- With *counters* you discredit and minimize what your competitors claim as strengths, their Aha!s.
- The surest way to a win is to identify your competitor's strengths and then counter (discredit) them. This is also the surest way to lose if you do a bad job.
- If you discredit a competitor's strong features, his Aha!s, you have mortally wounded him.

- The only time you ignore your key competitor's strengths is when you can't minimize or discredit them. Then you are probably in big trouble.
- *Exploiters* are theses that play on the customer's hopes, fears, and biases by showing that your approach solves them.
- In a tight competition, the competitor who responds best to the customers' hopes, fears, and biases will get the edge.
- Make your fears and concerns the customer's fears and concerns. Then present your unique solutions.
- The fundamental rule in winning is to give your customers what benefits them, not just what you think they need or what you have to offer.
- It is the height of marketing arrogance—or brilliance—to believe that you know your customer's business better than he does.
- Usually what benefits the customer and what he wants are one and the same.
- Don't try to pass your hobby shops on to your customers.
- Through competitive convergence, evolve the superior approaches that implement the benefits your customers seek.
- Technology transitions offer opportunities. You can go from last place to first place if you forecast the transition.
- Where customer benefits and desires diverge, you have a moment of opportunity—or disaster.
- A good winner knows the relative merits of all the alternate approaches because that's what is required to evolve the superior approach.
- If you believe the customer is wrong and you can't change his thinking, no-bidding is the smartest thing you can do.
- Winning without any benefit to yourself is just as bad and probably worse than losing.
- Do a complete job. If there are ten ways to prove your point, use them all.
- If your cost is high, then the approach you selected is too expensive. Change your approach.
- Arrogance has lost far more competitions than incompetence.

- If you can't figure out why your customer doesn't like your approach, don't bid. You don't know enough about the competition either to change his mind or to evolve a winning approach.
- It doesn't do you any good to be right if you allow yourself to lose. You can't help anyone as a loser.
- It is infinitely more important to win than to earn the customer's affection.
- You don't have to relax your discipline very much to slip from the winner's circle into the also-ran category.
- Listen to the ultimate experts—your customers.
- Substantiate every claim you make. If you can't prove it, don't claim it.
- Achieve accountability for completing action items by requiring documentation of results.
- The best leader and a committed management are going nowhere if they don't have the resources to do the job.
- Totally committed management is required for effective top-down direction.
- The first prerequisite for top-down direction is a strong and innovative leader.

PROPOSAL-DEVELOPMENT AXIOMS

- A proposal is a collection of substantiated claims that respond to the request for proposal.
- Use a competitive thesis, or white paper, to present your story, claims, and propositions. It presents the challenge that your proposal team validates.
- Use a proposal scenario to give the plot of the approach. The scenario shows the proposal's development, chapter by chapter, and gives essential details for writing.
- Use argumentative headlines and themes to claim how your approach implements benefits to the customer.
- Without a disciplined approach, proposal teams write mostly about what they know, and what they do best, not necessarily what the request for proposal asks for.

- Designate the innovator of the subject matter as the proposal leader. Give him an experienced proposal specialist to act as his alter ego.
- The first proposal draft is always bad, no matter how long you have worked on it. The purpose of an early first draft is to flush out the deficiencies so that you can do what the RFP asks for, before it's too late.
- Don't wait to get everything in before you publish the first draft. If you do, your first draft will be your last.
- The big value of the early draft is that the functional supervisors of the authors can see the parts that are missing.
- Don't leave anything to chance. Don't make assumptions. Check everything.
- Every proposal effort is different, unique to itself. So don't ever assume that you can relax your discipline. Each start is a new ball game.
- Lower-level claims must support higher-level claims so that all claims track and present a vectored approach to the RFP.
- Top-down direction is the means of assuring that you turn in only one proposal, the one that supports your proposal theme.
- Make it clear to the customer at the start of every chapter how your approach implements benefits to him.
- Everyone has to know that your proposal leader is the alter ego of your top management.
- If you have a proposal team that is easy to manage, you had better take a hard look at its members. They probably aren't your best people.
- If you want to win, you have to sacrifice your best-qualified leader to the proposal.
- Alternate proposals succeed only when the customer doesn't understand his problem. Anyone ought to be able to come up with a winner if allowed to rewrite the ground rules to favor his approach. But that normally leads to a protest.

Appendix

Discriminator Exercises

To complete your understanding of discriminators and develop your skill in writing competitive theses, you should go through a series of exercises similar to those presented in Chapter 3. We have created three competitions for this purpose, with three competitors per competition. Each competition is structured to produce numerous discriminators. Pick a competition and develop a list of discriminators for each competitor. Then write a competitive thesis for each. You might be startled by the number of discriminators you can identify, and you might be more surprised that you can establish a good competitive thesis for each competitor. If you work your way through all of these, you will certainly know how to maximize your strengths and neutralize your weaknesses, and you'll also learn how to attack the competition on all fronts. If you find that you need a little help, review Chapter 3.

SUBJECT: The City of San Diego requests proposals for commercial buses to transport its citizens throughout the greater San Diego area. The bus routes will be the freeways throughout the city and the outlying areas. Buses will stop at each on/off ramp and at intersecting freeways. Boarding areas are now being prepared at each stop.

This is a long-range plan designed to replace commuting automobiles with their one- and two-passenger loads. The service is intended to operate continuously from 5 A.M. until 10 P.M. every day except Sunday. The intent of the plan is to:

1. Reduce the congestion on the freeways at all hours, especially during the peak morning and evening rush hours.
2. Reduce the energy required to transport the San Diego work force to and from work.
3. Reduce the pollutants resulting from moving the San Diego work force to and from work.

This transportation system is based on the premise that most people can walk to work from the closest freeway off-ramp. And in those cases where the walk is excessive, our survey shows that the biggest companies will provide shuttle service for their employees during peak hours.

REQUEST FOR PROPOSAL: This RFP is for the buses we will buy to serve the transportation system. We will consider sizes that can carry from 25 to 200 passengers. We will consider new and used buses. Buses will have to meet standard Department of Transportation safety and environmental standards. Our demand delivery schedule is as follows:

1. First bus to be delivered in 6 months
2. Buses with seat capacity of 20,000 delivered by 12 months
3. Buses with seat capacity of 40,000 delivered by 18 months
4. An optional number of buses whose additional seat capacity equals 40,000, to be delivered by 24 months
5. An optional number of buses whose additional seat capacity equals 40,000, to be delivered by 30 months.

We encourage bidders to be innovative in their offerings. All designs that meet standards will be considered.

PROPOSAL INSTRUCTIONS: Bidders will submit a technical/cost proposal that describes the buses they propose. Of particular interest are the following characteristics:

1. Subsystem/System Integration: subsystem descriptions, loading, unloading, safety, comfort, fare collection
2. Performance characteristics: passenger load, speed, range, braking distance to stop
3. Cost of buses: purchase, service, parts, operation, fuel
4. Suitability of buses to freeway traffic and intended application
5. Supportability considerations: service, parts, equipment
6. Supply of buses
7. Bidder support capability (although this is a subject for later procurement)

EVALUATION CRITERIA: In descending order of importance:

1. Suitability of the buses to the commuters, freeway traffic, and the intended application
2. Projected costs per passenger mile and for typical trips
3. Performance characteristics
4. Supportability
5. Passenger comfort
6. Other factors including the bidders' ability to support the operation with service, parts, and personnel

Description of Competitors

Big New Bus (BNB) Competitor: BNB is a foreign firm with an excellent reputation. It produces a big 100-passenger air-conditioned bus that is modern in every respect. Riders love the bus because it is quiet, fast, comfortable, roomy, and environmentally controlled. In addition, its efficient diesel engine gets reasonable gas mileage. The bus is expensive, but upkeep is fairly reasonable because of excellent engineering of all the subsystems. Parts are manufactured abroad and shipped to the United States. The company supplies its own (foreign) service people, who do fantastic work.

Old Reconditioned Bus (ORB) Competitor: ORB is a Texas organization that specializes in acquiring and reconditioning used buses, and it does an excellent job in reconditioning these buses. It has cornered the market on the most popular bus of the past decade. This reconditioned 60-passenger bus is reasonably comfortable and air-conditioned, but its noise level is high. The engines burn gasoline and the gas consumption is high, but within the DOT specifications. The bus has adequate performance and is ordinary in appearance. Costs to the purchaser are low, and upkeep is reasonable. The engine and transmission are common to many vehicles in the United States. Parts are easy to acquire, and most mechanics are familiar with the engine and able to maintain it.

New Little Bus (NLB) Competitor: NLB is an American firm that has developed a small 25-passenger bus with many innovative features. One feature is that it can pull a walk-through trailer that increases its load to 50 passengers. The bus is light and easy to assemble, but it is noisy and not air-conditioned. It is also austere and only marginally comfortable. The advanced, lightweight gasoline engine gets excellent mileage. The cost of the bus is moderate, but its upkeep, while easy to accomplish, is extensive because of its light weight. The engine and all parts are manufactured in this country. The engine requires special attention for best performance, but the company has a good maintenance force of trained mechanics.

Assignment

Draw up a list of discriminators and write a top-level competitive thesis for each of the competitors. If you haven't read Chapter 2, go back and do so for guidance.

TENNIS RACKETS FOR ABC
DEPARTMENT STORE COMPETITION

SUBJECT: The ABC department store chain is looking for a new line of tennis rackets to sell under its trademark. ABC serves the broad market of middle- and lower-class America. It would like to capture the upper-class market with a quality product. But primarily it wants an affordable racket that will sell well and produce few complaints. And they want to make a good profit.

REQUEST FOR PROPOSAL: This RFP is for the purchase of 100,000 tennis rackets. That quantity is negotiable depending on price. ABC will consider any material, including composites, wood, and metal. The preliminary delivery schedule is as follows:

1. 100 test rackets to be furnished with the proposal, due three months from the RFP date
2. 30,000 rackets within the first month
3. 40,000 rackets within the second month
4. 30,000 rackets within the third and last month

Bidders will provide their own specifications and warranty. ABC encourages bidders to offer innovative and attractive rackets. All rackets from reputable domestic and foreign manufacturers will be considered.

PROPOSAL INSTRUCTIONS: Bidders will submit a technical/cost proposal that describes the tennis racket they propose. Of particular interest are the following characteristics:

1. Materials, construction, appearance, and durability
2. Performance under usual weather conditions
3. Performance under unusual weather conditions
4. Purchase cost per item
5. Service cost
6. Cost of parts
7. Suitability to clay, grass, and hard courts and for all tennis balls, domestic and foreign
8. Supportability: parts and service
9. Producibility
10. Management of bidder
11. Financial stability of bidder

EVALUATION CRITERIA: Same as the proposal instructions. All items are of equal importance.

Description of Competitors

Composite Racket (CR) Competitor: CR is a new commercial division of a well-financed aerospace company. It produces exotic racket frames made entirely of a composite material that is feather light and amazingly strong. The racket operation is unaffected by playing conditions, and it can be painted, just like metal or wood, or the color can be molded in. CR sends its rackets out to be strung and to have handles put on. Originally quality control of the frame, string, and handle was a problem. However CR appears to be getting these problems under control. The racket is the most expensive. CR initially attempted to market the racket themselves and then through a small outlet, but both efforts were unsuccessful. The parent company was on the verge of dropping this product line and closing down CR when the ABC RFP was released. After considerable study it decided to let CR go all out one more time and bid the ABC job. The parent company agreed to help fund a three-shift operation until the production-line capability could be built up.

Wood Racket (WR) Competitor: WR has been in business for a long time, producing a line of wood-laminated rackets from the inexpensive to the high priced. It has a very experienced work force, but its equipment is outdated and inefficient. Its products, even the inexpensive ones, are attractively painted and finished. You get exactly what you pay for when you buy a WR racket. The least expensive ones last for a while and then break, and they don't hold up well in rain and extreme humidity. The most expensive rackets have a reasonably long life with no problems even under adverse weather conditions. When rackets need to be repaired, WR can recondition them within a day for less than 50 percent of their original cost. But metal and fiberglass rackets have eaten into WR's share of the market, and inflation has driven the price of even the inexpensive rackets closer to the higher-quality ones. WR sees the ABC RFP as a way of maintaining itself as the highest volume producer of tennis rackets. WR's decision to bid was automatic.

Metal Racket (MR) Competitor: MR enjoys a good reputation and is a leader in its field. Five years ago, in an expensive operation, MR converted its product line from wood to metal rackets. MR had many difficulties and at one time almost went under. But now it has emerged with a quality racket, although the finances of the company are still shaky. MR's metal frame is rugged and virtually indestructable. It performs well under all conditions, although it does get hot or cold to the touch in weather extremes. It is a moderately high-priced racket. MR does all of its furnishings and service work, and the cost of parts and extras are in line with the industry. The racket has good producibility, but to reach the quantities ABC is asking for will require more capital investment.

Assignment

Draw up a list of discriminators and write a top-level competitive thesis for each of the competitors.

BULLDOZERS FOR XYZ CONSTRUCTION FIRM COMPETITION

SUBJECT: A national construction firm, XYZ, has decided to buy 100 new bulldozers. The firm studied the trade periodicals and determined that three companies have new, modern dozers that exceed XYZ's requirements. XYZ will use the bulldozers on construction jobs throughout the fifty states to move dirt, dig ditches, and do limited grading and hole drilling.

REQUEST FOR PROPOSAL: This RFP is for 100 bulldozers in excess of fifty tons. XYZ will buy these to replace its aging forty-ton dozers. The new dozers must exceed the performance specifications of its current forty-ton dozers. The demand schedule is as follows:

1. The first 2 dozers to be delivered thirty days after contract award
2. The remaining dozers to be delivered at 5 per month until the quantity of 100 is reached.

PROPOSAL INSTRUCTIONS: Bidders will submit a technical/cost proposal that describes the bulldozers they propose. Of particular interest are the following characteristics:

1. Subsystem/System Integration: subsystem descriptions, controls, earth-moving subsystem, ditch-digging subsystem, safety, comfort, auxiliary subsystems.
2. Performance characteristics under ideal conditions: earth-moving ability, rate that ditches can be dug, number and size of holes per hour
3. Performance characteristics in degraded environment and in rocky, muddy, and steep terrain.
4. Purchase cost of bulldozers
5. Service cost
6. Operational costs
7. Parts costs
8. Suitability to the types of surfaces, soil, and weather conditions in the fifty states.
9. Supportability: loading, unloading, transportability, training of operators, ease of service
10. Ability to meet delivery schedule
11. Stability and financial standing of bidder
12. Standardization of parts and subsystems

EVALUATION CRITERIA: Same as the proposal instructions. All items are of equal importance.

Description of Competitors

Big Capable Dozer (BCD) Competitor: BCD is a large American firm with an excellent reputation. It produces a seventy-five-ton diesel dozer that has great capability. It carries all subsystems at all times and can, without any shutdown for change, shift from moving earth to digging ditches or drilling holes. BCD's dozer is the most advanced manually-operated dozer on the market from the standpoint of capability. It performs well under all weather conditions and on all soil conditions. However, that capability is accompanied by a degree of complexity: the BCD dozer uses a large number of specialized parts, and when breakdowns occur, it takes time and skill to get the dozer operating again. It is also expensive. Service and parts are fairly expensive. The dozer can be rapidly loaded and unloaded, but its size and weight require extreme care and prior arrangements for transporting on roads and freeways. BCD can meet the delivery schedule with an extended work day.

Big Simple Dozer (BSD) Competitor: BSD is a large American firm with an excellent reputation. Its sixty-ton diesel dozer uses attachment tools, so its design and operation are simple. However, the dozer can do only one job at a time. To change from moving earth to digging ditches or drilling holes requires changes of equipment. This takes time, but it reduces the weight by fifteen tons and greatly simplifies the design, making repairs and maintenance much easier. It also allows for the use of standard parts. BSD's dozer has acceptable performance: it performs well under standard conditions and under adverse conditions because it is light and simple. It is moderately priced in all respects. Because of its light weight, it can be rapidly loaded, and it's easily transportable. BSD can meet the delivery schedule without extending its work day.

Advanced Technology Dozer (ATD) Competitor: ATD is a medium-size Italian company with an innovative, revolutionary fifty-ton dozer. Actually the dozer is slightly less than fifty tons, but by adding lead weight (an acceptable practice) ATD can get its dozer up to the fifty-ton lower limit. The ATD dozer uses a lightweight, powerful gas-turbine engine. But what really makes it revolutionary is that it can be operated by remote control. All of the sensors, power-supply systems, and actuators are minimum in size and very powerful. It carries all subsystems at all times and can, like the BCD dozer, shift from moving earth to digging ditches or drilling holes without shutting down for equipment changes. The ATD is without a doubt the most advanced dozer on the market. It outperforms every other dozer under normal conditions and on all kinds of soils. It performs adequately under degraded conditions, but using remote control becomes more difficult. If its computer or electronic parts get wet or contaminated, however, they have to be cleaned and dried before the system will accept and perform commands correctly. The dozer is complex and requires ATD specialists to maintain it. It uses specialized parts, and the initial and service costs are high. Because of its light weight, it can be rapidly and easily loaded and transported from site to site after the lead weight is removed. To meet the delivery schedule, ATD will have to add a second and third shift. However, the company is subsidized by the Italian government, which will invest in capital facilities to increase production if the contract is awarded to ATD. In fact, the Italian government and ATD are determined to give special considerations to this competition in order to win it.

Assignment

Draw up a list of discriminators and write a top-level competitive thesis for each of the competitors.

Positioning to Win
Seminar

Would you like to attend a Positioning To Win seminar/workshop conducted by the authors? Seminar attendees first receive a full course in the operational theory of the Discriminator Discipline, the nature and necessity of Substantive Marketing, and the tremendous leverage available from Competitive Convergence. Then, under the authors' expert guidance, they get practical, hands-on experience in putting this philosophy to work. Attendees enter group-effort mock competitions, using the Discriminator Discipline to develop their themes, competitive theses, executive summaries, and oral presentations. They face critiques of their own efforts and critique others, then graduate with another full set of mock competitions that demonstrate the extraordinary power of Competitive Convergence.

For further information, contact:

Positioning To Win
P.O. Box 1928
La Mesa, California 92041
or call (714) 462-5536

ABOUT THE AUTHORS

James M. Beveridge was graduated "With Distinction" from Cornell University, where he later taught. He joined Bell Telephone Laboratories as a member of the Technical Staff, continued his graduate studies, and then went on active duty with the U.S. Army. After seven years with Hughes Aircraft Company, where his last position was Manager of Advanced Program Development for Aerospace Group Marketing, he formed the management consulting firm of JMBeveridge and Associates, Inc. in the fall of 1963.

Jim travels some 100,000 miles each year in an active international consulting practice, and his clients include over thirty of Fortune's Top Fifty. His proposal development seminars have been delivered to over twenty thousand people. Jim has served as a principal consultant to the executives of essentially every major U.S. aerospace company as well as some of the largest in Europe, and he has been the marketing consultant for the successful contractor on several dozen major competitive defense/space programs. He is the author of two books (*The Anatomy of a Win* and *What's Happened to Our Economy?*) and co-author, with E. J. Velton, of two other books, including the present volume. He is a frequent writer and speaker on a wide range of topics including interpersonal dynamics and engineering and marketing management.

Over the past twenty years, Edward J. Velton has performed every role in proposal development, including that of the Program Manager and Proposal Leader. More than a decade ago he established the Proposal Development Group of the Convair Division of General Dynamics Corporation. He regularly worked with the other divisions of the company to set up proposal groups and procedures, review plans and proposals, and to act as the Program Director's alter ego in writing Executive Summaries and Overviews. General Dynamics submitted the better part of one hundred competitive proposals each year, many of which he personally worked on, and all of which he monitored. Under his direction, they achieved a win record which averaged over 70% for the last seven years.

Ed is the greatest pickpocket of proposal development techniques in the business. What consistently worked, he logged in the "do" column; what didn't, he put down as a "no-no." In the winter of 1977, after years of practicing the philosophies and disciplines first developed by Jim Beveridge in his consulting relationship with General Dynamics, he co-authored with Jim *All You Should Know About Creating Superior Proposals But Somehow Never Fully Understood,* which quickly became the aerospace industry standard manual on proposal development. In 1981 he co-authored the present volume, this time taking early retirement from General Dynamics to join Jim in an association to teach these disciplines in an international seminar series.

Index

Page numbers in **boldface** refer to illustrations.